Unequal Partners

Unequal Partners

**Philippine and Thai Relations
with the United States
1965-75**

W. Scott Thompson
Fletcher School of Law
and Diplomacy
Tufts University

Lexington Books
D.C. Heath and Company
Lexington, Massachusetts
Toronto   London

SOC
E
183.8
PS
T45

Library of Congress Cataloging in Publication Data

Thompson, Willard Scott, 1942-
　　Unequal partners.

　　1. United States—Foreign relations—Philippine Islands. 2. Philippine Islands—Foreign relations—United States. 3. United States—Foreign relations—Thailand. 4. Thailand—Foreign relation—United States. I. Title.
E183.8P5T45　　　327.73'0593　　　74-27747
ISBN 0-669-97758-6

For Nina

Contents

List of Figures and Tables

Preface

This book was completed at a time when Thailand and the Philippines were in the early stages of making the most profound changes in their foreign policies and internal structures in a generation. When research was begun in 1969, Thailand was a military-ruled autocracy depending on the United States for her security. The Philippines was a rambunctious and somewhat ill-disciplined democracy, talking much about lessening her dependence on the United States but doing little about it, with a similar approach to socioeconomic reform. In 1974, although still very much a bureaucratic polity, Thailand was in a state of ebullient upheaval. Democracy had come to the kingdom, perhaps not permanently, but in a more sophisticated form, and with a firmer base of support, than in the previous false starts in that direction—something to which some further support was added by the 1975 elections. American withdrawal from Viet-Nam and lingering resentment of the excessive involvement the larger power had had in Thai affairs was forcing a rapid change in her foreign policy, and the newly powerful students, along with other emergent social groups, were demanding radical restructuring of the polity. In the Philippines, following threats from the far left and far right and amidst growing anarchy, President Marcos declared martial law in September 1972. He continued to rule in a twilight zone of legitimacy under a new constitution after the term to which he had been elected was concluded in December 1973. During 1974 and 1975, he and the technocrats running the government sought to legitimize their rule through both extensive internal reform and through a sharp break with past diplomatic patterns—including a new self-confidence in dealing with the United States. In effect the two countries reversed roles during the period examined in this book.

The project of which this book is an initial product had as its intent the disaggregation of the various sources of foreign policy of a developing country, roughly divisible between those that are external and those that are internal. With few exceptions, developing states have complex and dependent relations with some great power, making the external sources of their foreign policy particularly important. But by virtue of the process of development the state witnesses rapid changes in its own sociopolitical institutions, and in addition must often cope with domestic insurgencies or at least ethnic cleavage; processes of which foreign policy must take account, to which it must relate, and from which it often derives. The external cluster of policy sources raises the interesting question of what combination of political and social structures in the developing state strengthens her resistance to external influences, or which are correlated with greater bargaining power with stronger partners. Is democracy or autocracy the better way to protect the state's interests, other things being equal—or do the circumstances determine which is more pertinent? The answer to the last question appears, on the evidence of this comparative study, to be yes.

The internal cluster of policy sources, i.e. the existing political and social structures, raises the question of how states and institutions adapt in a period of rapid change, given great external pressures. How governments reform themselves, how foreign services become more professional, how societies develop new institutions (and *which* institutions), are among the important questions raised in considering the state's adaptation to new trends in its environment. It is difficult to deal with one cluster of foreign policy sources without the other, but in practice we must often separate complex questions if we are to give them adequate attention. This volume focuses primarily on certain external sources of Philippine and Thai foreign policy, specifically, those which emanate from these states' lengthy and complex ties with the United States, and it looks at this interaction in terms of given internal sources of foreign policy. The domestic sources of foreign policy will be the subject of a subsequent work.

The notion of adaptation,[1] a controversial one in recent literature, brings us to another pattern of interest, and to the interface of foreign and domestic policy, with which we are concerned in this book. The term "adaptation" in essence refers simply to the success of policies. It must be applied not just at the systemic level of national performance, but at the subsystemic level as well. In the larger, systemic sense, "national adaptation" implies a continuum of measurable performance, with the maladaptive end indicating a loss of national existence; something that was more than a theoretical possibility in the region of interaction studied in this book. At the subsystemic level, we are interested, however, in what group or institution has benefited, at what cost or with what benefit to the state, through given clusters of foreign policies. The study of statecraft is the study of political elites within nations searching, ideally, for the optimal mix of structures, people, and policies, both internal and external. Statecraft has too often been considered merely in terms of single factors, such as leadership: great crises produce a more powerful leadership, which calms the nation or stands up to foreign demands. But the process is more complex, for all the constituent structures of foreign policy play a role in the nation's attempt to improve its prospects. Social groups tire of their nation's low status and work to raise it; governmental organizations find new relationships so as to increase stability. Superficial changes can sometimes adjust processes adequately. Diplomacy is the art of trying to do precisely this in the external system—finding a new relationship between contending pressures with the smallest possible shift in the nation's commitments or obligations.

The ideal in statecraft is seldom encountered. Groups or elites whose interests are prejudicial to the successful adaptation of the state as a whole can rule, often by virtue of unspoken alliances with external powers, so as to preserve group privileges, and in the process severely damage the survival prospects of their state system. This happened in Thailand under the old regime, particularly between

1971 and 1973, and many would contend that it is precisely what has happened in the Philippines under martial law.

How do we characterize the different patterns or stances that a state may effect to bring internal and external needs into harmony? Put another way, can we categorize the patterns of policies at the interface of states' internal and external policy? Rosenau's fourfold taxonomy of "acquiescent," "intransigent," "promotive," and "preservative" foreign policy moods is useful.

Only the last two of Rosenau's taxonomy need concern us here. A state in a mood of promotive adaptation is in the relatively rare situation in which leaders have considerable freedom of choice, where demands from neither the populace nor from outside powers are sufficiently powerful to affect more than marginally a governmental strategy of, say, economic development (or of immense personal enrichment). Preservative adaptation is where intense demands come from both within and without, while the leadership walks a tightrope between the two. "A strong sense of national identity inhibits acquiescence and resource limitations curb the emergence of intransigent and promotive orientations."[2] Although it is easy to see large powers in one mood and not another, because their size tends to preclude predetermined acquiescence toward any particular powers, it is difficult to see how most small and poor states can be categorized so simply. Thailand at one time might have been "promotive" in relation to Asia (and in relation to domestic development as well), while at the same time "preservative" in relation to the United States. States can try to be promotive internally and preservative externally, as was Thailand between 1971 and 1973, by ignoring mounting internal demands; this is likely to prove counterproductive, as the Thai case shows. Yet Rosenau's taxonomy has an important heuristic function, for in any system of interaction there must be some observable mixture of properties, and all states, in all their mutations, must be classifiable into a small number of basic types.

The most likely transformation of foreign policy mood is from promotive to preservative, particularly in the developing world. The circumstances wherein a leadership has both the self-confidence and the possibility of altering both its internal and external environment are rare. What is required for a transformation to a preservative foreign policy is for forces other than the leadership—ranging from political or social groups to foreign powers—to reassert themselves, forcing the leadership to contend with them until it is fashioning its environment less than it is reacting to these other demands.

Thailand is a good example of such a transformation. Under Marshal Sarit, who ruled Thailand after 1958 as singlehandedly as did kings prior to 1932, wide-ranging economic development programs were undertaken, and the kingdom worked closely with the United States to secure a new strategic balance in Southeast Asia—or to prevent further deterioration in the one that had existed. Sarit also accumulated a fortune in excess of $140 million. After his death in 1963, external pressures became stronger: such as an increasing need of the

United States for Thai facilities in the Vietnamese war, growing Pathet Lao contingents in Laos after the collapse of the Geneva accords, and finally, Chinese and North Vietnamese support to insurgents within Thailand itself. As the Vietnamese war became increasingly unpopular in the United States, American diplomats nudged the regime toward greater democratization so that the close association of the two allies would look better at home. Later it was necessary to withdraw part of the American forces in Thailand for the same reasons, while withdrawing military forces generally from all of Southeast Asia. Societal pressures also became far stronger, partly as a result of the foreign training of a large number of Thai students and the consequent influx of foreign notions. To garner more support and develop more capabilities, the regime encouraged this process; for the same reasons, plus American pressure, it eventually promulgated a constitution, and in 1969 it reopened the parliament. When these societal forces were perceived by the regime as having achieved *real* competing power, they were closed off, in the internal coup of 1971. The regime argued that the important demands coming from without and within the kingdom—the pressures from China and North Viet-Nam and dissidence within—necessitated their own greater freedom of action, and hence closed the parliament down and silenced the press. The government was simply blind to the dangers inherent in returning to straight military rule, and intolerant of criticism. Thus it tried to return to promotive adaptation, which proved impossible. The regime was not harsh enough to keep the emergent social forces bottled up; it had lost, perhaps through bewilderment at the changes taking place, the self-confidence that had usually characterized Thai military regimes. Thus it was possible for a student movement to catalyze its overthrow. The new government, which the king appointed on 14 October 1973, had compelling internal pressures on it, preeminently from the student reformers but also from laborers of all sorts, disgruntled businessmen, and, in effect, from communist insurgents in the far reaches of Northeast Thailand. China's increasing pertinence to the balance of forces in the region meant that external pressures were great also, necessitating a return to preservative behavior.

The case of the Philippines is not dissimilar. President Macapagal, a reformer by origin and temperament, following the most corrupt Philippine president up to that time, set in motion great changes in both the foreign and domestic sectors, in such a way as to reinforce each other. Land reform and decontrol of the peso signaled to the Kennedy administration that the new Philippine government meant to be not only humanitarian, but pragmatic as well. It achieved reform not only through positive acts (land reform) to redress iniquitous situations but also through essentially negative acts (ending the control of the peso, wherein more corruption had flourished than anywhere else in the country thus bringing law and human nature into accord). Therefore the American government extended massive financial assistance to Macapagal's administration shortly after it took office. A *démarche* in diplomacy in Asia alerted everybody to the Philippine attempt to be her own mistress.

Intrenched elites frustrated Macapagal domestically, and, as the Vietnamese war heated up, external demands on the Philippines mounted as well, drastically limiting her maneuverability. Ferdinand Marcos, Macapagal's successor, began under the same limitations, although he probably had no genuine intention of undertaking social reform or foreign policy change in his first term. He concentrated on administration of the state, particularly the military, and on the consolidation of his own political position. In his second term he might have been able to undertake social reform and to refashion foreign policy on his own schedule, using the substantial power he had accumulated and the skill in statecraft he had learned. A tremendous growth in dissidence, reinforced and given momentum by his own failings, forced him to take more drastic action than President Magsaysay had when the Hukbalahap rebels were on the outskirts of Manila. So caught was he in the web of his own corruption that, to recreate the possibility of reform and modernization of the archipelago, Marcos had to freeze the situation and silence former accomplices. On 22 September 1972 he declared martial law and began jailing politicians, firing civil servants, and collecting loose weapons, and he started the reorientation of foreign policy by breaking the bottleneck on the development of relations with communist states. Promotive behavior domestically was reinforcing, and was reinforced by, promotive behavior abroad.

Thus here, too, Thailand and the Philippines reversed roles at the interface of foreign and domestic politics. Thailand's regime in the early 1960s was developing a close and self-serving relationship with the United States, responding to that power's urgings as well as those of her own bureaucratic elites to develop the kingdom's resources and institutions. A decade later Thailand was responding to powerful internal and external forces, seeking to perfect her domestic democratic institutions, and to find a way to appease Hanoi while slowly but deliberately phasing out security links with her old protector. The Philippines had gone from the position where dominant political elites had made the nation's relationship with the United States increasingly cramped and tricky, but where, ironically, little foreign policy existed beyond the conducting of relations with the old colonial power, to a reverse situation by the mid-1970s. The old politicians were in jail, a new self-confident technocratic elite was ensconced in power beside Marcos and the military; relations with the United States were intimate, but the regime promotively sought a new set of relationships between domestic and various foreign fronts.

Why these two states? "What damn good is this country—you can't compare it with anything!" David Wilson said of Thailand.[3] A "premise of the uniqueness of Thailand," in Herbert Phillips's words, has underlain much work on that country, often resulting in a "scholarship of admiration."[4] The Philippines is no easier to compare, exceptional as the Republic is for her position as the only Christian state in Asia, with the many resulting cultural implications, and for her geographic position as an archipelago. Indeed, the Philippines comes out on some cross-national factor analyses as a Latin American state.[5] Yet "the comparative method consists of identifying similarities and differences. The process is pervasive in political inquiry as in all [scientific] inquiry."[6]

Although states hardly need to be similar in any overall sense before some common, but unequally shared, property is compared in them, the range of differences must be relatively narrow in the comparison of a few units if we are to shed light on a small number of questions. For our purposes, these two states are about as similar as states tend to be. Their population is almost the same—38.3 million Filipinos and 35.9 million Thai in 1970. In land area they are both medium-size countries, though Thailand, with 514,000 square kilometers, is almost twice the size of the Philippines, whose seven thousand islands total approximately 300,000 square kilometers. Both countries fall into Russet's "Stage III"—transitional societies—based on GNP per capita (a range of $108 to $239).[7] For purposes of comparing foreign policies, states can be categorized, following Rosenau, into "genotypes," according to level of development, size, and governmental accountability. (Clearly a fourth category is emerging, owing to the fourfold rise in oil prices: rich, but underdeveloped states have emerged, easily distinguishable from rich, industrialized states.) Underdeveloped and developed states, and very large and small states, have fundamentally different foreign policy problems; therefore states in the same genotype, as far as size and level of development are concerned, were chosen. For just over a year after Marcos proclaimed martial law in September 1972, Thailand and the Philippines were in the same genotype on all three counts.

There is also a surprising amount of data on, and a fair number of good studies of, each of these countries, as well as several comparative studies of the two.[8] In the case of Thailand, this is partly owing to the substantial research effort undertaken or sponsored by the American government in the 1960s; in one year the Advanced Research Projects Agency of the Department of Defense had a budget in Thailand of $10 million, or fully a quarter that of the entire American aid program in the kingdom. In the Philippine case, the wealth of data is the result of the research capability of several universities—particularly the very distinguished Institute of Philippine Culture at Ateneo de Manila University.

Finally, both states have had a lengthy association with the United States. True, the Philippine's relationship with America is vastly different from that of Thailand's in character. But the ties of both states with the U.S. were roughly equally complex, sensitive, and important to their own respective futures. Most pertinently, although both states in legal terms may be said to be "equal" to the United States, in wealth, military power, bureaucratic capability, in all the fixed factors that bear on relative bargaining strength, they were both manifestly unequal to the United States. Some factors, like the will of the leadership and the question of which partner, the greater or smaller, needed the other more in a particular situation, were changeable, and often worked to compensate for the inequality in fixed endowments.

In Part I of this book, "Interacting Partners," we look at the patterns of relations between Filipinos and Thai, on the one hand, and Americans on the other, and between their respective institutions, having in the introductory chapter briefly reviewed the background of American military, economic, and political ties with these two Asian states.

In Part II we look at one particular issue, where the United States pressed a specific case on both allies, namely that they send expeditionary forces to Viet-Nam. Both the Philippines and Thailand had had alliances with the United States for over a decade when the latter introduced ground forces into the war in Viet-Nam. But these alliances had been in the process of maturing. Relations between each of the Asian powers with the senior partner were becoming more even keeled, less crisis ridden. The Vietnamese war changed all that. Therefore, we examine the process by which each of these two states decided to involve itself with the United States as that power became so deeply enmeshed in Viet-Nam; and consider whether Thailand's military-autocratic structures or the Philippines' democratic institutions proved more efficacious in coming to terms with the United States on the issue of Viet-Nam.

Great powers can shift direction, with uncertain consequences for the unequal partner. "History, particularly of recent times," foreign minister Thanat Khoman wrote prophetically in 1964, "is strewn with examples of lesser nations being sacrificed by their allies on the pretext of preserving the peace of the world, but actually because the national prestige and vital interests of those allies were not directly affected."[9] As the United States partially withdrew from Asia, owing to her disastrous involvement in Viet-Nam, both Thailand and the Philippines had to adjust their foreign policies; more pertinently, though not as a direct result, they had to remold their polities. The collapse of the non-Communist Indochinese governments in the spring of 1975 added to the urgency of these tasks: though there was a pronounced tendency in both countries to change foreign policy quickly, and to consolidate domestic reforms, even to backtrack somewhat, as the news from the region became grimmer. In Part III we examine in detail the process by which the two states reacted to these great changes, and consider what form of governmental structures proved more efficacious in this period of contraction, so different from the expansionary one of the mid-1960s.

Acknowledgments

The genesis of this study and associated work and the bulk of its support came from the International Development Studies Program at the Fletcher School. Few scholars have made as profound a contribution to the understanding of the way developing states relate internal and external policies as its director, Robert West, who provided the initial focus and continuing support.

A semester's leave in the first half of 1970 allowed me to conduct the Philippine component of the project, under the auspices of the Asian Center at the University of the Philippines, led by Dr. Reuben Santos-Cayugan and Dr. Josepha Saniel. Mr. David Sternberg, General Carlos P. Romulo, Captain and Mrs. Carlos Albert, Executive Secretary Alejandro Melchor, General Fidel Ramos, and Mr. Francis Sionil-José are thanked for their assistance and many kindnesses. Prof. Mary Hollnsteiner and Father Lynch, of the Institute of Philippine Culture at Ateneo de Manila University, kindly permitted me substantial use of highly important data produced under their auspices. Diplomats at the American embassy were also helpful; I especially thank Ambassador Henry Byroade and Mr. William Piez. From my first expressed interest in the Philippines, Eduardo Lachica provided an invaluable combination of camaraderie and criticism; my debt to him is too great to be repaid.

My research in Thailand in 1971, during another semester's leave, was funded by the SEATO fellowship program in combination with continued support from my home base. I am grateful to SEATO not only for the funds but also for almost daily assistance, in particular to M.R. Subidja Sonakul and Mr. Hugh Docherty. Professor William Klausner, whose scholarly knowledge of, and love for, Thailand is exceeded by few people, was enormously helpful. While in Bangkok, I was affiliated with the Institute of Asian Studies at Chulalongkorn University. Hardly a day went by there that Dr. Kusuma Snitwongse did not provide advice and assistance in my research, and her colleagues joined her in their helpfulness. Dean Kasem Suwanakul of the Faculty of Political Science was especially helpful. I also had the benefit of research assistance from two young "Chula" graduates, Mr. Pratheep Nakornchai and Miss Ratanawan Lauhabandhu. No librarians have ever been so helpful to me as those of the Thai Information Center. American embassy officials were unfailingly helpful in Bangkok, and my thanks go to Ambassador Leonard Unger and to his successor, Dr. William Kintner, for their many kindnesses. Dr. Thanat Khoman, for so many years Thailand's foreign minister, was unfailingly courteous. I alone must be responsible for all the conclusions drawn herein, and any mistakes of judgment are despite the substantial efforts made by my talented friends in the Thai foreign service to set me straight on their diplomatic tradition. Though he will doubtless disagree with many of my conclusions, no one could have been more helpful in providing insight on Thai foreign policy than M.L. Dr. Birabongse Kasemsri. He and his colleagues symbolize the enormous effort, in the tumultuous period which this book covers, to preserve the kingdom's autonomy.

Thanks to support from the International Security Studies Program at the Fletcher School I was able to make a final research trip to Bangkok and Manila in December-January 1973-74, which made substantial revision of the manuscript possible, and led me to see where revision of some of my earlier assumptions and conclusions was in order.

Few people are experts on both the Philippines and Thailand. Jerrold Milsted is a happy exception, and for his help in reading several drafts and in adding to my data, I am indeed grateful.

Research assistants and secretaries carry much of the burden of a book like this, and at various times a host of different ones worked on different parts of this book. I am particularly grateful to Gail Fillion and Sylvia Noel, who typed the manuscript several times, and to Richard Kessler, James McCarthy, Charles Lotspeich, and Brian Flora.

My greatest debt of all is to my wife, who collected data, prepared the index, and even more important, took good care of me throughout, and shared the good and bad times that go into the preparation of a book. In the final analysis, she alone saw me through it, and for that I dedicate the book to her.

Unequal Partners

Part I:
Interacting Partners

1 Historical Background

The history of Thailand as an independent and relatively integrated[a] nation-state goes back at least seven centuries. Originally the Thai had emigrated from Southwest China where similar peoples still remain. The fascinating struggle of the Thai against the Khmers, then against the Burmans, as well as against many lesser peoples, has been often and well told elsewhere. Briefly, the Burmese sacking in 1767 of Ayutthaya, the Thai capital, almost destroyed the demoralized and feuding Thai state. A general who emerged from the disaster with a small army and great determination proclaimed himself king and built a new capital at Thon Buri, across the Chao Prya river from present-day Bangkok. King Taksin reunited the country, but after fourteen years of rule his madness led to his execution, and the establishment, by a brilliant general named Chakri, of the present reigning dynasty. For over a century Chakri's line provided the kingdom with wise leaders, at a time when, throughout Asia and Africa, the European colonial powers were expanding their empires rapidly on the map, if not always at a similar rate on the ground. The establishment of a modern bureaucracy in the fifth reign, toward the end of the nineteenth century, is an important example of self-imposed political development in a traditional regime. The kingdom improved provincial administration and extended it beyond its traditional confines, so as to avoid giving the ever-advancing British and French colonialists any pretext for taking control of more than the bare minimum of Thai territory; nonetheless, the European powers took possession of, or began administering, fully a half of what had previously been considered to be under Thai control or suzerainty.

Administrative development did not keep pace with demands after the death of King Rama V (Chulalongkorn) in 1910. The two succeeding kings were relatively weak, while notions of democracy and modernization in a variety of areas were spreading rapidly. In 1932, a group of worldly soldiers and bureaucrats, who knew Thailand could not afford to slip further behind the rest of the world, ended the absolute monarchy in a coup d'état, the first of many. Among the "promoters," as they were called, who made the coup, were groups tending in at least two directions. Political descendants of these two groups would, in one form or another, contend for power right up to the present. Luang

---

[a]The term is used in the sense given to it by Fred Riggs—"to designate the extent to which the actual performance levels of a given social system are adequate to maintain the system at its established level of differentiation." *Thailand, Modernization of a Bureaucratic Polity*, Honolulu, East-West Center Press, 1966.

Phibun Songkram, later field marshal, was the classic praetorian modernizer of the right. By 1938, he had assumed both de jure and de facto power, and brought to government policy a nationalism similar to that in Japan. Pridi Phanomyong, a lawyer and intellectual who, like Phibun, was educated in France, symbolized the quest for democracy and opposition to the Axis during the Second World War. Regent during the war, he became preeminent in 1944 with the waning of Japanese power. While prime minister he was discredited, owing to the mysterious death of the young king, Ananda Mahidon. Eventually Pridi went into exile, first to Paris, later to Peking. Toward the end of 1947, the military seized control of the government; by 1949 Phibun was once again well ensconced in power. As so often happens, a period of weak leadership led to a strong leader's seizure or assumption of power.

The Philippines, in contrast, had no independent existence as a nation prior to the modern era. It got off to a good start maintaining its autonomy as a cluster of only very loosely connected islands and peoples when Lapu Lapu, a chieftain in the Cebu area, killed Ferdinand Magellan on 17 April 1521. But the Spaniards kept coming, and fifty-one years later had established a capital at what is now Manila, from which they ruled north to the tip of Luzon and south through Cebu and Panay down to Mindanao, where Islam reigned. Three hundred fifty years of Spanish rule Christianized most of the non-Muslim Philippines, and beyond that imparted an inchoate sense of nationality, mostly as a reaction to the not exactly enlightened rule of the governors and friars. Not much in the way of economic development and education was done for anyone other than the *ilustrados*, the small landowning elite; which after all was not too different from what went on in Spain.

In the 1890s, a great cultural and political awakening took place, coinciding with, and in part prompted by, growing difficulties between a declining Spain and an expansionary United States. In the Philippines, rebellion grew apace after the founding, in 1892, of the Katipunan, a revolutionary society, to which the *ilustrados* gave no support. Skirmishes between rebels and Spaniards grew larger, but Spain was on the verge of winning when, after the outbreak of the Spanish-American war in 1898, Commodore Dewey entered Manila Bay and destroyed the Spanish fleet. The Americans did not just help the rebels and leave, as the rebels had understood would happen. They stayed and fought for two years, in one of America's bloodiest wars, until they had put down all resistance to their exercise of sovereignty over the archipelago, which they had purchased from Spain for $20 million. President McKinley prayed, he said, that he was doing the right thing in bringing Christianity to the "little brown"—but very Catholic—brothers. Thus what had started as Asia's first modern revolution had become a conservative partnership between the Americans, who needed a competent group with whom to work, and the *ilustrados*, who were capable, and quick to take up the opportunity of sharing power—and privileges—with the new conquerers.[1]

Without a great deal of delay (at least compared with what was happening in British, French, and Portuguese colonies), the Americans got down to the business of political development, at least for a good-sized elite, and education for a relatively vast segment of the population. Her educational policy was to be America's secret weapon in the Philippines up to the present day. She developed and sustained an image of benevolence that was to make her so popular in the villages that through the 1960s no election could be won if it was perceived that the candidate did not have American backing. In 1935, the Philippines attained Commonwealth status, which gave her self-government in almost every area except foreign affairs. This status gave way to independence in ten years. President Quezon contracted the services of General Douglas MacArthur, a retired officer of the American Army, to prepare the country militarily for the responsibilities of nationhood. Everything seemed to be on course.

But much had been left undone, and much had been done badly. American colonial policy had favored an old, rich, and powerful elite which would continue to stifle real social and economic reform for a long time to come. American strategy, such as it was in the interwar years, did not do enough for the defense of her Pacific ward—a "vast debit item," Theodore Friend wrote, though bickering between the elite Filipino groups was equally unhelpful in constructing a realistic defense posture.[2] When the Japanese invaded the country, although there were many collaborators, there was no lack of Filipinos ready to die fighting beside the Americans. There was much heroism, but little help from "Mother America," as the colonial power was known to many Philippine leaders.

Nor did the Philippines, having been an ally, enjoy the benefits of enmity conferred on Japan after the war by the Americans. General MacArthur was to have his finest hour in carving up the Japanese monopolies, redistributing wealth, and, in general, through social and economic reforms, laying the basis for Japan's spectacular postwar surge. It was never likely that the Philippines would be so favored; General MacArthur's aide there was, after all, Andres Soriano, one of the most successful businessmen. Don Andres, though one of the most innovative entrepreneurs in Asia, had no more interest in social reform than had any other of the principal American allies in the Commonwealth.[3]

The Philippines took its independence in 1946, the glory clouded by the devastation of war, the feebleness of her institutions, the unlikelihood of reform, the unsettled issue of collaboration with the Japanese of many of the elite; but the little Philippine boat, to use the metaphor of President Roxas in his inauguration in 1946, knew which great ship to follow. The other colonies that gained their independence at the end of the war got it from declining powers; but America's day had just begun. What was obvious, as far as Philippine foreign policy is concerned in the immediate postwar era, is that the disparity between the little boat and the big ship was to increase, which it continued to do until the late 1960s.

The differences, then, in how the two countries entered the postwar era are obvious. Thailand had gone through the hard school of adversity to learn how to maneuver internationally. Thanks to European imperialism, she had lost control over roughly half of her territory. She had never had a protector, and had faced her gravest crisis—that of the Japanese invasion of Southeast Asia in 1941-42—as an independent state, unlike any other state in the region. It is important to note that the Philippines had no similar freedom of action in finding an inexpensive path to salvation. Fighting alongside the Americans in World War II was making a virtue of necessity, not the best way to learn the lessons of self-reliance.

This brief historical overview helps show why, in developing or sustaining ties with the United States, the two countries were to behave so differently. The Philippines relied on her excolonizer to pave the way for her internationally and to set a lead on numerous critical issues, not just because of her perceived dependence, but because the Americans, peculiarly among colonial powers, had not foreseen the importance of training their wards in diplomacy at any level. America had not herself fully accepted the responsibilities attendant on a nation her size in the international arena during the interwar years. Given America's growing preeminence, it was an understandable conceit that relations with the colonial power, even after independence, were all that was necessary for a Philippine foreign policy. Hence, Filipinos, and Americans to an extent, would see the United States always ready to bail the country out financially, in return for Philippine cooperation on American foreign policy initiatives. Thailand moved just as close to the United States in diplomatic and military arenas but always *appeared* better able to call the shots herself.

In looking at the ties the Philippines established with the United States at independence and thereafter, the crucial point is the weakness of the Philippine bargaining position. It must be remembered that the Philippines had been a very special responsibility of the United States as her colony. Some great Americans took part in her administration and service, ranging from such governors as Cameron Forbes and William Howard Taft to military advisers like Generals MacArthur and Eisenhower. However, Philippine independence in 1946 coincided with the greatest increase ever of American diplomatic involvement with the rest of the world; and consequently, the Philippines dropped dramatically in American priorities. As this was unperceived by the Filipinos, they thought their hold on America was much stronger than in fact it was. For another two decades there were to be many "old Philippine hands" in Washington in the successive American administrations, to whom appeals could be made for special favors and considerations, although such tactics became increasingly marginal to the success of Philippine policy.

Thai-American relations had a more auspicious background. American missionaries and teachers played a respected role during the fourth reign, that of King Mongkut. Formal relations were established in 1856, and, though extraterritoriality was included, the Americans were never considered as demanding as the Europeans.[b] In 1882, the United States was the first country to raise her mission from consular to ministerial level, and, after World War I, was the first to abolish extraterritoriality. The Americans refused to acknowledge the Siamese declaration of war against them in World War II. This was partly owing to Roosevelt's profound condescension, but also to the fact that the Thai minister in Washington shrewdly omitted to deliver the note informing the American government of the declaration. This action, their ensuing wartime cooperation at the intelligence level in the China-Burma-India theater, and their mutual opposition to the return of European colonial rule to the area after the war all led to an American position toward Thailand diametrically opposed to that of Britain, who wished to chastise and severely punish the Thai for their alliance with Japan.[4]

American interests were simply different. A new and friendly regime, composed of the same people with whom America had worked throughout the war, had established itself in Thailand. Sensing the growth of instability in the region, thanks to independence and communist movements, America wanted friendly relations with a continental and Southeast Asian independent power, of which Thailand was the only one. So the Americans forced their allies to lower their demands; however, Thailand did have to disgorge the territory which by Japanese grace she had nibbled off her neighbors. The Americans, then, were friends, something reinforced by the missionary-educational hue of the American presence in Thailand in the past.

Let us now look briefly at the ties established in the military, economic, and political arenas between the United States and these two Asian allies. In the 1930s, the chief issue between the two contending leaders of the islands, Sergio Osmeña and Manuel Quezon, was whether America could hold on to her bases after independence. Although Quezon, the first president of the Commonwealth, did not favor retaining the bases, while in exile in America during the World War, he "granted" the president of the United States, through negotiations, the authority "to withhold or to acquire and to retain such bases . . . as he may deem necessary for the mutual protection of the Philippine Islands and of the United States."[5] Though it has been argued that Quezon's volte-face resulted from his newfound realization of the island's vulnerability, it might be more pertinent to note that few negotiators have ever argued from so weak a position. The Americans used the agreement to keep their established facilities and to add to them a vast number of properties, the most important of which in the resulting network were Clark Air Force Base, with 131,642 acres, and Subic Bay Naval Base, with 36,124 acres.[6] The term of the lease was ninety-nine years.

[b]But not all Americans were in the favored category. A missionary, in 1886, wrote that there were actually "two kinds of Americans who came to Siam, one to Christianize the natives and the other to liquorize them . . . In fact, the missionaries feared to unfurl the stars and stripes because the natives thought that it was the sign of a liquor store." See Virginia Thompson, *Thailand: The New Siam* (New York: Macmillan, 1941), p. 203.

The Americans committed themselves to the defense of the Philippines, which, of course, they also did by merely holding bases on the islands, to serve, depending on one's political persuasion, as a magnet for, or a deterrent to, an attack. The basis of the commitment was first the Military Assistance Agreement of 1947, which in effect committed the Americans not only to sustaining the security relationship, but also to developing an internal Philippine security capability and what in seven years was to become a region-wide capability for the Republic's SEATO responsibilities. A great deal of military-aid money flowed thereafter, $20 million a year in the 1960s and early 1970s. The keystone of the partnership was the 1951 Mutual Defense Treaty which, in its most pertinent passage, stated: "Each party recognizes that an armed attack in the Pacific Area on either of the Parties would be dangerous to its own peace and safety and declares that it would act to meet the common dangers in accordance with its constitutional processes."[7] What that meant was to be the subject of further negotiations and Philippine demands in the future, but it is fair to note that even as ambiguous a commitment as this was unprecedented in U.S. diplomatic history.

The military ties with the United States were very thick—indeed, so much so as to compromise seriously the republic's autonomy in the first decade of cooperation. The Joint U.S. Military Advisory Group (JUSMAG) openly campaigned for Defense Secretary Magsaysay against President Quirino in the 1953 elections, having decided that Magsaysay was the knight in shining armor that the Philippines (and they themselves) needed.[8] As the republic weathered her early crises—rebuilding the economy from the wreckage of war, holding off the Huk rebellion, combatting fiscal insolvency, and so forth—she slowly began to assert her own rights. In 1956, this led to her demand for renegotiations of the military ties. This, the first of many renegotiations, was marked by such rigidity on both sides that the talks failed. President Magsaysay had thought he could easily renegotiate the agreements, but, in order to pay off political debts, he was forced to put several senators on his panel known for their opposition to the Philippine-American defense ties. The Americans saw no point in continuing to negotiate in such an atmosphere. True, a Mutual Defense Board was established, at least symbolizing an American attempt to deal with the former colony on the basis of equality, but it had no real power. Three years later, new talks got much further. However, the principal American concession—to shorten the base lease from ninety-nine to twenty-five years—was not then implemented by the Philippines.

In Thailand, the United States had no such privileged position. Especially with the overthrow of Pridi's liberal regime and the subsequent return to power of the military, the Americans were in no position to expect full cooperation. A turning point in relations came in 1950. President Truman's special envoy in Asia, Ambassador Phillip Jessup, found Luàng Phibun in the same frame of mind with regard to Asian security problems when they met early in the year. Four months later, when North Korea attacked South Korea, Thailand was the first Asian state—over a month earlier than the Philippines—to offer a contingent to fight alongside American forces. The ensuing October, the two powers signed an Economic and Technical Assistance Agreement and a military assistance agreement. Ten million dollars of the latter came in 1950 alone; its peak was over $75 million in 1967. It was not until 1959, when events in Laos scared both Thai and American leaders, that cooperation complemented the military-aid program. From that time cooperation increased for ten years, before it began, ever so slowly, to taper off.

Mutual ties became very solid in this period. Based as they were on cooperation between a militarily expanding superpower and a military oligarchy in a smaller country, these ties were to have a very profound effect on the course of Thai history, determining events far more than similar ties would do in the Philippines. Generals in political positions who maintain their military roles have a strong tendency to let their desire for equipment and their military relations with cooperative allies determine their overall stance, or so it would seem for the Thai case.

Philippine economic ties, for several reasons, are of a different order from those of Thailand with the United States, American policy toward Thailand was always based on security considerations, while the Philippines, trade and American investments there, as well as security, have had a very considerable input on policy. From the other side, Thai policy toward America has been based partly on a desire to obtain economic aid, but this has been less important than the goals in the military-security area. In the Philippines, economic considerations for the Filipinos in relation to the United States have weighed more heavily in national decision-making than is true in reverse; military-security considerations have always been relatively more important to the Americans than to the Filipinos. This is easy to understand when one compares the proportion of total American investments (as Table 1-1 shows) and trade accounted for by the archipelago to the proportion of Philippine trade accounted for by the United States, as Table 1-2 shows.

Although the American business community is hardly without influence in Manila, until 1970 and the advent of martial law, it was unsuccessful in stymying the onward thrust of economic nationalism. Nor has it been able to prevent such specific legislative acts aimed against it as the Retail Trade Act, limiting American participation in various sectors of the economy. There is also much evidence to suggest that until the late 1960s, the embassy and the American government generally was American business's least-used route to influence Philippine decisions. It was a frequent complaint of the business community that the embassy gave American investments a fairly low priority, at least in comparison with military-security questions. Indeed, several high-ranking American diplomats were known to take a condescending view of the pressures of

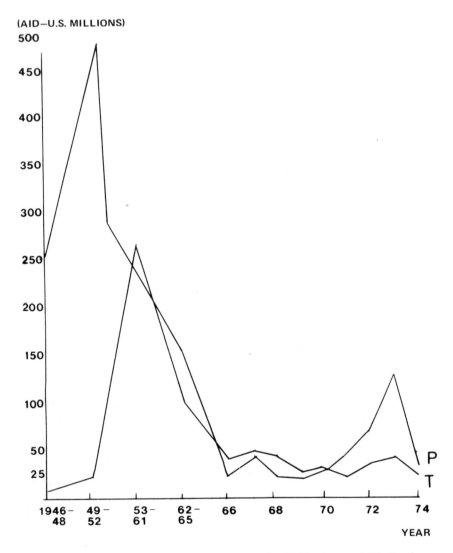

(AID—U.S. MILLIONS)

Figure 1-1. U.S. Economic Assistance to the Philippines and Thailand

American businessmen; Henry Byroade, the ambassador in the early 1970s, who was immensely popular with the American community in Manila because he fought for its interests whenever they were threatened, is a conspicuous exception. Within a year of his arrival in Manila, Byroade had established a reputation as one of the best diplomats ever to be accredited to the Philippine Republic; he thus had more than sufficient personal diplomatic capital with which to protect what were secondary American interests in the Philippines—

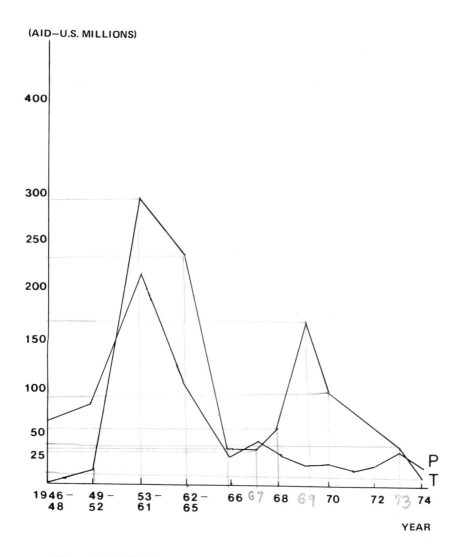

Figure 1-2. U.S. Military Assistance to the Philippines and Thailand

namely American investments. The difference in timing is also pertinent. By the time of Ambassador Byroade's arrival, time was running out for renegotiations of the Laurel-Langley Trade Agreement, through which American investments in the Philippines enjoyed certain types of protection that would expire in 1974. During the tenure of ambassadors G. Mennen Williams and William McCormick Blair Jr., in the mid- and late 1960s, this was less pertinent.

The other side of the coin, Philippine perceptions of which American

Table 1-1

Capital Investments of Newly Registered Business Organizations in the Philippines, 1963-1972

| | (Thousand Pesos) | | | | |
| | Paid in Capital | | | | |
Year	Total	Filipinos	Chinese	Americans	Others
1963	373,524	320,996	44,643	5,048	2,837
1964	340,500	292,290	37,613	9,343	1,254
1965	327,267	268,835	36,641	17,776	4,015
1966	388,009	354,292	27,994	4,066	1,615
1967	419,182	381,802	28,962	2,599	5,817
1968	470,815	426,691	29,811	6,121	8,192
1969	410,024	391,272	13,115	4,539	1,098
1970	437,967	425,018	9,576	1,928	1,445
1971	670,179	645,108	8,230	814	16,027
1972	604,273	577,887	12,079	2,764	11,543

Source: *Statistical Bulletin*, vol XXIV, December 1972, Central Bank of the Philippines, Manila.

interests count more, is understood easily with reference to the nature of the ruling elite. Either implicitly or explicitly, Philippine leaders (and particularly those of wealth), saw their own developing position on the American base lease and defense ties in general, during the 1960s, as a function of the American position on the sugar quota and related questions.[c] Considering that, until the early 1970s, the American consumer paid four times the world price for sugar and that a substantial percentage of the Philippines' $200 million annual sugar bounty went almost straight into the pockets of the central elite of the country; and that the bases are, in fact, a considerable source of foreign exchange ($148,543,596 in 1969, employing ultimately 40,500 people, including contractors and concessionaires), it is easy to see why Filipinos would not want to be rid of the bases as long as the sugar market in the United States remained good, and as long as the bases were bargaining chips for use in trade negotiations.[9]

But the situation is more complicated. Publicly, and amidst a significant segment of the governing elite, American economic ties with the Philippines have been subjected to more abuse, perhaps justly, than any other aspect of the relationship. It was hardly the policy of colonial powers to promote industry in the colonies; that was not what the relationship was about. How free trade between colony and metropole develops the colony as a market for industrial goods and as a supplier of primary products has skewed most relationships

---

[c]A point made by numerous members of the Philippine elite with connections in the sugar world, but in particular by Senator Benigno Aquino.

between former rulers and ruled. Nowhere is this more so than between the Philippines and the United States, where free trade obtained from 1913. Radical groups have a war cry, and nationalistic groups, who have an economic interest in catalyzing a fire sale of American businesses, have lots of kindling.

Moreover, the Americans made an expensive mistake at independence. It was the American calculation that American business would not invest in the Philippines after her independence, given alternative opportunities, unless they had equal rights with Filipinos in certain areas. Nor did it appear that existing American industry in the archipelago would wish to reconstruct their plants unless the climate was favorable. The Philippine constitution, as the Americans saw it, prevented precisely the type of access needed if cooperation were to ensue and American money and expertise to come back to the new republic. Backlogs of demands for equipment in America added to the difficulty of procuring needed industrial goods in Manila, which further added to the urgency of some sort of political guarantee to American industry. Meanwhile the Philippines was seeking vast war-damage claims. The two issues were linked together by the Americans; the Philippines would get American rehabilitation funds, only after it had passed the Trade Act, which *inter alia* gave America parity with Filipinos in the exploitation of natural resources and operation of public utilities. The act also provided for eight more years of free trade, after which gradually diminishing American preferences would be the rule until 1974, when all American preferences in the Philippine market, and those of the Philippines in the American market, would end. The Trade Act required a constitutional amendment, painfully but dutifully supported by the Philippine leadership and resented ever after. In 1954, the treaty was updated and improved so as to confer more benefit to the Philippines; the United States gave up her de facto control of the peso and provided for a faster diminution of American preferences in the Philippine market than of Philippine preferences in the American market—all of this ending in July 1974. As it turned out, the concessions themselves were never to be a significant economic factor in encouraging American investment, after the initial postwar period drew to a close, but they grew in political significance, with the Philippine sense of grievance increasing faster than American concessions could be made.

The Philippine-American aid relationship as seen in Table 1-3 has gone through at least four phases. The first, rehabilitation, brought almost $850 million in loans and grants between 1946 and 1952.[10] A new phase got under way in 1950, with the Bell Mission to the islands sent by Dean Acheson, who was appalled by the lack of discipline in the government there. American aid as intervention, as David Wurfel points out, really began with this mission, as aid for subsequent institutional developmental programs was tied to wide-scale reform—particularly in the areas of taxation (nobody paid any income tax) and labor (there was no minimum wage and much exploitation).[11] Much came out of this, though the epochal attempt by an American advisor to effect a

Table 1-2
Direction of Trade for the Philippines

(value of trade in millions of U.S. dollars)

	1966		1967		1968		1969		1970	
	Exports	Imports	Exports	Imports	Exports	Imports	Exports	Imports	Exports	Imports
DoT Total	842.70	956.90	813.30	1171.80	848.80	1457.60	827.40	1260.55	1042.70	1206.20
Developed Areas	785.20	812.10	736.80	992.00	768.40	1096.10	721.40	1074.30	952.70	1023.10
of which U.S.	332.70	325.10	350.70	402.30	383.30	415.30	343.60	357.90	433.30	354.90
LDCs	57.0	144.30	76.10	179.80	80.40	361.50	106.00	186.25	90.00	183.10

	1971		1972		1973		1974 (Jan.-Sept.)	
	Exports	Imports	Exports	Imports	Exports	Imports	Exports	Imports
DoT Total	1120.80	1329.90	1068.70	1365.00	1886.30	1789.70	1933.10	1585.50
Developed Areas	1015.40	1071.80	985.40	1107.80	1700.30	1454.90	1783.20	1907.80
of which U.S.	452.90	330.60	434.20	352.10	686.70	506.70	847.80	619.70
LDCs	105.40	258.10	79.40	255.40	171.50	309.00	124.90	651.10

Source: International Monetary Fund, IBRD, *Direction of Trade*, monthly bulletin.

Table 1-3
American Aid and Aid from International Organizations to the Philippines and Thailand

Philippines

(U.S. Fiscal Years—Millions of Dollars)

U.S. Overseas Loans and Grants—Obligations and Loan Authorizations

Program	Post-War Relief Period 1946-1948	Marshall Plan Period 1949-1952	Mutual Security Act Period 1953-1961	1962-1965	Foreign Assistance Act Period 1966	1967	1968	1969	1970	1971	1972	1973	1974	Total FAA Period 1962-1973	Total Loans and Grants 1946-1973	Repayments and Interest 1946-1973	Total Less Repayments and Interest 1946-1973
I. Economic Assistance*—Total	256.7	564.2	286.0	158.4	14.6	44.2	19.2	18.7	25.1	40.5	69.9	124.0	60.2	514.6	1,582.5	180.1	1,402.4
Loans	69.2	34.0	75.8	13.9	–	26.2	4.4	–	10.3	20.7	53.6	46.9	37.7	176.0	332.1	180.1	152.0
Grants	187.5	530.2	210.1	144.4	14.6	18.0	14.9	18.7	14.8	19.8	16.3	77.1	22.5	338.6	1,250.4	–	1,250.4
II. Military Assistance—Total	72.6	80.2	218.2	108.6	29.0	42.3	34.2	24.5	25.8	17.1	19.3	37.7	n.a.	338.5	709.7	–	709.7
Credits or Loans	–	–	–	–	–	–	–	–	–	–	–	–	–	–	–	–	–
Grants	72.6	80.2	218.2	108.6	29.0	42.3	34.2	24.5	25.8	17.1	19.3	37.7	n.a.	338.5	709.7	–	709.7

Table 1-3 (cont.)

Thailand
(U.S. Fiscal Years—Millions of Dollars)
U.S. Overseas Loans and Grants—Obligations and Loan Authorizations

Program	Post-War Relief Period 1946-48	Marshall Plan Period 1949-1952	Mutual Security Act Period 1953-1961	Foreign Assistance Act Period										Total FAA Period 1962-1973	Total Loans and Grants 1946-1973	Repayments and Interest 1946-1973	Total Less Repayments and Interest 1946-1973
				1962-1965	1966	1967	1968	1969	1970	1971	1972	1973	1974				
I. Economic Assistance*—Total	6.2	16.1	257.2	112.9	46.7	55.9	49.3	37.4	29.0	24.3	34.0	39.1	25.2	428.6	646.1	45.4	600.7
Loans	6.2	–	49.2	31.6	–	3.5	–	–	–	14.0	23.0	11.9	13.3	72.1	103.1	45.4	57.7
Grants	–	16.1	208.0	81.3	46.7	52.4	49.3	37.4	29.0	24.3	20.0	16.1	13.3	356.5	543.0	–	543.0
II. Military Assistance—Total	–	17.0	299.4	244.6	31.4	33.1	59.5	170.5	102.5	78.9	73.8	42.2	n.a.	836.5	1,152.3	–	1,152.3
Credits or Loans	–	–	–	–	–	–	–	–	–	–	–	–	–	–	–	–	–
Grants	–	17.0	299.4	244.6	31.4	33.1	59.5	170.5	102.5	78.9	73.8	42.2	n.a.	836.5	1,152.3	–	1,152.3

Assistance from International Organizations
(Millions of Dollars)

Country and Program Contd.	1946-1948	1949-1952	1953-1961	U.S. Fiscal Years 1962	1963	1964	1965	1966	1967	1968	1969	1970	1971	1972	1973	Total
Philippines	–	0.1	25.0	43.3	25.6	4.5	27.7	7.9	51.1	3.9	20.5	72.9	67.6	80.3	106.4	536.7
IBRD	–	–	18.4	40.8	18.3	–	25.5	5.0	36.9	–	12.5	58.2	22.3	29.5	11.6	279.0
IFC			–	–	4.4	–	–	–	12.0	–	–	7.4	8.0	15.1	17.2	64.0
IDA			–	–	–	–	–	–	–	–	–	–	–	10.0	12.7	22.7
ADB											5.0	2.5	31.1	23.4	63.0	125.0
UNDP		0.1	4.6	1.9	1.9	3.4	1.3	2.0	1.6	3.1	2.1	4.2	4.1	1.1	0.9	32.3
Other UN			2.0	0.6	1.0	1.1	0.9	0.9	0.6	0.8	0.9	0.6	2.1	1.2	1.0	13.7
Thailand	–	25.7	106.4	2.1	41.1	4.9	25.4	34.6	13.6	57.3	46.1	60.7	28.7	67.2	132.0	645.8
IBRD	–	25.4	95.5	–	36.9	1.0	22.6	31.1	11.0	48.9	20.0	46.5	12.5	42.4	80.6	474.4
IFC			0.3	–	–	0.2	–	–	–	–	22.1	–	0.2	–	–	22.8
IDA															25.0	25.0
ADB										5.0	–	10.0	14.5	18.0	23.0	70.5
UNDP		0.3	9.2	1.6	2.6	2.8	1.9	2.5	1.9	2.1	3.0	3.4	1.0	4.4	3.4	40.1
Other UN			1.4	0.5	1.6	0.9	0.9	1.0	0.7	1.3	1.0	0.8	0.5	2.4	–	13.0

Source: Statistics and Reports Division, Office of Financial Management, AID, *U.S. Overseas Loans and Grants and Assistance from International Organizations*, May 1974.

land-reform program was doomed.[12] From 1952 to 1965, $317 million was given, much less than had been envisaged for this second phase. From 1965, a third phase began with a "more qualitative" approach; which is to say that a much smaller program was run. Aid

began to be systematically concentrated in those key sectors where Filipino initiative and leadership, combined with AID financial or technical assistance, showed great promise of significant economic breakthrough. Thus, in a sense, the "Guam Doctrine" with its emphasis on local initiative . . . reflects not only the direction of AID's programs here in the Philippines . . . but also coincidentally reflects the directions of that program during the closing years of the sixties.[13]

Such diminution of the program, however, reflected a lack of confidence that large programs would accomplish anything, given the mess in which the Philippine government was considered to be. Still, the successes of the third phase were highly important—including, as they did, the "SPREAD" program which "packaged" "miracle rice" with a plan for its effective utilization by farmers throughout the archipelago. From about 1971, the program began to increase substantially, reflecting a growth in American confidence, especially considering that American aid worldwide was declining.

Aid as foreign-policy input was more pertinent in Thailand than in the Philippines in the 1960s. In the Philippines, for reasons already briefly mentioned, the aid program though large in comparison with aid programs elsewhere, was relatively small especially compared with all the other inputs from American money—namely veterans' benefits, military aid, and military spending at the American bases. Filipinos, moreover, have always considered aid part of a sacred debt, as the discharge of American obligations, whereas in Thailand, American aid has always, from its start in 1950, been a function of American, and to a lesser extent Thai, security preoccupations in the area. Aid in Thailand means the Operations Mission, USOM (the name a holdover from earlier days), and denotes a powerful institution that could take part in the bargaining process among institutions in Bangkok.

Especially in the 1960s, Americans felt a sense of urgency about aid to Thailand; three-fourths of it in 1969 was, ultimately, for counterinsurgency purposes. More basically, American aid to Thailand has always been a function of the American conviction that the Thai did not realize how serious was the threat to them—especially in terms of the degree of domestic mobilization perceived necessary to counter the perceived threat. According to an official American paper, the objective of the program was "to build a bridge between the people and government."[14] This is not exactly the way the Thai would have put it, and in the 1970s, it sounds strange indeed, as the objective of the American government in a foreign country. For the Thai, aid programs were accepted because they got a great deal of money for things they wanted to do—and so they put up with the rest of the programs. There was always close cooperation between the Royal Thai government and USOM, if only because the Americans required that the Thai put up a substantial share of every program—often 50 percent, which globally amounted to 8.9 percent of the budget by 1970.[15] Networks of associations were created through membership of American officials on Thai development-oriented committees, and, at the highest level, there has always been a considerable amount of bargaining over aid terms.

In the nature of the Thai and American objectives, with all their differences, the American aid effort has gone toward identifying and supporting those elements it thought would be interested in modernization per se, thus providing those Thai "with a source of influence relatively independent of the power structure of Thai society,"[16] as one former USOM officer wrote—meaning, with a source of influence independent of the *established* power structure, but one intended in part to replace the established power structure. It was this—American support of the modernizing elements—as much as anything that limited the overall importance of aid as a political input, but that from the opposite point of view made possible any progress at all.

In the political realm, to the extent that it is separable from the military and economic areas, we find a difference in the extent of involvement of the Philippines and of Thailand in America's affairs, and of America's in theirs, prior to the mid-1960s. Thanks to their historic relationship with the Philippines, the Americans had innumerable frameworks of influence in the archipelago with which to influence elections, senate votes, or whatever. This relationship was not entirely one-sided. A former high official of the state department commented that General Romulo, while ambassador to the United States, "came close to being declared *persona non grata*" a number of times as a result of his interference in American politics: "Whenever Romulo sensed that he was in trouble with us he would deliver a rousing anti-communist speech to a Rotary Club somewhere so as to make any action against him exceedingly expensive." The Thai-American relationship was, in contrast, a "hands-off" affair. Thai diplomacy in Washington never even attempted to exercise any influence on the American political process, and American diplomacy in Bangkok, perhaps reflecting the fascination and awe with which Americans have always held the Thai, always dealt at arm's length, at least through the mid-sixties, when relations were so complex and close that such could not continue to remain true.

In both Thailand and the Philippines, some elements sought less dependence on the United States, which was always a factor in the political relations of each country with Washington. In Thailand there was, first of all, the restraining influence of the professional diplomats, who were generally anxious lest the generals in power exhibit excessively close ties to Washington. One distinguished Thai diplomat commented:

Thailand almost became a satellite, a client of the United States. At the U.N. if there were no clear-cut instructions, Bangkok would respond to our query: "ask our friends how to vote"—i.e. the United States. But Thailand and the United States did not have an identity of interest on all issues. On some, like South Africa or Israel, America's position would be conditioned by its global responsibilities or particular historic ties. On the Israeli question, Thailand's interest was to have friends in the Arab world, but we often compromised our real interest.

Political ties also varied with the stability of the regime in power, as one faction maneuvered to increase its strength by shifting the balance of the kingdom's relations to the United States. (Even as late as 1970 factions in the cabinet considered using the embassy to redress the balance of forces in the cabinet. Representatives of General Prapat made inquiries at one point as to whether the embassy would recognize [i.e., implicitly support] a new government headed by Prapat following a coup against the premiership of Marshal Thanom.)

To the Philippines, the question of the alliance to the United States was, until the late 1960s, a touchstone of political faith. One was either pro-American or anti-American. The latter included both those genuinely opposed to the alliance on ideological grounds and those simply wishing to diminish their country's dependence on its former rulers. The dispute in 1954 over the slogan "Asia for the Asians" illustrates how central was America's position in relation to the maintenance of an equilibrium in Philippine politics. It all started when a somewhat radical official of the foreign office proposed endorsement of the slogan as a basis for Philippine policy. Benign and obvious as it sounds, the issue nonetheless divided the Congress and many of the politically sophisticated Filipinos into bitterly opposed groups. Those opposed to its use thought it anti-American by implication. Moreover, as a young congressman, Ferdinand Marcos argued, it would ally the Philippines with Communist regimes in Asia.[17]

There was a great similarity between the political objectives of Philippine and Thai diplomacy in Washington. Both wanted an upgrading of the American security commitment to their country and the region in general. But whereas for the Philippines it was more a question of self-esteem, for Thailand it was perceived to be a question almost of survival. Filipinos, for example, were always convinced that the American commitment was less automatic than that of the United States to NATO countries, making the Philippines something of a second-class ally, although American officials always denied it. As late as 1970 it was possible for senior Filipinos to argue that an automatic retaliatory commitment similar to that of the United States to NATO countries should be included in the language of their defense treaty.

Initially, Thailand's diplomacy was entirely within the SEATO framework. Together with the Philippines she pressed for a NATO-like organization and the commitment of troops within the framework of the treaty, but the United

States consistently held back and stalled on the Asian request. In August of 1954 the joint chiefs of staff, for example, recommended that the United States not enter into combined military planning with Manila Pact countries, and not make known to them the details of unilateral American contingency plans to deal with communist aggression.[18]

There was, nonetheless, considerable close cooperation between the three parties. Right from the start, however, Thailand had a higher status in Washington than the Philippines. Too often American policymakers held an underlying contempt for the Philippines hardly in keeping with the closeness of the two parties. Luckily for the alliance few Filipinos ever sensed the essence of the American attitude, though all were aggravated by one or another of its symptoms.

The foreign policy of states is most obviously affected externally by direct relations with other powers, alliances, requests for assistance, economic demands, and so forth. Foreign policy is also affected by the very state of the world as perceived in the given country, which Rosenau calls the "systemic variable." The American role in the international system as a whole, for example, was so substantial in 1965-1975 that her relationship with her adversaries had great effect on smaller third parties, like Thailand and the Philippines. The extent to which the world was seen in Bangkok or Manila as polarized between the super powers inevitably conditioned foreign policy freedom of maneuver.

Consider the security position of our two Asian states in terms of this consideration in 1951 and 1971. The international system, in 1951, was more sharply polarized than it has ever been. Communist forces had seized power in China through military victory, as the Vietminh were attempting to do in Viet-Nam; in Europe, apart from the Baltic republics long since gobbled up by the Soviet Union, six states had fallen to local communist forces, with the help of the Red army. In Korea, United Nations forces were attempting to repulse a North Korean invasion of South Korea (and return to the status quo ante). Whether in fact the picture was less black and white is not pertinent. Thai and Philippine leaders perceived the world in precisely such terms. (Nor is it pertinent in this context to inquire into the extent to which the two leaderships were representative, enjoyed popular support, and had good or bad reasons for fearing the intrusion of communist notions in their countries.)

In Thailand, an insecure military-dominated and conservative regime, whose country had not exchanged relations even with a capitalistic-conservative China, now had, just to its north, a Chinese regime proclaiming world revolution. Whether it could have accomplished such a revolution (as Frank Darling asks)[d] is

---

[d]See Frank C. Darling, *Thailand and the United States* (Washington: Public Affairs Press, 1965), pp. 83-85. Darling's thesis is that both American and Thai leaders overreacted to the threat from China, and that America, in so doing, helped the new military rulers of Thailand to consolidate their position.

irrelevant in this context, because the Thai government perceived China as capable of interference. It is one thing to make a deal with, or practice clever diplomacy toward, a state whose interests are opposed to one's own but whose internal system is similar enough not to pose a threat to one's own existence; the Thai had traditionally tried this with the European powers. It is another thing to cope with powers whose professed goal is not only to replace the leadership in one's state, but also to change the entire structural system there and everywhere else as well. Small wonder, then, that the Thai leadership looked for friends, the only possible one of which, of any relevance, was the United States. For the next fifteen years, the "systemic variable" as it affected the formation of Thai foreign policy remained relatively constant. To be sure, the Thai were aware of other forces in the world and made some minor efforts to act on them; hence various talks and moves with the Soviet Union, and, as time went on, with the North Vietnamese and the Chinese. Given not only the fundamental weakness of a rootless regime trying to rule a kingdom that had for almost its entire history been an absolute monarchy, but also given the state of the world, the regime's desire for as strong links as possible with America is understandable. As a result of their perception of the world, the Thai's overriding objective was a clear American commitment to aid them if they were attacked. The Americans could no doubt have exacted much more in return for what they granted the Thai in the way of promised protection; but as we shall see, both parties were to elicit a fair amount of cooperation and were to practice, consciously or unconsciously, a fair amount of deception.

The Filipinos felt the pressures of the Asian communist victories less compellingly, but they intuitively agreed with the American view, and adopted the American position on international matters as forthrightly as did the Thai. The Huk campaign in their own country reinforced their fears: in 1950, the Huks were on the outskirts of Manila and, had an eleventh-hour effort of great drive and genius not been launched, it is questionable whether the young republic would have averted revolution. Both powers saw the possibility of communism advancing to their respective front doors for a long time thereafter. Thailand, by a process of elimination, and the Philippines by history and choice (reinforced by domestic events), pursued increased security ties with America as the best remedy to their vulnerable positions.

America's East and Southeast Asian allies were throughout the 1950s and sixties the most fervent anti-Communists anywhere; it is in the nature of being a less equal partner to be more papist than the pope. This pleased Washington, and had the intended effect of pushing the Americans in the direction of stronger security commitments in Asia. The dangers from a revolutionary international system to a conservative small power are far greater than to a conservative great power. America's two Southeast Asian allies were consequently more enthusiastic about American participation in the Vietnamese war than was most of offical Washington.

Similarly, being more vulnerable to China than to America, Thailand and the Philippines were slower to appreciate the new configuration of forces emerging in the late 1960s and early 1970s. A "multihierarchical" or polycentric and emergent multicentric world, to use Stanley Hoffmann's terms,[19] replaced the harsh bipolarity of the early 1950s. With a resurgent Japan that, by 1970, could replace America as the Philippines' most important trading partner; with a strong Europe investing and trading in Southeast Asia; with a victorious India possessing strong leadership and unlimited confidence; the point was eventually driven home in Manila and Bangkok that in a less polarized world Washington might need their cooperation less. Consequently the position in the early 1970s was the reverse of that two decades earlier. The United States was withdrawing its military presence from the region as rapidly as the situation in Viet-Nam would allow, and felt encumbered by her treaty obligations to Thailand and the Philippines. In East Asia, the United States concentrated on building ties with China, rather than putting restraints on her. Thailand and the Philippines would have to make their separate peace, so it seemed, with local great powers: but in the meantime, they had made grave choices.

As the period covered in this book drew to a close, the very end which American, Philippine, and Thai policy and cooperation had been intended to prevent, namely Communist rule throughout Indochina, came about. Both Asian allies publicly called for an examination of their relations with the United States, and the Thai even set a deadline for the removal of the United States bases, but both hedged as much as possible in private. Neither precluded the development of new forms of military cooperation. Despite the débâcle in Indochina, Washington had new strategic reasons for holding on to the bases and sustaining the alliances. It was by no means clear how far cooperation could go in these circumstances, but it seemed certain that subsequent chapters to the evolving relationship between the United States and her two Southeast Asian allies could be as interesting as those of the past.

2

Dealing with a Foreign Presence: Filipinos, Thais, and Americans

Diplomacy, foreign policy and international relations result, at a primary level of analysis, from the interaction of people in various roles, acting to advance the interests of different types of systems—self, group, ministry, clan, state, region, alliance. Particularly between unequal partners, differences in customs, morals, or standards of performance may make a vast difference in the success of the relationship, and affect the bargaining power and ability of the parties.

The role of foreigners in the decision-making process of a state, widely discussed in recent years usually under the term *penetration*, has rapidly increased with the growth of interdependence in the postwar era. Every state is a penetrated system, but there is great breadth to the continuum, with China or Albania at one end, where ideology conspires with culture and geography to insulate the state; and Niger or Senegal at the other end, where colonial history and economic vulnerability make *conseillers techniques* or businessmen from the former metropole enormously influential. True, large states have historically been involved in the decision-making process of smaller states whose affairs interest them. The difference lies in the increased participation in governmental affairs of a growing variety of people, not just foreigners. The transnational linkages of business in particular, but also of semipublic agencies, grant to the foreigners accordingly greater access to the decision-making process.

For this more complex modern period further distinctions are in order. Clearly the ability of one country to influence the decision-making of another would appear to vary directly with the disproportion in their fungible power, with the openness of the penetrated state, with their proximity, and with the amount of historical interconnection; and inversely with the homogeneity and coherence of the penetrated nation-state.

On each of these dimensions (except size and proximity, where our two countries are roughly equal in relation to the United States), we could expect the Philippines to be more vulnerable. Openness refers to the lack of governmental strictures against advocacy by citizens; historical interconnection tends to result in shared norms, mores, customs, and the like. The two together in the Philippines mean that American interest groups, including those of the government, can take an active part in the polity's decision-making process, from lobbying efforts by American oil companies to pressures on Malacañang, the presidential palace, by the American ambassador.

The question of language illustrates the importance of shared customs. In

Thailand, the fact that both former premier Thanom and deputy premier Prapat felt uneasy with English made them less accessible to American influence. The embassy in large measure has always worked through intermediaries, not themselves the decision-makers. When American pressure is applied, the Thai often use their unease with English as an excuse to back off and give themselves more room in making a decision.

In the Philippines, the American ambassador can and does take problems directly to the president for long, wide-ranging discussions. Nowhere would the ease of a diplomat's relationship with his counterpart seem of greater import. In early May 1970, Ambassador Byroade took a six-day cruise with President Marcos in the latter's yacht. They only talked business for four and a half hours—yet for Byroade the rest of the time must surely have been ideal for developing and sustaining a position of influence on a foreign head of state. What they talked about most was the impasse over the respective Philippine and American positions on the military bases. The Americans were convinced that this discussion brought to Marcos's attention for the first time data that they felt had long been ignored.

The more different a homogeneous state is from all others—that is, the more idiosyncratic—the more it can and will institutionalize barriers between its citizens and organizations on the one hand and foreigners on the other. If this proposition is true, we would expect American-Thai interaction in Bangkok to be very difficult indeed. There is, for example, a widely noted tendency of Thai society to "punish" a member who participates too intimately with outside powers. But given the parallel interests that the two powers identified in the 1960s and the consequently vast involvement of the United States in Thailand, the old rules were bound to vary. Many Thai found that working closely with the Americans was a shortcut to power in their own bureaucracy: by coordinating with the Americans and fulfilling an important function in that country's programs and objectives, a Thai could quickly gather a staff about himself and move up several notches in the hierarchy. But such beneficiaries only got so far before they got their wings clipped.

The role of the foreign ministry is an example of an institutionalized safeguard against penetration. In a more open society, the foreign ministry might be expected to see its role as one of looking outward for cooperation and, generally good relations with other powers. In Thailand, it was the foreign ministry that tried to keep a good front up for Thai independence; it tried to make the degree of cooperation between Thailand and America in the 1960s seem far less than it was, and to keep American officials at arm's length from all Thai institutions. It played the opposite role of the foreign ministry in Manila. However much the importance of Thanat Khoman as foreign minister may have been qualified in this study, the fact remains that he was allowed to remain in power for about thirteen years, most of which time he spent helping to keep the Americans off guard and at a distance.

It is important to note the differences in penetration between different state systems; apparently similar processes can have quite different effects. When one examines the nature of cooperation between the United States and her two partners, the actual institutions of cooperation may or may not facilitate cooperation. For Thailand cooperation, in reference to her internal decision-making, implies giving away part of one's power. Hence, the joint committees— such as the important one established in the early 1960s to see through the American-instigated programs of economic and social reform—achieved little. If anything, they provided the smaller power with opportunities to penetrate the larger power. For example the aid director could be pressed to elicit more money from Washington and his pleas for reform could be ignored. For this reason, one USOM director shrewdly tried to extricate himself from as many committees as possible. In the Philippines, cooperation can be the cover for American domination and penetration. The Mutual Defense Board, on which the top Philippine officers sit with the commanders of Subic Bay Naval Base, Clark Air Force Base, the ambassador, and several others, makes Filipinos feel part of the American process, and is a useful communications link; but it is peripheral to American policy. Communication between Americans and Filipinos is pertinent only when it is done between powerful individuals.

The implications of how a country deals with a foreign community in its midst are substantial. Given the amount of dependence obtaining between developing countries and one or the other major powers, we can assume that the foreign group in a developing country's capital—the diplomats, military attachés, businessmen, economic advisers, and technicians—are at the crossroads of both the internal and external sources of foreign policy, and of the host country's domestic policy. Robert L. West has argued that differences in the "preferred roles" of foreigners in developing countries "is very frequently at the heart of political conflict between significant opposition groups and the regime, and is also frequently the issue most forcefully articulated."[1] West is concerned with the amount of resilience a host country has in dealing with foreigners, and with the clusters of policies devised to cope accordingly. Countries having institutionalized and depersonalized the management of the foreign presence, "with relatively unfavorable resource endowments, without significant colonization experience, not oil countries, and with a mode of political style providing unusual institutional strength in dealing with the foreign presence tend to have low dependency ranks."[2] This description fits Thailand.

In contrast, countries that manage relations with foreigners in a "highly personalized and particular way,"[3] and in which the "dominating presence of foreigners defines the most widely held perception of dependence, tend to be countries with structural characteristics resulting in high values of the classical indicators of dependence; they are likely to be small countries, to enjoy relatively favorable resource endowments, to have had a significant colonization experience, to include the oil industries, and may have a personalized political mode of dealing with foreigners."[4] This description fits the Philippines, placing it at the opposite ends of a continuum from Thailand.

"Opposition" to a regime must not be construed literally. In most developing countries the pertinent opposition function is that of factions within the regime. Thus in the case of Thailand, while it would be true that, with respect to American aid, the "donor seeks to employ economic resources as an instrument of its foreign policy, frequently to collaborate more or less purposefully with the aid-receiving government in altering domestic structures,"[5] it is equally pertinent to try to determine which segments of the government wished to alter which structures. Some just wanted the money. Others wanted new organizations to buttress their own positions, others wanted nothing.

In the Philippines, prior to martial law, the foreign presence was a fundamental issue between government and at least part of the opposition—namely the uninstitutionalized opposition (students) and the illegal opposition (Huks, Maoists, Muslim sucessionists). The formal opposition, save for the early postwar elections,[a] did not differ on the American role.

The Thai have many advantages for coping with a foreign presence. Pride in their seven hundred years of continued sovereignty gives them "the unquestioned assumption that they run their own affairs,"[6] something quite different from an ex-colony. It was therefore always important to the regime to play down the role of Americans in the kingdom.[7] The average citizen, who thinks little about politics, would not take kindly to the notion that his country depended on some other country for anything important. Much effort has gone into the management of the American role and its image in Thailand.

The kind of confidence the Thai have in dealing with foreigners can result in strategies designed to keep the great power off balance. A USOM memorandum, for example, remarked that in

some important instances, major program decisions have been taken and finalized within the Thai CD [Community Development] organization without USOM or concerned ministries of the RTG [Royal Thai Government] being aware that these decisions were under consideration. . . .

USOM would then be confronted with a fait accompli and deprived of the usual opportunities for negotiation and expression of opinion before major policy decisions affecting joint operation . . . are taken. Obviously such a situation also has destructive effects on coordinating relationships involving concerned Thai ministries.[8]

---

[a]"The influence of the sugar bloc was enhanced in the early postwar struggle between the Liberal party and the Nacionalista parties in which the Liberal party, with strong participation and financial support by the sugar industry came out on top." Frank H. Golay, *The Philippines; Public Policy and National Economic Development* (Ithaca, N.Y.: Cornell University Press, 1961), p. 135, fn. 26. The issue, of course, was policy toward the United States and its lucrative sugar bounty.

The Thai have also been able to minimize the importance of advice while maximizing total amounts of aid. Advice was sought quite pragmatically in the old days: no *farang* (foreigner) is more honored in Thailand, for instance, than Francis Sayre, who negotiated the extraterritoriality clauses out of existence for Thailand in the 1920s. M.R. Kukrit Pramoj, a most distinguished Thai, has noted that it traditionally was prestigious for ministers to have *farang* advisors–but that it became increasingly important, as time went on, to humor them to keep them irrelevant.

By the 1960s it seemed that enough Thai were trained for experts from abroad to be unnecessary. Then, why keep them, George Tanham recounts asking a Thai. Because they were free, was the response. And, far more important, "a lot of aid came with them."[9] Whenever advisors began to become relevant, they were negotiated out of existence. Originally, for example, an American advisor was assigned to every provincial governor in the "Accelerated Rural Development" program ("The Governor continues in his failure to delegate authority commensurate with responsibility, despite lip service to the contrary")[10], but they were progressively weakened in position and finally removed.[11] As one USOM official noted, new arrivals there usually had to get slapped down at least once by a Thai counterpart before realizing that aid to Thailand was very different from aid to any place else. As American aid began its rapid decline in the 1970s pressure mounted for an equally rapid demotion of American advisors.

The negotiation of the status of American forces (SOFA) indicates another aspect of how Thailand handled the vast intrusion of Americans, which compares very dramatically with how functionally equivalent problems were handled in Manila. In 1967, when the build-up of the bases had already begun, discussions were held attempting to find a satisfactory way of handling the perenially complex problem of legal rights of forces stationed away from home and country. The first round of discussions was abortive–largely because the Thai really did not wish to have legal agreements about something so sensitive. Without agreements the existence of a problem could be denied. If the commonality of interests that brought the troops there dissolved, the troops could be asked to leave. A SOFA probably would give Americans rights they could not expect under Thai law. The Americans wanted an agreement; long experience in dealing with host governments convinced them that even a short stay necessitated clear and binding understandings as to whose law would apply in which sort of cases. They quickly realized they could not get an acceptable agreement, so they tried devising with the Thai a peculiarly Thai solution. The fact that the American negotiator was Ambassador Leonard Unger, who well understood Thai sensitivities and sensibilities, made this possible. Working with the military and with Thanat in one of the few instances where the foreign ministry became involved in such matters, Unger arrived at this solution: Thanat, a lawyer, recited to Unger everything in Thai law that applied to foreigners–

particularly to servicemen stationed in Thailand charged with commission of a crime. This recital stated precisely what their courts provided for in general, but was not a commitment that Thailand would abide by those regulations. The American position was very simple; it was politically unacceptable for Thai courts to try Americans for on-duty crimes. Most of these involved automobile accidents; so the Americans hired Thai to do almost all the driving. The solution worked well. When serious crimes were committed, the Americans, with Thai agreement, quickly and quietly shipped the offender home for trial.

With all this, it is small wonder that Herbert Phillips could argue that

on balance there is much greater adaptation on the part of the Americans to [informal] Thai political processes . . . than there is political adaptation on the part of the Thai to the availability of American largesse. . . . Although American financial power obviously influences in some ways the Thai decision-making process and the fortunes of some individual Thai leaders, the Thai political system has a powerful historical and institutional integrity of its own . . . which results in American deferring to Thai demands far more frequently than they dominate them.[12]

But as will become increasingly evident, the American return on the investment of its deference was certainly deemed sufficient.

The American presence is nowhere more evident in the Philippines than at the bases; the biggest uproars are always over jurisdictional problems there. The ruckus caused by these disputes is astonishing. Clearly the question of jurisdiction is symbolic of the whole issue of sovereignty, and particularly critical in relations with the former colonial power. To the average Filipino the U.S. was virtually a coexisting, and often competing, sovereign in the archipelago, and his sensitivity to the American role can be indicated statistically. In countries where the United States stations forces it is customary for American commanders to request waivers of jurisdiction for their men charged with crimes that come under local law; in the U.S.-Philippines bases agreement, the Philippines agrees to give favorable consideration to American requests, except where the case is considered important. The reason for this is obvious: if American military courts can try the case, it is handled expeditiously at no expense to the host nation, and there is no bilateral diplomatic problem. Presumably in most cases justice is done. The percentage of waivers granted is:

NATO	94.8%
Worldwide	83.5%
Philippines	00.9%[13]

The most difficult problems in Philippine-American relations have been over crimes at the bases, or committed by American soldiers off the bases. In

1965 panels of Americans and Filipinos negotiated a new agreement regulating responsibility and jurisdiction: the Mendez-Blair agreement, unlike the original 1947 agreement, conceded to the Philippine side jurisdiction over "off-duty" offenses committed inside U.S. military bases, and deprived the U.S. of jurisdiction over Filipinos "unless they are in the U.S. military service."[14] The trade-off, which brought the agreement into line with American agreements elsewhere, was that thenceforth the determination of whether or not a crime was committed on duty was no longer for the provincial "fiscal" (the prosecutor) nor even ultimately for the secretary of justice, who previously had had the option of trying off-duty cases in Philippine courts. It was to be determined by the base commander; which in 1969, however, he was to do in only 3 percent of the cases.

The year 1968 was a difficult one in Philippine-American relations. Some of those whose powers had been diminished by the 1965 agreement began questioning whether the Mendez-Blair agreement were even in force; on 14 November Justice Secretary Teehankee ruled that it was not, and so informed the Department of Foreign Affairs.[15] The motive for disagreement is not clear, and no doubt varied from group to group. Some certainly felt that the agreement had never been legally ratified, and others resented its disadvantageous aspects. Within the American embassy, it was felt in certain offices that the Justice Department's reversal also derived from the quite separate desire to get rent for the bases. (Rent has always in effect been paid in the constant $20 million in military assistance, but it is not rent in the sense that the American government pays for Spanish bases.) They suspected that the Filipinos wanted to exploit existing irritants in order to increase their bargaining power in negotiating rent.

A case of murder was at issue at the time. Corporal Kenneth Smith had killed a Filipino at Sangley Point Naval Base, and the Americans asserted jurisdiction. The Filipinos apparently fearful that Smith might escape conviction, did not wish to try him in any case; an innocent verdict would look worse coming from an American court. To make certain of avoiding jurisdiction they disavowed the Mendez-Blair agreement and claimed that the 1947 agreement was still in force. They did not attempt to get rent, though in the ensuing spring the new justice secretary, Juan Ponce-Enrile, sustained Teehankee's opinion that the 1965 agreement was not in force. By this time another American had killed a Filipino, at Subic Bay, and inflamed public opinion still further by testifying that he thought he was shooting at a wild boar. Jurisdiction in this case went to the Americans, as the Filipinos did not assert it soon enough. The accused was acquitted in his court-martial. Relations at the public and judicial level sank to a new low.

By early 1970 the situation had changed, and there was new harmony in Philippine-American relations at the top, following riots and troubles that frightened Marcos and led him to strengthen ties with Washington.[16] It had been agreed to renegotiate the military bases agreement once again, so in March 1970 the Philippine government reversed its position and decided that the Mendez-Blair agreement was in force. According to an embassy official, "We agreed with President Marcos that there was no point in negotiating in the circumstances previously prevailing, or until we knew what we wanted to end up with."

But now a very ticklish problem presented itself. The case this time involved forcible abduction with attempted rape, charged on 21 September 1968. The defendant, Sergeant Bernard Williams, who had first appeared as a witness for another person originally charged, was tried in 1969, with the prosecution resting what the court eventually found to be a very weak case on 15 July. Williams's tour ended in November, and because the Filipinos had not taken the normal administrative steps to alert base authority that Williams must remain in the country pending the verdict, he was able to leave.[17] The officer responsible at the base, Lt. Col. Raymond Hodges, was relieved of his duties and reassigned before the case was resolved, and the ambassador began pleading with the Air Force in Washington to get Williams back to the Philippines. The Secretary of the Air Force so ordered on March 19, 1970, but Williams obtained an injunction from the U.S. District Court for North Dakota restraining the Air Force from returning him. The issue was headline material every day.[18]

The Angeles City Court judge, Ceferino Gaddi, "the short Pampango with a tough and uncompromising passion for justice,"[19] issued an order on June 19, finding Hodges—as well as the base commander, Colonel Averill Holman—in contempt of court, and ordered them to be " 'imprisoned in the Provincial Jail of San Fernando, Pampanga, to be released only upon their compliance with their undertaking in the custody receipt, that is, *upon the surrender to the Court of defendant Bernard Williams.*' "[20] The official American position was that it was not Holman's problem, but the U.S. government's. And since

Colonel Holman does not have the authority to order Sgt. Williams back . . . the Court's order . . . could be interpreted to mean that the Court is attempting, through the imprisonment of Col. Holman, to make him a hostage to compel the United States to take the action the court wants. This is obviously improper since, under the rules of international law, the courts of one sovereign state cannot assert jurisdiction over another sovereign state.[21]

Holman was doing whatever he was doing on duty, and under the Mendez-Blair agreement that was clearly for him to determine.

Ambassador Byroade and President Marcos, working closely together on many issues in this period, decided that they could not sustain an harmonious relationship between the two countries with such problems recurring. From the American point of view it was preposterous that base commanders should be in the position Judge Gaddi had put them. Byroade, it was claimed in the local press, asked for and got a de facto alteration of the bases agreement, making it impossible for local courts to discipline base commanders for their on-duty work, but this was denied at the embassy.[22] The Americans did manage to settle this particular case amicably. Marcos resented Judge Gaddi's attempt to make Philippine foreign policy for him, and dropped him as a fiscal right after martial law was proclaimed.

In effect this is how business was always done between the two governments in the first Philippine Republic. Popular resentment or feelings of one kind or the other poisoned the atmosphere; strong individuals attempted to interpret the law forcefully in a role-serving way; the impasse was resolved by the president and the ambassador.

Little directly comparative data on Philippine and Thai popular attitudes exist. Phillips's study of the Thai peasant personality, in which the sentence completion technique was used, was, however, replicated by scholars at the Institute of Philippine Culture, and the results were compared.[23] Whether a comparison of peasant values will shed light on differences in foreign policy is debatable. But to the extent that the peasant personality represents a "national personality," and to the extent that these subvariables compose part of the patterns of national adaptation, we are entitled to use the results cautiously. No one will object to the point that differences in societal attitudes and structures will have some effect on policy, however: how far we can take them is less clear. When Congressman Rivers publicly called General Romulo "ungrateful," because of some mildly anti-American remarks in early 1970, the reaction at every level of Philippine society was out of proportion to the insult intended. The charge of being "ungrateful" is possibly the most serious that can be leveled at a Filipino; it suggests that he has failed to do his part in the entangled game of life, *utang na loob*—the reciprocal obligations of leader and follower—in which he is enmeshed. Most Filipinos view their relationship with the United States in terms of the reciprocal benefits and obligations of follower and leader, and most feel that Washington has rendered insufficient benefits. Americans tend not to agree, which makes for trouble.

The results of the IPC tests are interesting:[24]

Filipino (N=80)   Thai (N=55)

2. When he is in the presence of an important person he feels . . .

Identification	10%	Esteem	64%
Elation	12%	Discomfort	25%
Discomfort	66%		

3. When his boss gave him an order which he knew was wrong he . . .

Do not fulfill	76%	Do not fulfill	53%
Fulfill	11%	Fulfill	36%

* * *

5. When he asked if he wanted to become boss he . . .

| Accept offer | 74% | Accept offer | 21% |
| Reject offer | 16% | Reject offer | 69% |

* * *

11. When he found that his best friend spoke against him he . . .

Anger	36%	Anger	66%
Confront	15%	Talk it over	10%
Hurt, silent	30%	Distress	10%
Avoid	12%	Counsel him	13%

* * *

16. People who never show their feelings are . . .

| Disapproved | 52% | Disapproved | 12% |
| Approved | Rare | Approved | 80% |

* * *

25. When he insulted me I . . .

Anger	14%	Anger	40%
Hurt, but smile	17%	Depression	13%
Avoid	39%	Improve self	14%
Retaliate	9%	Avoid	14%

Some of the inferences are self-evident. As the authors conclude:

Power and authority may be much more transitory among Filipinos and—cause or effect?—much more an area of emotional conflict. . . . The data suggest some differences in the role of friendship, with the possibility that Filipinos become more deeply involved in their friendships. They emphasize that a true friend loves and understands, and report more frequently than do Thais that they are personally hurt if a friend fails them. At the same time, they are less likely than Thais to respond with indifference to rejection by friends.[25]

Perhaps more interesting is the difference in reaction to important people. Combined with the historical effect of American colonialism, the discomfort which 66 percent of the Filipinos feel, and esteem that 64 percent of the Thai feel, surely explains in part the relative ability of an American ambassador in Manila and Bangkok to accomplish national objectives through personal diplomacy.

The other side of this coin is the American attitude toward her partners. The view of the dominant partner historically will have an important conditioning effect on the attitude of the smaller partner. In the mid-1960s, the United States clearly had far greater respect for Thailand than for the Philippines; almost until the end of our period Thai status in Washington was vastly higher.

Lyndon Johnson, then vice-president, returned from his Southeast Asia tour in 1961 speaking highly of Marshal Sarit, who was "more strongly and staunchly pro-Western than many of his people"; this while Sarit was busy accumulating his vast fortune, and his chief advisor was playing the American ambassador off against the Russian. Johnson's trip had, he observed, countered neutralism in Thailand and—note the change of tone—"anti-American election demagoguery in the Philippines."[26]

At one conference of American military planners, it was decided that the Philippines was not to be trusted in bilateral contingency planning over Laos, and throughout the Pentagon papers we find instructions that the Thai be briefed more fully and earlier than the Filipinos because the Philippines presented "a constant threat of untimely leaks."[27] This was a good reason, but not the real reason. Later in that decade, American policy-makers usually placed Japan, Indonesia, and Thailand ahead of the Philippines in importance to America in Asia, and some even interposed Singapore. Japan's place is unquestioned. But to place Indonesia (not to mention Singapore), solely for its importance as a growth stock, ahead of the Philippines, seat of the largest overseas American base in the world *inter alia*, highlights one of the obstacles that country faced in Washington—where, in the words of one official, "every day [was] dump-on-the-Philippines day." In testimony to Congress in 1968, cabinet officials spoke disparagingly of the Philippines, and referred to the lower stability of its political institutions as compared with those of other countries in the region! Thanat Khoman has noted his awareness of how familiarity has bred contempt in the American view of her former ward and of how—in his view—the United States cannot stand those who like her, much less those who do anything for her. A fitting amount of contempt was the remedy, which Thanat and other sensitive Thai were willing and able to apply, sometimes with success.

The American view in this period was also influenced by the comparatively greater sense of urgency felt to obtain Thai cooperation in the Vietnamese war. This also helps us to determine what the relative desire of each smaller party was to obtain the cooperation of the other, who is consciously more useful to whom, and thus which smaller party will have the greater bargaining power. It is easy to see how America held the upper hand in Bangkok when those two parties started a new intense phase of their relationship in 1950. In receiving American aid, the Phibun regime not only got help against the threat of communism, which America was also getting through Thailand, but it also got legitimacy for itself, which it badly needed. In contrast, as one of the best American diplomats dealing with Thailand has argued, the Thai got so much of what they wished in the 1960s because they astutely realized that at this later period it was more important for the Americans to have Thai cooperation, to keep Thailand as an ally in the Vietnamese war, than it was for the Thai to have America's; the Thai thus only had to play hard to get.

By late 1960, Washington had become obsessed with the importance of Laos; President Eisenhower thought it so important that, if others would not move with them, the United States would " 'intervene unilaterally,' " Arthur Schlesinger records.[28] Thailand was one key to Laos, particularly if a neutralist solution were ruled out, and as long as Marshal Sarit, a relative of the then Laotian prime minister, maintained his very close links with Vientiane. The concern for Laos was symptomatic; the ultimate concern was the fate of countries like Thailand and South Viet-Nam. One part of a very high-level official American study of Thailand in 1969 concludes that, at least by the autumn of 1960, the Thai had already discovered how much bargaining power they had, at which point they began pressing—through the American Embassy in Bangkok and Ambassador U. Alexis Johnson—for a clearer security commitment than that in SEATO. They wanted one which would not wholly be bogged down either in America's "constitutional process," with discretion left to the executive whether or not to respond to aggression, nor, more pertinently, left in the hands of the other SEATO allies who might or might not go along.

By 1962, South Viet-Nam still had not become stage center for American policy. There remained a near equivalence of American concern for Thailand, Laos, and Viet-Nam, even as she became more anxious about events in the latter two, for then Thailand's cooperation became all the more necessary as a backup. But no matter to what extent Bangkok saw friendly regimes in Vientiane and Saigon as her front lines of defense, she, unlike those two neighbors, was not directly threatened. Her own insurgency consisted of a few cadres. The Pathet Lao and Vietcong were a long way from digesting the entirety of their respective target countries. The long-run threat to Thailand was of course far greater than any threat Asian developments could hold for America. But the shorter term needs and capabilities in the context of a policy in a given place defines bargaining power—"in the long run, we are all dead." Had the threat been direct, Thailand would surely have mobilized and given far more aid to Laos than she had been giving through some minimal cooperation, for example, in intelligence. To be sure, Thailand had watched Tonkin become a Communist state and was now witnessing the crumbling of the South Vietnamese regime. There was plenty of room for anxiety, and planning, in any event, had to be done on a "worst possible case" basis, which meant America had to be tied down far, far more.

The Thai succeeded in this stage. In 1962, President Kennedy airlifted 12,000 troops into Northeast Thailand to bolster her defenses (and, more importantly, to demonstrate the American readiness to help) as the Laotian situation deteriorated, and Secretary Rusk signed an accord with Foreign Minister Thanat Khoman affirming that the United States would act unilaterally in the SEATO framework, without fear of veto from France or Pakistan, if Thailand's defense required it.[29] As the war in Indochina escalated and in discussing contingency plans to bolster Laos in June 1964, a consensus was reached at an American strategy conference in Honolulu that the starting point for our bilateral consultation should be Thailand, since that government's confidence in the sincerity of the U.S. commitment seemed particularly needful of being shored up.... Ambassador Martin echoed the themes which he had reported earlier in cables—that the Thais were not convinced that we meant to stay the course in Southeast Asia and probably would not participate in or permit allied troop build-ups in their country without firmer assurances than had been given in the past.[30]

At least in part this was bluff on the Thai part. Thus, Washington was not reluctant to pay the price exacted by the Thai. It made additional requests of the government almost daily in 1964, so that, in the view of many policy-makers of the day, the United States was very indebted indeed to the Thai.

Seen from Washington, the focus of Thai-American relations from the early 1960s was also what may be called "the problem of the Northeast," though as time went on, the problem concerned much more than just that part of the kingdom. The Northeast has always been something of a Thai stepchild: though Northeasterners are unquestioningly Thai, and see themselves as owing loyalty to the Thai state, some central Thai admit it only reluctantly. The dryness and location of their region has kept it economically far behind the central kingdom throughout modern history, with the gap widening in recent years despite fairly extensive efforts recently to narrow it as shown in Table 2-1. The presence of 50,000 or so Vietnamese refugees, most of whom emigrated after 1954, and the proximity to Viet-Nam, made New Frontiersmen nervous about the possibilities for insurgency there.

This concern had a respectable history; the American-financed Friendship Highway, completed in the 1950s, was built to open up the kingdom, strengthen the army's forward posture in the region most strategically vulnerable to the new communist state of North Viet-Nam, and make control of potential insurgencies possible. Ambassadors Alexis Johnson and Kenneth Young in the period 1958-62 were both highly concerned about the Northeast, and the latter spent considerable time in 1960-61 educating official Washington about the problem. In 1961, a SEATO study committee with much American participation con-

Table 2-1
Per Capita Production by Region, Thailand (in dollars)

Year	Region			
	Central	South	North	Northeast
1961	159	125	76	61
1967	222	150	100	69
Increase 1961-1967	40%	19%	32%	14%

Source: Address by Puey Ungphakorn, Bangkok, May 28, 1969.

cluded, after quite systematic examination of the possibilities for insurgency throughout Southeast Asia, that the Northeast would be likely to have an insurgency within two or three years.[31] Although Marshal Sarit, himself a northeasterner, was increasingly concerned about the region's development, the fact was that the government generally discounted the possibilities for a real insurgency there, and, when one began in 1965, a little behind SEATO's schedule but perhaps a bit ahead of its own, the Thai continued to discount it. The Americans, who by late 1962 had devised a plan of action for dealing with the Northeast, had to find a way of awakening the whole of Thai society to the challenge to it, if the plan were to be used. In time, insurgencies developed in the North, and in a slightly different way in the South; that, and the development of a much worse one in South Viet-Nam to the East, broadened American involvement in Thailand all the more—for the Americans began trading off Thai help (or at least their symbolic involvement) on the latter in return for their own continued help to the Thai on the former. The Thai, however, were usually unenthusiastic about helping Viet-Nam, and apathetic about help from America in solving or even recognizing Thai insurgencies; indeed they sometimes suspected the Americans of inventing the latter as a pretext for supplying aid, and thus having a basis for expecting help in Viet-Nam. As the Americans began to withdraw from Southeast Asia, in the late 1960s, their leverage for accomplishing those changes in Thai society, without which they could not envisage its survival in its existing form, declined further. Their continued need for an "unsinkable aircraft carrier" near Viet-Nam into the 1970s made the Thai bargaining position even stronger.

In the case of the Philippines, the administrative machinery was so weak and corrupt (the Americans assumed), and the rot in the social fabric of the land so pervasive, that the destruction of democracy (and perhaps, of the American alliance) would come from within. During the Macapagal administration (1961-65), the failure of land reform and the generally low level of political performance in that period, as assessed by the Americans, followed by a resurgence of the old Hukbalahaps in central Luzon and still later by the birth of the Maoist New People's Army, along with student riots, strikes, and an astronomical crime rate in Manila, all tended to reinforce this image, however inflated.

The worry was never excessive, for aid levels remained low until the early 1970s. Both because the Philippines was further from Viet-Nam and because her general cooperation could be assumed, Washington could give it much lower priority, though oddly they considered it to be in much more serious trouble of its own making. "For some years now, we have carried out limited training and institution-building programs only in the Philippines, to prepare for the day when a purposefully directed national will for economic and social development would emerge," was the rather artful and euphemistic way in which American policy was rationalized in 1967.[32] The assumption was that the Philippines could not absorb more than the small amount of aid it was getting, several million dollars a year, until it "straightened itself out"; the absorptive capacity of a country was hardly an important criterion of aid policy elsewhere in Southeast Asia in the 1960s, however.

3 Interstate and Transnational Interaction: Parallel Hierarchies in Bangkok

Relations between countries, as we saw in the previous chapter, are mediated through individuals, and the attitudes citizens bring with them to the process of interaction, greatly affect the pattern of relations between two powers. *States* interact most obviously internationally; that is, as sovereign states respecting each other's legal equality. Such interstate interaction is generally handled by prime ministers and foreign ministries. *Nations* interact transnationally—that is, to use Samuel Huntington's definition, through large, hierarchically organized, centrally directed bureaucracies, performing a set of relatively limited and specialized functions across boundaries "and, insofar as is possible, in relative disregard of those boundaries."[1] In this chapter we will look at examples of interstate and transnational interaction of the United States with Thailand, as, in the ensuing chapter, we examine the Philippine case. We start by examining the American hierarchy, with which both Southeast Asian states must deal, and the pattern of interstate diplomacy between the two parties.

The United States has complicated problems of coordination as she tries to influence her partners in Bangkok and Manila along desired directions, and many of these are built into the situation bureaucratically. The American embassies in Bangkok and Manila, among America's five biggest in the entire world, are vast establishments. In some areas of common interests, the American department is as large as that of the host government, and, very often, subsystemically, more efficient. But an embassy and all its ancillary agencies together is not a corporation susceptible to leadership (much less efficiency) in the organizational sense. The leader is the ambassador, whose job is diplomacy. There is never time to coordinate, as one mission coordinator put it; and there are always deadlines for achieving a goal—with the result that the individual agencies procure the same items from different suppliers or compete to do the same job in a given area. Programs are seldom budgeted in terms of priorities.

Much has happened since Kennedy's 1961 memorandum giving the ambassador the power he needs to contain the feudal lords of the country team. But given the speed with which the American presence increased in Thailand in the 1960s, it was inevitable that problems of coordination be acute. The conflict between General Stilwell, the chief of the Military Assistance Command (MAC-THAI), and Ambassador Graham Martin is legendary. Martin's ultimate success in bridling Stilwell was achieved at great cost (including considerable noise). One very senior official commented that such friction "is usually the case where you have a military assistance program in a country run by a military junta."

The problems existing between the United States Operations Mission, (USOM), the local AID agency in Bangkok, and the embassy were usually even greater. Because AID missions are usually in separate buildings from the embassy, an organizational *esprit* usually develops, further hindering good relations in the American community. In the mid-sixties, USOM was directed by a strong-minded official named Howard Parsons, himself a former economic counsellor at the embassy. The supervisor of the economics office at the embassy, J. Robert Fluker, a high-ranking official by the time of Parsons's arrival at USOM, insisted that all programs be channeled through his office. USOM simply refused; Parsons is said to have instructed his staff to have nothing to do with Fluker's office. The problem persisted for their successors; the economics section of the embassy would ask for monthly accounts of activity, which would come the month after the request and not thereafter. (The ambassador could have easily corrected such a situation—so it would seem—through his power to approve the annual program review, but the multiplicity of the demands on him made such a review difficult.)

Despite the many permutations of AID since its beginning, its officials have developed considerable identity in their roles as development-oriented experts. Although they are sent abroad explicitly to serve American interests as defined by the president and his advisors, it is easy to see why most should come to see economic development, per se, as the single American interest—and to consider the embassy ill equipped to advise them on their mission. AID officials will often distrust colleagues who appear to work too closely with the embassy, or who do not instinctively rebel against embassy direction. Members of AID in the country bureaucracy will often work to isolate coworkers who associate too closely with the embassy. Such individuals will resent the fact that their foreign counterparts appear less interested in economic development than they themselves. Samuel Huntington has astutely noted that as donor agencies (like AID) have economic development as their *raison d'être,*

and since governments are inherently multi-purposed, this situation should cause neither surprise nor alarm. It does mean, however, that the economic development goal which may be the be-all and end-all for donor agency officials is only one of several targets for the harassed and cross-pressured political leaders of the recipient government.[2]

Fred Von der Mehden has suggested that no group of people in the American community abroad has closer working relations with local officials than the AID group, and none has less understanding of its own purpose.[3] The misdirected idealism and occasional ignorance are often staggering.

The embassy is in something of the same position as the host government, pressed on different sides by people with different role-derived views of the function of various American programs, and of the whole American objective. Thus with economic assistance: while AID officials will see it as the allocation of resources to affect changes in the socio-economic structures of the host country, military attachés will see it in security terms, and the ambassador may see it as a simple payoff; which it may be, with unintended economic consequences.

Having declined in the early 1960s to the point where AID promised Congress to phase it out, the program in Thailand suddenly shot upward. A former AID official wrote:

It seems therefore somewhat unlikely that American concern for insurgency in Thailand would have been the sole, or even the primary, reason behind the complete reversal in aid plans. . . . There was in 1964 little generally available evidence of communist activity in rural Thailand; and the U.S. military was not overly concerned with the possible development of guerrilla warfare either. It does not seem probable that, only on the basis of what was known about communist activity in 1963 and 1964, plans would have been laid, as they were, for such a radical increase in aid. Numerous audits and evaluations in recent years have shown that aid increased much more rapidly than normal AID procedures would have permitted, to the extent that the absorptive capacities of recipient agencies were seriously strained. It has been not implausibly argued, therefore, that the rapid increase in American economic aid to Thailand represented at least in part a form of rent for American use of Thai air bases in conjunction with the Vietnam war.[4]

In such a situation, the managerial objective of the embassy must be to maintain enthusiasm among people, like the aid technicians, who often have little understanding of the broader political interests they serve.

At the other end of the continuum from AID are the intelligence operatives of the United States in both countries. The Thai are particularly suspicious of foreign intelligence, owing to their sensitivity and experience on the issue of sovereignty. Intelligence is sub rosa and no host government is likely to believe an embassy's protestations that the objectives of mission operatives are wholly benign and innocent. Thai skepticism, it was often claimed by Americans, compromised the possibility of solid professional assistance offered to them. But small wonder; American intelligence agencies persistently attempted to increase their number, increases which were resisted with equal persistence by the more politically tuned ambassador, who knew how strongly Thai heads of government felt on this issue.

In Bangkok the CIA is CAS, or Controlled American Source. The multiplicity of its functions almost ensured that it would eventually create problems for American policy as a whole. There are eighteen or more Thai intelligence agencies, depending on how they are classified, and CAS developed special lines with many of them. Its most important function became that of liaison and cooperation with those agencies dealing with the various Thai insurgencies—principally CSOC, or the Communist Suppression Operations Command. Theoretically such came under the Counsellor for Counterinsurgency (later renamed the Office of Development and Security), but that office had no funds of its own, and few officers not seconded from the CIA. Its impact and ability to control CAS depended purely on the variable skill of its head. CAS had a front at USOM, in the police training program. It had what were called CATs, Census Aspiration Teams, which in fact were village intelligence. CAS was operational. It ran a joint interrogation center with the Thai. The wonder is that it managed to stay invisible for so long.

Diplomacy, which has become the tip of the iceberg of the interactional process between states, has always been a special talent of the Thai; Filipinos, living in an archipelago, and with a traditionally close relationship to a superpower, never thought they needed to develop diplomatic skills. Nonetheless, certain traditional roles of diplomacy between unequal partners generally pertain in these two cases. For the small power the object of the game is to use the larger power's ambassador as its lobbyist in his own capital. Any diplomatic representative must report to his government the position, anxieties, and proposals of the host government. Surely this requires sensitivity and understanding, particularly with subtle people like the Thai. It seems to be a natural tendency for those capable of understanding to sympathize as well, but this endangers the diplomat's standing with his own government. It is the old problem of diplomats becoming representatives of, rather than to, the governments to which they are accredited.[5] American ambassadors to Thailand have often been accused in Washington of taking a "Thai line." Reasons beyond the general, transnational one makes the problem particularly acute in this case.

Thai diplomacy is Bangkok oriented. As an object of diplomatic pressure, the United States, to all intents and purposes, is the American embassy on Wireless Road; until the early 1970s, the Thai embassy in Washington was little used, other than as an intelligence center for keeping tabs on Thai students. A very important study was done by the American government in 1969 on its own commitments to Thailand. It argued that the de facto upgrading of the SEATO commitment embodied in the Rusk-Thanat memorandum of 1962 came about in considerable measure owing to sustained and compelling pressure on the embassy in Bangkok, particularly on the ambassadors of that period, U. Alexis Johnson and Kenneth Young. Ambassador Young considered this inaccurate, but there probably is some truth in it.[6] American ambassadors also have often publicly priased the Thai for their cooperation in Viet-Nam, especially after Senator Fulbright and others began to lambaste them for their allegedly mercenary motives there.[a] The stranger the host country behavior seems to his home office, the more expensive such praise becomes for the diplomat. There are more differences between Thai and neighboring peoples in diplomatic style

[a]*Prachatipatai*, in quoting from a speech by Ambassador Martin, used the occasion to make a few additional points as to how great the Thai contribution to the Vietnamese war effort was. "In other countries there would have been opposition voiced openly [to participation], or even processions . . . staged" (May 16, 1967). See also speech by Graham Martin to the Overseas Press Club, 3 May 1967, "The United States and Thailand," in *Department of State Bulletin*, 56, 5 June 1967.

than between most peoples; making their behavior the more difficult for the home office of the great power's ambassador to understand. Thailand's reluctance to admit that her bases were being used for attacks against North Viet-Nam, and her hostility to foreign correspondents wishing to visit bases, seemed disingenuous and short-sighted (as indeed they turned out to be) viewed from the United States. But no American familiar with Thai customs had any difficulty understanding why they behaved as they did. In addition to the traditional hostility towards the press and the desire on the part of the Royal Thai Government not to underscore the presence of bases to its own people, there was the obvious additional factor of not wanting to give the North Vietnamese an additional card at the negotiating table. Just as the North Vietnamese did not admit to having troops in South Viet-Nam, so the Thai could deny ever having helped the Americans in this particular way.

Diplomats always have an advantage on their home ground: their hospitality, their rules, their culture prevail. The Thai have been quick to utilize these advantages, and have historically striven to impress *farangs* with the righteousness of their point of view. Like scholarship, diplomacy in Thailand has been a diplomacy of admiration. The very survival of the Thai state compels, peculiarly, respect in the diplomatic sphere.

The American presence in Bangkok, overall, is multihierarchical. But so too is the royal Thai Government. It would be in the interest of a great power to gear its diplomacy to such, and through its ambassador coordinate all mission activity. In the case of Thai-American relations in the 1960s, possibly because of the rapid pace of expansion of the American involvement in Thailand, one of the principal patterns of the policy process between the two powers is however one of American hierarchies interacting directly with parallel Thai hierarchies, and countervailing ambassadorial attempts to achieve coordination.

The vastly increased international interaction of the postwar world has produced a new mutation of interaction, the most revolutionary sort, if we follow Huntington, namely transnational interactions. With the important exception of the Roman church, these until recently have been mostly American creations and mostly businesses. Now they are also Japanese and European businesses, governmental organizations (like AID offices), and at times "international" organizations, such as the World Bank. In countries interacting intensely with the United States in the postwar world, it follows that there usually has been an additional foreign policy source to the smaller country's foreign policy, deriving from transnational forces. Thus, when great division existed in the American community in Bangkok as to where to channel funds for an acceleration of rural development efforts, the existing Thai Community Development Department played one American hierarchy against the other, to prevent the emergence of a new coordinating mechanism other than itself—unsuccessfully, in the event. Conversely, functionally similar groups from separate nations, like the military, often find their common organizational interests as great as or greater than their own state's avowed interests, and line up against other similarly paired groups to make policy. The purpose of this section is to explore how the Thai achieve their purposes in their relations with the United States, and, necessarily, to look at the other side of the coin, American attempts to influence them. American *policy* despite all its ambiguity in this period is considered a given.

In the late 1960s, the involvement of Americans in Thailand was first and foremost concerned with the build-up at the five great bases used for the bombing of Viet-Nam. The most significant interaction of Americans and Thai, however, was in the general field of counterinsurgency (CI). When CI was popular in Congress, it was generally claimed that three-fourths of American aid was CI-related, broadly construed, which was pretty much true. We shall consider several aspects of CI work that developed in terms of parallel hierarchies.

The basic tenet of Thai CI activity was—in theory—coordination between civilian, police, and military (C-P-M) units for a concerted, multifaceted attack on the problem.[7] C-P-M came to be thought of as doctrine. How it was to work in practice was always less clear than the theory, as the attempt to develop village security forces suggests. As with all such programs designed to deal with security problems, or problems generally related to the development of the Northeast, the main question was what Thai hierarchy would supply which part of the general effort. The military favored letting the police handle it, freeing themselves from the responsibility, provided this did not let the police grow too large, and so long as the villagers were given the kind and size of weaponry and funds the army wished them to have. Civilian organizations wanted only minimal cooperation from either the police or army. There had long been a Volunteer Defense Corps (VDC), under the Department of Local Administration (DOLA) of the Ministry of Interior, a militia formed in 1954 which existed to supplement the police force as an adjunct to the governor, though only down to the district level. In an emergency, the VDC would be mobilized and enlarged and placed under the Ministry of Defense, but in practice it never got off the ground. Energetic USOM and embassy officials looked for a program that would enlist citizens in the defense of their own villages at their own level, and which would stimulate a sense of responsibility at a level where little government-provided administration existed. In 1967 the ill-starred Village Security Force (VSF) was born, in which most villages were to receive arms for five or ten of their own men—sufficient protection, it was thought, against Communist terrorists.

The biggest dilemma was who would control it and that problem largely lay within the Ministry of the Interior, then headed by one of Thailand's two most powerful men, General Prapat Charusathien. The ministry itself is broadly divided between the police, then headed by General Prasert, over whom Prapat had little operational control (in the manner of the American FBI under J. Edgar Hoover and the Attorney-General) and, on the other hand, those aspects in charge of and concerned with welfare and the governance of the entire country. In the latter category is, preeminently, the Department of Local Administration (DOLA), which in effect governs the 71 *changwat* (provinces) and 520 *amphur* (districts) of the kingdom. Clearly this bureau had great power, particularly in an era of rapid political development with national elections in the offing.

Director-General of DOLA in 1967 was Dr. Chamnan Yuvpurna, one of the most efficient, energetic, intelligent—and, apparently, corrupt—of Thai. (After a period as mayor of Bangkok, Chamnan's alleged involvement in a scandal involving the sale of pork became so widely discussed that the regime in 1969 decided to ship him off to Argentina as His Majesty's ambassador.) The Americans had no anxieties about working with him. Little attention was paid to persistent rumors that he was benefiting more than was considered appropriate even in the Thai government of that era, because Chamnan was one Thai who could "get things done." As one official put it, Chamnan had done more than anyone else in recent Thai history to stimulate and develop local administration throughout the kingdom. The parallel hierarchy within USOM, the office of rural affairs, was most enthusiastic about Chamnan, as was most of USOM.

DOLA and Chamnan naturally welcomed the VSF. It would strengthen DOLA's influence at the village level, where previously the police had been preeminent (to the extent that any officials had been involved). There would obviously be considerable benefits of a "pork-barrel" nature. It can hardly be proved, but it certainly was on the minds of the American officials and some Thai that, with elections promised, and Prapat less than enthusiastic about them, the VSF represented an important new channel of influence through which Prapat's forces, headed by Chamnan, could work. Power in Thailand flows from those controlling the guns; should the VSF succeed, DOLA would be transferred from an object of policy to a policy-maker. DOLA lobbied intensively to obtain large-scale American financial support for the new project, which had started off on a small scale. Its American allies were almost all USOM, save the Division of Public Safety and the mission director. Much of the embassy, including the ambassador, also supported it.

Ranged against it were, firstly, General Prasert and the police; the VSF represented not only an organizational threat, but a political threat to his wider ambitions. The police were already responsible for village security. The army— save for General Prapat—was solidly against this proposal; like the police, they were deeply concerned with the effect of so many loose weapons, and about the conditions governing their use and the pay of the villagers.

Parallel to these opponents was, firstly, Public Safety at USOM. Its programs, increasing the size and scope of the police and its activities, were the largest single component of American aid. They had good working relations with the Thai police, and thus no reason to rock the boat. Beyond these were whoever in the American community (and in Washington) wished for one reason or another to avoid further building up Prapat. These people tended to know little of the contemporary alternatives within the existing order; their objections tended to be on moral grounds, while their Thai counterparts objected to the increase of Prapat's power on intensely personal, self-interested grounds. Among many American officials was a consciousness of past mistakes, of how American aid had "created" strong-men before. One quoted a Thai friend as saying, "You Americans were responsible for Sarit in the 1950s—so we are watching you very carefully now." George Tanham, the recently appointed minister for counter-insurgency at the embassy, was from the first instinctively opposed to the project, and worked out the practical consequences of the proposal: what it might eventually cost to arm five men in every village (about $50,000,000), and what risks would be run. "We supplied the Vietnamese three times over. The arms went right to the Vietcong. The Malaysian and British on the other hand never let a single weapon get out of control," Tanham said. He wore down the supporters and helped to get a negative report to Washington.

The program itself had not, in the meantime, made impressive progress. Groups from one village were reinforcing themselves by getting together with groups from others, defeating its purpose; weapons were getting into terrorist hands, or, were being used in other ways against those supplying the weapons. AID in Washington refused to fund the program any further, and on 30 June the embassy had to inform DOLA that there was no more money for it. At the highest level, Ambassador Unger had to inform an embarrassed Prapat that the American government could not support it, inasmuch as DOLA and the police could not agree on a unified program, even though Prapat offered to sign for both the police and DOLA. The implication was painfully obvious—either he could not effectively control his own ministry, or he was not willing to pay the price that controlling both departments would have entailed. It is said that, for the two ensuing years, there was hardly any communication at all between DOLA and the police; and that relations between the Public Safety program at USOM and the other parts of the agency took a long time to heal as well.

In the meantime, there was no agency to coordinate the various new programs pertaining to village security, and there was no agreement as to what mix of police and civilian effort should exist. To be sure, "village security and development units," a rather minor compromise, were authorized, which would train villagers in paramilitary and psychological activities, but it was on a small scale—$1,000,000 spent in 1970. This was a neat way of pretending to solve a problem that was unsolvable as long as the political balance of the country (and, more particularly, in the Ministry of Interior) remained as it was.

A variant on this type of interaction is where one hierarchy attempts to strengthen an existing counterpart hierarchy's position within its own government, which we see in the development of the Communist Suppression

Operations Command (CSOC) as it was called then.[b] In response to the outbreak of the insurgency in 1965, the government created CSOC late in the year, giving it full responsibility in the CI area. "More specifically, it [CSOC] was to support and encourage the various agencies in their counterinsurgency mission, to order and institute coordination when needed, and to carry out counterinsurgency operations when asked to or when it saw fit."[8] CSOC's commander, General Prapat, and chief of staff, General Sirikit, had parallel roles in the army. The Director of Operations, who was in charge on a day-to-day basis, was a dynamic and relatively young—but somewhat controversial—army general, Saiyud Kerdphon. If he was to have any special role at all, then a C-P-M approach was necessitated; otherwise, he would only be going along with what the army would be doing anyway. General Saiyud's inclination was to emphasize the civilian aspects of CI work in any case. Alas, "The Thai initial suppressive reactions to the outbreak of open insurgency in 1965-1966 were actually a lashing back at the enemy rather than a reflection of their more serious thinking about counterinsurgency. Air and artillery as well as large sweeps were used to strike at guerrilla bands."[9] The *New York Times* began to report incidents where villages had been bombed indiscriminately upon discovery of insurgent elements, leading to increased alienation from the Thai government.[10] Saiyud obviously was winning neither the bureaucratic war, nor that against the terrorists.

Ambassador Martin, already quite disturbed by what he considered the mistakes in Viet-Nam, namely overmilitarization and inadequate civilian effort in combatting an insurgency, established in mid-1966 a counterpart office in the embassy, officially to coordinate American CI inputs in Thailand, but also to try to guide the Thai along the desired channels. The holder of the new office, Peer de Silva, was a C.I.A. official who had held a similar post at the embassy in Saigon.

For all the American efforts, the Thai army in practice was unwilling to take orders from a civilian bureaucracy like CSOC, and in October 1967, the Second Army Forward took over CI work. In civilian quarters, particularly among Americans this was considered a coup. This left CSOC something of an empty shell, whose function, of coordinating efforts, is not an easy task in Thailand.

The American response was to upgrade the office of the special assistant for counterinsurgency to the level of minister-counselor, something bureaucrats understand. Into the office was placed George Tanham, a distinguished student of guerrilla warfare[11] who, as an added qualification, possessed a sense of style, a highly important commodity with form-conscious Thai (and one too often lacking in Americans in Bangkok). His grasp of the situation, combined with his

---

[b]The name was changed to the "Office of Communist Suppression and Prevention," in 1969 after the promulgation of the new constitution but "CSOC" stuck as the name to which it was commonly referred. George K. Tanham, *Trial in Thailand* (New York: Crane, Russak and Co., 1974), pp. 71-93. In 1974, in reaction to the period of close collaboration with the U.S., the name was changed again, this time to 'ISOC', or Internal Security Operations Command.

standing among many Thai leaders, gave him some clout in the pursuit of his objectives, preeminent among which was the support of CSOC, and the C-P-M doctrine it symbolized. As it developed, Tanham sometimes had more influence with CSOC's senior masters than its own coordinators. At least on the issue of civilian input, the CSOC bureaucracy often tried to use Tanham to increase their support from the cabinet and senior ministers. It also used him to get information about what was occurring at lower levels of the CI effort. As one Thai official put it, "There is no two-way communications in our government; orders go down but nothing comes up. This is where the Americans are crucial."

American interest flagged with the growing resistance in Washington to involvement in CI work anywhere. With Tanham's departure in 1970, his office was downgraded and renamed "Development and Security," to deemphasize its prime function. Saiyud lost his chief backer, the C-P-M cause was hurt, and the insurgency continued to increase in seriousness.

There was another dimension of the problem of parallel hierarchies. For those like Tanham trying to prevent "another Viet-Nam," the chief lesson from America's Vietnamese experience was the importance of avoiding participation in CI activities themselves, lest the host country become psychologically and militarily dependent on American aid. It was clearly the short-term interest of the Thai army to draw American forces as deeply into the insurgency as possible. This was, of course, always denied, and it was of course true, in theory and in practice. Thai encounters with the enemy often ended in recriminations against the Americans for having been insufficiently helpful.

In fact, the American military assistance command and the Thai military may have become the most important parallel hierarchy of all (though their interaction is more difficult to examine). This is always the problem in countries with military juntas, it is often said, and the problem in Thailand was exacerbated by the fact that the ambassador did not have complete operational control over the commanding general of MACTHAI. American officers in Thailand were often eager to help out, according to any number of reliable sources.[c] This perceived identity of interests between Thai and American armies was strong enough for

[c]The difficulty in establishing the extent of such cooperation derives from the defensiveness of Americans involved in Thai counterinsurgency work. These Americans knew well that any information about their activities in the public arena would not help their continued effectiveness.

It is claimed in some Bangkok circles that American fire and manpower were used to punish Thai dissenters directly. Whether Americans ever did partake in such work is not clear, although it is difficult to believe that there were not a number of borderline cases where the Americans were involved. An article by a former American intelligence official, writing under the pseudonym "Winston Pack" in *Ramparts* magazine, purports to describe airborne, electronic sweeps by the CIA from Udorn to punish Meo tribesmen who had clashed with Thai government forces over control of their traditional areas: this sometime in late 1968 or 1969. (See *New York Times*, 16 July 1972.) There is undoubtedly some hyperbole in the claim of the study, however: senior officials working in the embassy during that period in interview made a compelling case against the conclusions of the study, though they were interested parties.

Tanham to draw up—and relentlessly enforce—explicit guidelines preventing the involvement, or even the appearance of involvement, of American forces in Thai work below battalion level.[1][2]

This policy bred considerable resentment among the Thai. To the extent that they were prepared to admit the existence of the insurgency and not blame Americans for stirring it up directly, they often considered it as part of the cost of doing business with the Americans. Unlike the Philippines and Malaya, Thailand had not suffered a Communist insurgency in the late forties and early fifties. Only when they became deeply involved in an American war in Viet-Nam did Thailand's traditional enemies begin to retaliate, or so went the argument. That the Americans were now reacting against the consequences of their very own policies, penalizing their allies for their own change of heart and changing their policies across the board in the process, was considered, not unreasonably, deeply ironic. The Thai, making a virtue of necessity, began insisting rather loudly that the Americans never be allowed to take part in CI efforts. This had the additional benefit of helping convince American public opinion (and several senators) that the Americans truly were not "creating another Viet-Nam." (Such was the principle burden of many of Thanat Khoman's statements in the 1968-70 period.)

The other side of the "parallel hierarchies" coin is the attempt by governments, organizations, or powerful individuals involved in statecraft to induce coordination among competing hierarchies, either cross-nationally or nationally. The more an administrative structure is composed of competing and parallel hierarchies, the greater the need for coordination in fulfilling inherently cross-ministerial objectives. The more disinterested the observer, the more apparent the need for coordination will be. In practice, this means that a foreigner who has no stake in ministerial struggles but has a stake in (for example) successful CI work, will be quick to see where the local effort could be improved if better coordinated. Embassies will almost inevitably be more flexible than ministries. Their officials turn over rapidly, and define success in terms of completely different peer groups from those right around them. But the local officials will, as Herbert Phillips has noted of Thailand,

resist foreign innovation in their administrative arrangements, and from their point of view, the resistance is quite justifiable. To them, a government agency exists not only to get a job done, but to provide the people in the agency ... with status, power, and influence. To them, coordination with, as contrasted to domination of, other agencies is the first step in the relinquishment of one's own power and influence.[1][3]

The type of resistance met by the Americans in their attempts to secure coordination can be seen in an early case, where USOM had been eliciting a statement of policy from the Thai government defining and directing the new Community Development Department. "This need was commented on in a strong letter from Ambassador [U. Alexis] Johnson to the Prime Minister," the aid director wrote to the ambassador. "Three separate drafts of a policy statement have been considered by the Cabinet and the National CD Committee but as yet none has been approved. Without such a statement, the coordinating relationships and responsibilities of the various ministries concerned in the CD Program will remain unclear."[14]

Officials may feel that certain policies advocated from outside are intrinsically good, but if fully implemented would slow down their program as a whole. They will react against such advice. The point is that one part of each ministry's brief—in this case development in the Northeast—may be the kingdom's most vital problem (though the Thai would not grant even that). Such does not mean that an agricultural ministry official will have a role-derived incentive to accelerate his programs in that region. Tracy Park, the USOM director in the early to mid-1960s, had a frustrating life trying to get line agencies to do precisely this, with little success. The line agencies' resentment knew no bounds, when AID as a result of this lack of success started working with the Thai to create a new conduit, and a new organization, for American money. Such would require, of course, the enthusiasm—and vested interest—of a strong figure in the government, who could use the opportunity to bring agencies from other ministries under his sway.

The creation and development of the Accelerated Rural Development program (ARD) illustrate these problems. Americans in AID often debated the wisdom of "building up Prapat" by continuing this particular program. Prapat's power greatly increased in this period. One AID official noted that "we used to work through the Ministries of Agriculture and Education. Now we work through DOLA"—which meant aiding General Prapat. We have already seen that some AID officials opposed a particular program (the VSF) largely on the grounds that it would further build up Prapat's power. From Prapat's point of view, his growth in power resulted in greater efficiency in the government.

The ever-expanding aid mission in Bangkok prodded the royal government in the mid-1960s to initiate an overall plan for development of the Northeast, particularly of roads, in the first instance. Most basically, they sought a decentralization of government functions down to the *changwad* (provincial) level. The Laotian emergency of 1962, the growth of insurgency in Viet-Nam, the arresting of North Vietnamese and Thai Communist agents in the region, and the continuing hints of American largesse, finally led to the creation of a "subcommittee for coordination and operational planning," bringing representatives from throughout the government together to deal with the snowballing emergency. The notion of "accelerated rural development" began taking hold, and the *farang* initials were adopted. A pilot program was started in six border *changwads*, with a brief to open them up quickly to modern influences. USOM made a grant of approximately two million dollars available. In 1964, the subcommittee became a committee, and at the end of that year, Dr. Chamnan

Yuvpurna was made chairman, which ensured the cooperation of DOLA, as well as administrative efficiency and the backing of General Prapat; the notion was becoming institutionalized. Work grew so rapidly that there was a further upgrading, to a "Central Committee for Accelerated Rural Development" in the prime minister's office, where, it was thought, coordination could best be stimulated. The chairman, however, was the deputy prime minister, General Prapat.

There were a number of reasons for not putting what was becoming a high-powered department into the ministries of the Interior, Agriculture, or Education, the appropriate line ministries. As ARD's job was to accelerate things that theoretically were the brief of these ministries, how else could one get special emphasis and acceleration unless the new organization were outside the line agencies? Because the organization was to be transitional, it would be easier to eliminate if not incorporated into a line ministry. Resentment grew in these ministries; all community development programs were, in effect, being slighted, and Agriculture considered USOM as having betrayed its years of cooperation.

The problems that were always to bedevil the ARD were apparent from the beginning. First, the Americans and Thai differed in their sense of urgency. Secondly, said a "joint" evaluation of ARD in mid-1966 (obviously written by and for Americans), there was a confusion as to basic objectives—meaning that there were different objectives altogether. There was, thirdly, inadequate coordination, and a low level of efficiency. The report noted the importance of not appearing (sic) to be in command over Thai, and that "there is a real need for a strong bond to be established between the Thai and U.S. personnel and that the concept recommended by USOM advisers should not only be clear and concise, but fully and without reservation accepted by the Thai counterparts."[15] The Thai made their own evaluations of ARD. One, sponsored by DTEC (the Department of Technical and Economic Cooperation, which theoretically coordinates the aid-giving process), caused resentment at USOM. As Alexander Caldwell writes, "This reaction was due in part to the fact that DTEC had not adequately explained the purposes and approach to USOM and ARD before undertaking it, and in part to the fact that ARD was at that time having some serious problems in absorbing U.S. aid, and such a study could therefore have proved embarrassing."[16]

The basic problem was that, although the ARD concept—accelerating change—was formally accepted at the top, by the prime minister and by General Prapat, it was neither truly digested there nor, more pertinently, lower down. The government never really took it on as its own responsibility, a USOM official commented. "ARD falls between two stools. It should either be responsible to the province governor or to Bangkok, but it has cooperation from neither and loyalty to neither." It was a nice way of getting a lot of American money in to build many new roads, which were seen as a good thing. But the program was an American program—"ARD" programs, with the same initials, existed elsewhere in the world under the American aegis. It was impossible to find a concept which could symbolize for the villager even what the leadership sought, let alone the Americans. When the prime minister spoke of development, and the villager understood only new toilets or new roads, then development obviously became associated with these. The notion of accelerated rural development, in the absence of new peasant attitudes, naturally became synonymous with the building of new roads. (There was, nonetheless, an objective security component to the roads, whatever the subjective understanding of them.)

Problems at the staff level compounded general difficulties. Some officials working for ARD were seconded from Interior, where their loyalties remained; those who were ARD officials alone were ineligible for appointment to positions outside of ARD and could not rise to higher positions within the *changwad* to which they were appointed. There were no long-term opportunities for advancement of the most competent officials, as ARD officials were quick to point out. All were sensitive to the charge that ARD was an "American tool"; this belief made it that much more difficult to elicit cooperation from the rest of the government. ARD people had no security backup in the provinces either, yet as time went on and more precise knowledge was available as to where the main CI threat existed, they were expected to go into increasingly vulnerable positions "stark naked," as one American advisor put it. As the army was hardly willing to defer to ARD officials on the timing and direction of thrusts, the dilemma was unsolvable. Nor was it easy to assimilate the new ethic of achieving a better relationship between government and people, the ultimate end (for the Americans) of the whole exercise. "It was learned that some staff sent to do development work created the misunderstanding among the natives by making a scandal with the native girls. The people might have a bad impression of government officials as the result of a feudalistic relationship pattern."[17]

When ARD was begun, the insurgency in the Northeast was only incipient. As its seriousness increased in 1965, the question had to be asked whether ARD activities should be geared to medium-long-range challenges of economic development, or to shorter term security needs in the most sensitive provinces. Obviously such raised very basic questions about the relationship of *development* to peasant *loyalty*. As more than one survey demonstrated, there was no clear relationship between improved services in villages and greater loyalty to the government.[d] If anything, the converse seemed truer.

All this posed problems of coordination at a higher level. ARD was designed to effect coordination of a number of functions, but, once established, it was simply another organization, and, as we have seen, a not very deeply rooted one. The basic question for the Thai government was how to coordinate security and

---

[d]George K. Tanham, *Trial in Thailand* (New York: Crane, Russak and Co., 1974). Indeed, it might be assumed that the relationship would be an inverse one, given the widely noted relationship between rising expectations and the propensity to rebel.

development activities in insurgent-ridden areas, and the basic objective of American policy in Bangkok was to get them coordinated. The question was discussed at one five-hour session of Thai ministers and generals in the presence of USOM officials. General Prapat outlined the problem very cogently; Bangkok must provide villagers with what they, not what Bangkok wanted. CI activity must be coordinated with development activity; "a joint plan for suppression and development is needed," the notes on his presentation said. Dr. Chamnan added that, in the ARD program itself "suppression and development cannot be separated." General Kriangsak of the National Security Command—definitely a competing organization—asked who was going to make the final decision in case of conflict between the two. General Prapat said that one man should head both development and suppression work.[18] No one doubted whom he had in mind. There was the rub, for giving anyone that much power would have disturbed the country's political balance. Effective coordination of these activities was achieved neither then, nor later.

Meanwhile the Americans found their man to direct the budding bureaucracy being set up to coordinate and implement ARD goals. Prasong Sukhum, well connected and able, was placed in the new headquarters and surrounded by American advisors who, prompted by the very highest authority, promised that "money is no object." By 1970, knowledgeable observers noted signs of Prasong's weakening position. Senior government bureaucrats even gave vent to their impatience with "that young man" for the record. And in knocking him down a few pegs, they were, of course, knocking down his true sponsors (it was a peculiar, if unconscious, American advantage often to be insensitive to this kind of subtle reproof).

Dennis Duncanson and George Tanham wrote of this general problem "resulting from accelerating the adjustment of the native culture, the native bureaucracy and traditional relations between administrators and administered to modern ways."

Modernization is made both more difficult and more urgent by the communist challenge. A remedy may be sought in setting up parallel government agencies alongside the traditional ones, to operate in fields and at a tempo designed to meet that challenge and make use of foreign technical advice. But the psychological result will be that the *impermanence of the operation will be emphasized in the public mind.* Two additional dangers are that the ad hoc agencies will encounter envious opposition from the traditional bureaucrats, and that they, themselves, will acquire a vested interest in the perpetuation of the insurgency they are being employed to terminate.[19]

From the point of view of the line ministries, the question was whether they could skew their entire program to the Northeast; their objective was entirely rational, if not productive in terms of the kingdom's most urgent needs. This also led to much duplication of effort; according to a joint evaluation, line ministries would go into a *changwad* with a program that competed with those of ARD. Thus it was commonplace in Bangkok in the early 1970s to hear ARD damned from all sides, accused of being a mere road-building agency (and an expensive one) that would shrivel along with the American presence.

Politically, this is what happened. Following the 1971 "governmental re-organization," or coup, ARD became a special target of the newly constituted National Executive Council. As a result in 1972 it was moved under the umbrella of the Interior Ministry where the Community Development Department could try to dismember it. Although Prasong himself largely succeeded in keeping the essence of ARD intact, the notion of ARD as a powerful stimulus of change and as a political force was dead.

Despite the criticism of it by the Thai, ARD had become a highly professional outfit utilizing advanced social science techniques and knowledge in its work; it had furthered comprehensive rural development planning as a technique. Most of all it had "fostered . . . decentralization and devolution so that technology and management can be effectively applied to meeting localized needs quickly," as its Planning, Evaluation, Research and Management team had put it.[20] ARD could celebrate its tenth anniversary in 1973, pleased that 5886 kilometers of roads had been built, that USOM's role had vastly diminished as the percentage of ARD's budget supplied by the Thai side increased,[21] and that it had developed innovative methods of evaluating *changwad* performance.

To be sure, it had had its weaknesses, as we have noted. According to an evaluation by David Wilson, Fred von der Mehden, and Paul Trescott, it was "weak or negative in economic distribution, political participation and security," but as they also concluded, it was quite effective in the areas of economic growth and administrative development.[22]

ARD, like CSOC, symbolized the problems of two unequal partners, interact-ing in the smaller power's country. It is difficult enough to define objectives, let alone attempt to implement them. The larger power will see the broader issues transcending the local theater; yet it is precisely those local issues that decide the fate of individuals and governments of smaller partners. Small wonder, then, that they resist the otherwise compelling advice of their more efficient, great-power ally.

4 Personal Centers in Manila

In the two years following the most radical changes in Philippine politics in a generation, it was not easy to see what would be the long-term patterns of interaction between Philippine and American institutions and people. It seemed clear that there would be more continuity than appeared on the surface, for societies usually change slowly. Changes in any event often begin unnoticed, and appear only after a certain lag. The increasing power of Philippine technocrats and of the military are examples, where the changes themselves began well before martial law and yet are commonly attributed to it. It makes sense to deal with the Philippines on the assumption that pattern maintenance will be found wherever old patterns have not already been destroyed.

As in Bangkok, there are American hierarchies in Manila interacting with Philippine hierarchies. But the American institutions themselves are substantially less interrelated than is the case in Thailand, which makes American diplomacy more difficult to conduct—or at least less easy to coordinate. Clark Air Force Base, seat of the 13th Air Force, has vast extra-Philippine responsibilities, from Taiwan to Thailand. The American naval commander, formerly at Sangley and now at Subic Bay Naval Base, is the representative of the Commander-in-Chief Pacific, giving him power that competes with the ambassador's in this area. The Joint U.S. Military Advisory Group (JUSMAG) competes with the military attachés at the embassy, and vice versa. Each of the American hierarchies, and particularly its leader, tends to develop cross-cutting and informal alliances with one or another of the Philippine strong men. For some time American diplomacy in the Philippines has been governed by the premise that objectives cannot be achieved through institutions, only through effective and powerful men.

The Manila diplomatic system develops "personalities" within the American community, which exacerbates the problem, which is only to be expected in such a personality-oriented system. The American ambassador has sometimes been the second most powerful man in the country, and fortuitously, a long line of distinguished men have occupied the post—Charles Bohlen, G. Mennen Williams, William McCormick Blair, Jr., Henry Byroade (who had been ambassador in Cairo at the time of Suez, where he started legends that never ceased) and, most recently, William Sullivan. And others in the American hierarchy became personalities. Wesley Haraldson, for several critical years director of AID in Manila, was a local hero in the provinces where his teams developed their miracle rice programs, as well as a power in Manila. And General Lansdale's role in the Philippines in the anti-Huk campaigns is well known everywhere.[1]

As in any diplomatic capital, and as between any two interacting powers, there are some parallel hierarchies in Manila which operate like those in Bangkok. Whether we characterize the interaction in terms of such patterns is a matter of degree. One obvious parallel hierarchy is at the top: the Philippine president and the American ambassador. The relationship is somewhat institutionalized. The American ambassador is expected to represent Philippine interests to his own government in Washington, or at least to make them known. This is not surprising, given the low status and capability of the Philippine foreign service, the psychological relationship between Filipinos and Americans, and the historical evolution of the relationship. For all that, there is a clearly demarcated line that American ambassadors do not cross. No one argued the Philippine case—for an upgrading of their ties with Washington and increased aid—more forcefully than did Ambassador Byroade. Nonetheless neither in Washington nor in Manila was he thought to have crossed the barrier, for no American envoy had ever worked harder to protect American interests in the Philippines, from military base rights to economic interests. Indeed, Byroade's forthright defense of American interests elicited more respect for him from Filipinos than any of his predecessors had gained. General Romulo, for instance, Foreign Secretary throughout Byroade's tenure in Manila, made his view that Byroade was "the best diplomat of any country ever assigned to Manila" widely known. The institutionalization of this arrangement is more reflective of history, and the colonial relationship that previously existed, as well as the way Filipinos manage the foreign presence, than it is of a system of interacting parallel hierarchies.

Thus we would characterize the interaction in Manila, in contrast to the competing and interacting hierarchies of Thailand, as one of uncoordinated personal centers of power being acted upon by and acting on American centers of power. What pertinent administrative hierarchies exist have always been the president's. In the actual process of decision-making and governance, the *bureaucratic* backup of a strong personality in the cabinet or at another level, on a particular issue, is relatively unimportant in comparison with Thailand. What counts is the reputation and strength of the individual at the top of the institution or department of government. Personal wealth always helped more than competent administrative support until recently, when the impact of the Presidential Economic Staff, and later, the Development Management Staff in the Executive Secretariat, began to make their impact.

In Thailand the programmatic interaction of the kingdom with the United States—for the most part that deriving from American aid—was characterized by the urgency and large scale of American intentions and programs, aimed at developing Thai institutions of governance in the provinces, at narrowing the income gap between provinces in the Northeast and those in the center, and so forth. The interaction was characterized by the resistance to change of line agencies, or hierarchies. In the Philippines, the equivalent programmatic interaction has been characterized by longer-term objectives of more basic social and administrative reform; the bottleneck has usually been the opposition of powerful individuals in or outside government. American programs have been successful when they have been relatively small and have worked through one or several key individuals. As we saw, "absorptive capacity" was never an important criterion for the amount of aid in Thailand. In the Philippines it was the converse. As Wesley Haraldson emphasized in testimony to the American Congress, "The forward movement of the Philippines is not impeded by any shortage of funds on our part. The critical factor is better government organization. When the Government gets better organized, more funds will be forthcoming from loan agencies and probably from U.S. aid as well."[2] Haraldson's great contribution during his stay in the late 1960s was to develop a program to supplement "miracle rice," the IR-8 strain developed in Los Banos that was to double output in the Philippines and revolutionize agriculture in Asia. SPREAD, the Systematic Program for Rural Economic Assistance and Development, "packaged" the technologies and administrative necessities required for efficacious use of the new rice strain—fertilizer, supervised credit, improved provincial governance. By Haraldson's own account it succeeded because he was able to find a couple of key individuals through whom to work, who would commit themselves to it as wholeheartedly as he was himself. The individuals were, most critically Raphael Salas, the executive secretary, but also Vice-President Lopez, the secretary of Agriculture. There was little opposition to the program because the objective was to increase productivity generally, without redividing the pie. When Ambassador Mennen Williams and Haraldson tried to tack land reform onto it, according to AID officials, they ran into stiff opposition and imperiled SPREAD.

Land reform (as an issue) in fact, has always been tied up with the Americans. That it has always been considered a crucial issue to more than just the Americans is indicated by the PAASCU/IPC elites study, in Table 4-1. Tenancy rates increased from 3 percent in 1903, at the beginning of the American period, to 50 percent in 1970.[3]

Following on the Bell Mission to the Philippines, which made large-scale economic aid dependent on wide-scale reform in the former colony, a report was written by an American, Robert Hardie, who had been involved in the Japanese postwar land reform. The report "was factual and informative, but its arrogance ignited sensitive Filipino nationalism. Public opinion was quickly aroused and easily manipulated by political leaders in Congress and the administration to kill land reform as a policy issue."[4] It was therefore 1955, after Magsaysay's election, before a land reform bill could get through Congress. Its efficaciousness was undermined by a series of provisions that made it easy for landlords to subdivide and retain control of estates. Another land-reform bill was enacted during the Macapagal period. It too was somewhat emasculated by the failure to pass a land tax. But as a later official American study suggested, "The balance of

Table 4-1

Percentages of 100 national and 248 local influentials who agree that selected national issues are crucial, classified by issue, cross-classified by respondents' reputed scope of influence (data gathered June-December 1969).

Average Rank Order	Issue	Respondents' Reputed Influence			
		National		Local	
		%	Rank Order	%	Rank Order
1	Implementation of land reform	82%	1	81%	1
2	Attracting foreign investments	66	3	68	2
3	Extension of Laurel-Langley	70	2	63	3
4	Breakdown of traditional morality	49	5	61	4
5	Philippine-U.S. bases agreement	58	4	51	5
6	Toleration of demonstrations against Catholic hierarchy	24	6	37	6
7	Philippine participation in Vietnam	22	7	31	7
8	Prosecution of Sabah claim	11	8	25	8
Number of respondents		100		248	

Source: Peria A. Makil and Frank Lynch *PAASCU/IPC, Study of Schools and Influentials*, Institute of Philippine Culture, Quezon City, 1972.

political forces had shifted sufficiently that a landlord resistance might have been overcome if the program had not been underfinanced, imperfectly administered and frequently used as a vehicle for political ends. . . . It finally broke down."[5]

After Marcos's election in 1965 land reform became a political football. For rhetorical effect Marcos would proclaim numerous districts "land-reform areas," but nothing was done to implement the program. As he often told his confidants, Marcos was more interested in productivity. Also, the enormous financial support with which he had won the election left some important political debts to be paid. Nor was Marcos "high on social consciousness," as one AID official put it. But circumstances called for another real try at land reform. Promptly after Marcos was reelected in 1969, a massive reaction set in against him, for the venality and arrogance of his campaign, and the lack of reform initiated in his first administration. Social reform then became politically more useful.

In February of 1970 a new AID director, Thomas Niblock, arrived, who had worked with Byroade in Kabul and who shared his interests in building a large, successful and reformist program in the Philippines. Before arriving in Manila, he had made his interest in land reform known. A review at AID-Manila of past land-reform programs yielded the conclusion that past attempts had been too ambitious. A small program was needed that could have a demonstration effect, which within two years, could result in "the development of effective operational systems which could provide the basis for an accelerated national program of agrarian reform."[6] Niblock soon learned the importance of finding key individuals, and was successful in working with them.

The disillusionment in the country at the time, as the "Spring Review" of land reform at USAID put it, "has meant a substantial augmentation of the power not only of the radical forces in the city and country, but the emergence of a small number but highly influential group of technocrats with no particular loyalty to the system as it operates at present or to the present occupant of the presidential office."[7] An example is Arturo Tanco, Jr., a Harvard Business School Graduate who was made under secretary of Agriculture in 1970 and later secretary. Niblock, Tanco, and others found a province (Nueva Ecija) where rice, not sugar, was the principal crop, for tenancy is worst with rice. The governor there was an opposition liberal, but they made what proved to be a sound decision to add a political constituent to the team, and to involve him at every stage.

By April 1970, they were surveying the proposed pilot province. The stumbling block was Marcos, down whose throat "they had to stuff the program," as an embassy official put it. But by enlisting several key officials along the way and pledging small sums of money the Americans were able to help get a program going. It became a joint undertaking of the National Land Reform Council, the National Food and Agriculture Council, and the Provincial Government. The team, representing AID, the National Economics Council, the Department of Agriculture, and the Land Authority, became a very visible group in Nueva Ecija. They commissioned a baseline survey of the economic, social, and psychological circumstances of the farmer and landowner population of Nueva Ecija; they began participant training; they made a Public Safety communications network for all thirty-three Nueva Ecija municipalities available to the land authority. The program was successful and had momentum. Its timing was also lucky. After the proclamation of martial law, two years later, Marcos saw the utility of a massive land-reform program, by which time Filipinos had developed a capability for it. Nueva Ecija, however, was by far the most successful province for land reform.[a]

Philippine-American transactions are not all American actions and Philippine reactions. Where important individuals have freedom of action within the Philippine context to pursue advantages in the American system they can be highly motivated and purposeful. An example is the sugar industry.

---

[a]In the fifty-four provinces involved in the land reform programs as of 31 December 1973, some 144,424 tenant-recipients of land transfer certificates had been issued; Nueva Ecija accounted for a vastly disproportionate 33,254, owing to its head start. See "Summary, Operation Land Transfer (As of December 31, 1973)" mimeo, Department of Agrarian Reform, Manila, 1974. See also "Land Reform—Integrated Development Program for Nueva Ecija," USAID Manila, n.d.

Philippine sugar exports to the American market go back a long way, to the administration of President Washington.[8] The marriage of convenience between high-priced American sugar producers and inefficient Philippine producers in the interwar years laid the foundation for the present basis of trade and bargaining. Also pertinent was the notorious stipulation of the Americans in 1946, that the Filipinos, in addition to granting the United States "parity" in the exploration for and exploitation of natural resources, must enact a prohibition against export taxes. This was one thing for the young republic in North America to have written into its constitution in the late eighteenth century, but quite another for it to require in a poor country's basic laws 160 years later, when the lucrative sugar trade was such a logical basis for social legislation. The American market, which required steady supplies, buys at what until 1973 was around twice the world market price in order to ensure a steady supply.[9] But as Frank Golay has written,

A major consequence of U.S. sugar price policy has been to subsidize the Philippine economy to the extent of the difference between the proceeds of Philippine sugar exports to the United States and the value of these exports in the world sugar market. During much of the postwar period this subsidy has amounted to 40-50% of Philippine sugar export proceeds. Currently [1960], it is 2-3 times the magnitude of the U.S. aid program. It is difficult to conceive of a less efficient way to subsidize the Philippine economy, which must rely on a trickling down process to diffuse the monopoly profits of the sugar industry to the rest of the economy.[10]

Out of such subsidies have grown the great Philippine fortunes—of the Lopezes, the Montelibanos, Teves, Cojunacos, Yulos, and others. Although most of these families diversified their interests in the postwar era, and some (like the Lopezes) got out of sugar altogether, the mutuality of interest prevailed and their enormous influence in the politics of the country continued out of all proportion to their actual economic importance, thanks to their concentration and tradition of working together.

Sugar is still vitally important to the economy, usually supplying about 20 percent of the foreign exchange the republic earns abroad, most of which—around $200 million—is from the American market. The way the sugar community has maintained this position at home and abroad is clear enough. At home political power in the Congress was sufficient to prevent all but the most indirect and minimal export taxes, and in Washington sugar has maintained a highly skilled and highly paid lobbyist, John O'Donnell. "Nondiplomatic representatives," Nicholas Berry points out in reference to O'Donnell, "because they are citizens of the state in which they operate, provide access to levels of government not normally available to diplomatic representatives."[11] There are limits, of course. So stung was Senator Fulbright and others at the sums of money contributed by the Philippines through O'Donnell to American congressmen prior to passage of the war-damages bill that increased scrutiny began to be given to all such lobbying.[1 2]

What we see in the sugar industry is a highly motivated, purposeful, and well-coordinated drive to maintain an advantageous situation. For many years sugar declined in relative importance to the Philippine economy, but in 1974 with its world price skyrocketing it came back into its own and the Philippines was no longer dependent on the American market for high prices. The benefits still went into the same pockets, and by 1975 few of the sugar growers' economic privileges had changed, despite Marcos's demolishing of their political power after martial law. It is interesting to note that progressive Filipinos in 1971, when the American sugar quota was up for negotiation, saw Washington not Manila as the place to lobby for their claims. For example, Francis Sionil-José, editor of the reformist journal, *Solidarity*, toured the United States that year, addressing himself to this question. Representatives of the sugar bloc amusingly thought that they should themselves finance the proposed trips to Washington of long-haired radical students.

In considering Philippine attitudes toward Americans and the United States, it is first important to keep in mind the lessons of the IPC/PAASCU study. (See Table 4-2.) As is evident, "two out of four primary reasons given as deterrents for an ideal relationship between the Philippines and the United States are psychological. Fifty-five percent of respondents think that RP-US relations are less than ideal because of 'Filipino colonial mentality,' or 'American colonial mentality.' " Overwhelmingly, Filipinos identify the ideal relationship as "one that characterizes equal sovereign nations. It should not be one of preferential treatment [between a developed and an underdeveloped nation] or any other kind of relationship."[1 3]

Substantive issues—like the existence of the bases—provide the irritants that cause "colonialism" to be so critical, and we will examine a case, the Customs and Payments Agreements negotiated in 1969, where Filipinos and Americans attempted to resolve problems in the military issue area so as to relax the underlying anxiety. This demonstrates, firstly, the difficulty of negotiating anything with the Philippines without domestic Philippine politics entering in at the start; the importance of personality; and finally, the security concerns of the American government.[1 4]

As in all of the negotiations between the two parties from 1956 onwards, it was assumed that problems flowing from the existence of American bases would be eliminated as a result of the final agreement—but the 1965 Mendez-Blair and 1966 Rusk-Ramos agreements could not resolve all the problems. From the Philippine side, the reasons for seeking a customs agreement was that vast quantities of American goods came into the bases, some in Navy ships, some in ships under the Navy's charter, and some also in Military Sea Transportation Service (MSTS) space charter shipments on other vessels. Enormous amounts of goods ended up on the black market. The Philippine government naturally

Table 4-2

IPC/PAASCU influential respondents classified by selected variables, cross-classified by four factors they more commonly mention as preventing an ideal relationship between the Philippines and the United States (1969-70)

Selected Variables	American Bases		Economic Treaties		American Colonialism		Filipino Colonialism		Total[a]
	N	%	N	%	N	%	N	%	N
Level of Influence									
National	25	27%	23	25%	41	45%	54	59%	91
Local	34	24	30	21	88	61	76	53	144
Total	59	25%	53	23%	129	55%	130	55%	235
Age									
25-34 yrs.	4	17%	5	21%	12	50%	13	54%	24
35-44 yrs.	12	24	10	20	32	65	29	59	49
45-54 yrs.	20	30	15	23	30	45	43	65	66
55-64 yrs.	15	38	12	31	24	62	12	31	39
65 yrs. and over	0	0	3	30	4	40	8	80	10
Age unknown	9	20	7	16	27	61	25	57	44
Total	60	26%	52	22%	129	56%	130	56%	232
Area of Influence									
Government	15	31%	13	27%	27	56%	26	54%	48
Economics	10	17	14	24	26	45	33	57	58
Education	11	38	12	41	16	55	15	52	29
Professions	14	27	8	16	26	51	26	51	51
Mass media	5	25	3	15	11	55	14	70	20
Social justice and welfare	3	17	1	6	15	83	10	56	18
Religion	1	10	1	10	8	80	6	60	10
Total	59	25%	52	22%	129	55%	130	56%	234
Occupational Area									
Government	24	36%	17	25%	36	54%	33	49%	67
Private	35	21	36	21	93	55	97	58	168
Total	59	25%	53	23%	129	55%	130	55%	235

[a]Total percentages are not shown since they add up to more than 100 because of multiple responses.

wished to control this flow, though not really to stop it. It had been an important objective of the new Marcos administration in 1966 to increase tax revenues by curtailing smuggling (which occurs on a vast scale—thanks both to the length of the coastlines and the low level of political development) and tax evasion at ports of entry. There was a dramatic increase in tax revenue in the first year of the Marcos administration. Ports of entry were tightened and smuggling was curtailed, thanks to the American-supplied fast patrol boats. It was their contention, on the one hand, that while stores entering in naval ships and chartered ships were not subject to examination under the existing agreements, MSTS shipments were; and, on the other hand, that inadequate controls existed overall for preventing leakage of desired goods onto the black market.

It was hardly inappropriate for the then commissioner of Customs, Juan Ponce-Enrile, a favorite of President and Mrs. Marcos, to wish to tax the MSTS shipments. From his reading of the working agreements—and he is an able lawyer—his government was entitled to this.[15] Sometime in 1967, the commander at Sangley Naval Base apparently (and unwisely, the rest of the American community thought) invited him to inspect the existing checks for himself. The rear admiral's office did not follow up on the invitation, probably as a result of pressure from the embassy, which irritated Enrile—who was then something less than the embassy's favorite. In the autumn of 1968, the United States made clear that, in its interpretation of the 1951 Mutual Defense Treaty, the Philippines was not entitled to American protection in her ongoing imbroglio with Malaysia over North Borneo (Sabah). Enrile, outraged, reportedly decided to exert pressure to get concessions from the Americans, and demanded, *inter alia*, lists of every item entering the ports.

The Americans publicly made known their resentment of the implication that anything untoward existed in their practice or methods. In the preceding years, they had tightened procedures up considerably, spending, by their own private estimate, as much as $100,000 annually to prevent any misuse of their tax-free privileges on the bases. But beyond that there were three substantive considerations. Firstly, some of the shipments included hardware under the Military Assistance Program (MAP) for the Philippine armed forces, and the Americans considered it inappropriate and ironic that such should be subjected to search, let alone port fees or duties. Secondly, considerable sensitivity as to some of the weaponry and hardware coming in caused a vehement reaction to the possibility of a search. When the original agreements had been negotiated in 1947, before the worldwide dispersal of American strategic arms, the question of what type of weaponry could be installed would hardly have existed. By 1959 the United States had agreed not to base bombers in the Philippines, nor to build missile launching sites there. Apart from these, however, nothing was excluded, and American policy after that was to refrain from discussing sensitive weaponry or stockpiling in any manner. The Filipinos never called them on it.

Beyond these two considerations, the Americans did not consider what the Filipinos were asking for all that unreasonable. The third consideration as one commented was that

It was inconvenient; it was more than what we had been doing for them, we feared that it was a foot-in-the-door request which would lead to more demands and restrictions later, and we doubted that they would put our import data to good use, but on the face of it, their request was reasonable. Therefore, we had to give in eventually. What we wanted was to do so in such a way as to discourage demands from them for more concessions later.[16]

By late 1968, however, relations had become so strained over the gap between the two positions that the customs commissioner was not going to allow ships to come in if they did not pay harbor fees and submit to examination. In response the Americans threatened to hold up the MAP supplies for the Philippine armed forces rather than submit to this. The Americans further insisted that their shipments were so computerized that they could not possibly comply with Philippine requirements.

Fortuitously, and fortunately, a basis for compromise emerged in the form of a new Philippine need of American assistance. On 27 November 1968, they made proposals for "channeling into the Philippine government banking system the United States expenditures within the Philippines so that the same might be availed of in the most advantageous and meaningful ways."[17] There was, at that time, great leakage of dollars to the black market, with the peso deteriorating, and dollars going into the economy from so many controllable sources, including veterans' and social-security payments to Filipinos in the Philippines, contractors on American bases, base expenditures generally, and "R and R" spending by servicemen. It was a legitimate objective for the government to wish to prevent such leakage. Channeling all such dollar expenditures through the Philippine government banking system would involve no direct costs to the Americans. It would, in normal circumstances, have been a helpful and economical gesture of a great power to a smaller one attempting to increase its low level of control. The Philippine request at first was very broad in its scope—for example, asking the embassy to do all its banking at the Philippine National Bank, which would have been very compromising, given the bank's bad reputation. The bank was popularly known, prior to martial law, as the "Milch cow for Philippine politicians." But it was narrowed, at the embassy's suggestion, to a request that the embassy restore "lipstick"—or overprinted—checks, which permitted encashment in pesos only (as, in fact, the U.S. government had done until the decontrol of the Philippine economy of 1962); and to a request that the government buy its pesos from the central bank, which American embassies often do in other countries.

The real problem was, What were the implications of "most advantageous and meaningful ways" of dealing with this problem to the Philippines in an election year—given the extraordinary costs to the nation and temptations to the politicians of elections in that country? Tens of millions of dollars were to flow through the national bank, paid out at the official rate of 3.9 to the dollar, while in Hong Kong, the rate fluctuated between 5 and 6 to the dollar. All those 3.9 dollars coming into the central bank, without a touch of illegality, could be sold to whomever the bank wished; and it had to be presumed in the embassy that the "whomever" would be contributors to Marcos's campaign, who could make a fifty percent profit on their money in Hong Kong. Such would clearly depreciate the currency, and in the past, this had meant trips by Philippine politicians to Washington after the election, asking to be bailed out. The excessive spending in the 1969 elections, at least in part accounted for by this windfall, did indeed lead to devaluation, as predicted by several officials in the embassy. The bargaining between embassy and government was implicitly over which group of Filipinos—Marcos or someone else—would benefit from this. The extent to which the Americans were prepared to go along with the Marcos administration, given how precisely this issue was understood, is a fair measure of how valuable the Americans saw their unimpeded base access to be.

As for the negotiations themselves, there was a characteristic lack of coordination on the part of the Filipinos. Undersecretary Ingles, at the Department of Foreign Affairs, was supposed to be in charge of the negotiations, but at first Enrile, and then his successor Geotina, attempted to run the show themselves; each was actively building up his standing in the government. The substantive discussions, however, were actually conducted on the Philippine side by Jose V. de Venecia, the minister in Saigon, who spent most of his time in Manila and had direct access to Marcos. In the end, the American negotiators did what they so often do in similar circumstances—left the final decision on the agreement for the ambassador and Philippine president to work out, on the grounds that nothing would be accomplished otherwise.

Clearly Thailand has been less penetrated by the United States than the Philippines, at least in a technical sense. The Thai have devised methods of institutionalizing barriers between themselves and foreigners, while the Filipinos have not only failed to devise any such methods, but also in relation to the United States, have suffered from a deep-seated inferiority complex. The ability of powerful Americans to take their case directly to the president of the Philippines, or to other powerful Filipinos in the hierarchy, and to develop close working relations with them, clearly made the Philippines far more vulnerable to penetration. The greater homogeneity and apparently greater coherence of Thailand further supports this conclusion.

Three factors vitiated these advantages. The first is the question of the parallel hierarchies that characterize Thai bureaucracy. The American establishment in Bangkok was large enough for each of its organizations to coordinate with counterpart organizations to its own advantages, which it found necessary in light of Thai behavior. It seems that parallel hierarchies tend to develop their counterparts. A foreign organization, for that matter, can be less formal, hence more flexible and adaptive, in a host city than the host government will be, which is certainly true of the American community in Bangkok. Americans who knew what overall American policy was could more easily achieve the first of their own national objectives in Thailand, namely, maintaining Thai cooperation in the Vietnamese war effort, because of the competing nature of Thai bureaucracies. Along with such knowledge much deference to the Thai was required; this was fairly expensive, psychologically, but in American circles hardly considered more than the traffic would bear. If American organizations could be played off one against another, so could Thai organizations. That is another story, and a fairly full one, the proof of which is in part in the continued willingness to grant virtually every request the Americans made with respect to cooperation in the war, despite much bluster by the Thai and much contortion of policy by the Americans. The American return on its deference to Thai and to Thai institutions was indeed deemed sufficient.

Secondly, in some areas and in some ways the traditional barriers between Thai and *farang* had broken down, something made evident by the *results* of Thai policy—the extraordinary intimacy of Thai-American relations despite Thai practice and tradition. A clue as to how this intimacy developed despite the traditional Thai reserve and distance came in several structured interviews held with Thai government officials. The decision-makers were provided an opportunity to develop traditional Thai views about dealing with *farangs*, something which, in most cases, they were quick to do—for it put the interviewer in *his* place too. But in several cases these views were not presented, and courtesy alone did not explain the omission. Rather, it seemed that some of the senior members of the old regime, those just below the handful of ruling generals, had been "co-opted" by the Americans from whom they had benefited and by whom they had been educated. While holding clear views about the difficulty of working with Americans, they took the relationship as an American would expect it to be taken, in the spirit of pragmatic problem-solving among friends. It was therefore all the more astonishing a testament to the success of the American effort in some areas. Change has occurred too rapidly for the traditional Thai system to acculturate its new elite members to traditional elite attitudes, which was bound to have some effect on the kingdom's overall ability to adapt to new challenges.

The third and final factor is much the most important. What was the overall nature and objective of the partnership between the unequal partners? Was the cooperation being used systemically for systemic purposes? As we shall see in successive chapters, nearly every facet of the Philippine-American relationship was being used by the Philippines to transform their diplomatic stance and bargaining position. If Marcos was personally benefiting, that was largely incidental in scope and size to the other changes occurring. In Thailand, the cooperation became increasingly subsystemic for subsystemic purposes, with substantial controversy building among the educated elite over whether Thai-American cooperation had gone too far. From the early days when Marshal Sarit had used American aid to help him start the economic transformation of the kingdom, members of the regime proceeded to a position where they were using American aid to develop and sustain their own hierarchies; there was now no common view or purpose. In effect the Americans had gained *substantive* access to the Thai regime, even though their *technical* access, to use Nicholas Berry's distinction,[18] was less than in the Philippines. Furthermore, the Thai refusal to coordinate its activities in a way that would advance America's secondary interest in Thailand, namely coping with Thailand's own insurgency, was far more costly to herself than to the United States. It is not necessarily a virtue to be resilient to outside advice, unwilling to perceive the grave challenges on a steadily encroaching perimeter, incapable of concerted action against threats to a kingdom. It was a Pyrrhic victory for powerful generals to weaken ARD, for example, when it was becoming effective in some areas, and when the insurgency was spreading deeper and deeper into the kingdom. Successive sections deal with these questions substantively.

Part II:
Sources of Decision:
Sending Troops to
Viet-Nam

Introduction to Part II

Heretofore we have been concerned with the background to, and the patterns in, Thai and Philippine relations with the United States. In the ensuing three chapters, we take up the specific case of a decision made by both Southeast Asian governments, and look at the differences in the input to the decision-making process.

The question of theoretical import that is posed by the case study is which of our two states, the military-run autocracy, or the open democracy, was more successful in bargaining with the United States when that power requested the dispatch of troops to aid her in the war in Viet-Nam.

This particular case was chosen not only because it was the most easily replicable between the two countries; but also because it was also the most momentous in the relations of each country with the United States in this period. As shown in Table II-1—the result of a poll taken among 500 Thai and Filipinos in mid-1965—relations with the United States were good on the eve of the decision by each country to involve herself in the Vietnamese war directly. Although no directly comparable data were available for the end of our period, it was obvious that the attitude had changed away from such an identification with the United States. To a degree this was related to involvement in the war.

Table II-1
USIA—Philippines and Thailand, May-June 1965 (c/c=500)

Ques. 5. In your opinion, are the basic interests of our country and those of the United
States very much in agreement, fairly well in agreement, rather different, or very
different?

	N Thai.	N Phil.	% Thai.	% Phil.
Very much in agreement	178	104	36	21
Fairly well in agreement	217	324	43	65
Rather different	12	47	2	9
Very different	7	10	1	2
Don't know	86	15	17	3
The Soviet Union?				
Very much in agreement	2	2	—	—
Fairly well in agreement	64	40	13	8
Rather different	140	153	28	31
Very different	111	216	22	43
Don't know	183	89	37	18
Red China?				
Very much in agreement	1	—	—	—
Fairly well in agreement	13	9	3	2
Rather different	89	121	18	24
Very different	236	296	47	59
Don't know	161	74	32	15

Ques. 9. How about the United States Government? Have you a favorable or unfavorable
impression of what the United States Government has been doing in international
affairs recently? Very or only somewhat?

	N Thai.	N Phil.	% Thai.	% Phil.
Favorable—very	225	175	45	35
Favorable—somewhat	182	142	36	28
Unfavorable—very	17	10	3	2
Unfavorable—somewhat	5	7	1	1
Don't know	71	166	14	33

Source: Roper Public Opinion Research Center, data collected for USIA sponsored
attitudinal study, 1965.

5 Pressures from Washington

When Philippine and Thai leaders decided whether or not to send troops to Viet-Nam, the configuration of the balance of forces internationally was characterized by the greatest polarity in a decade. Definitionally this means that "systemic" sources of foreign policy, or those derived from the way international currents indirectly affect a given country, were potent in affecting Thai and Philippine decision-makers. An incipient looseness in the system made it easier for the American president to reverse long-standing policy toward Communist powers. That is not what was perceived in Bangkok or Manila where Lin Piao's 1965 tract on revolution in the "country-side" of the world, which was followed by an increase in Chinese help, in word and deed, to dissidents in both of the Southeast Asian states was pertinent. Nor did the "Cultural Revolution" coming soon afterwards reassure them. Relevant also was the hardening line in the Soviet Union, and in its sphere of influence—where attempts at liberalization by one satellite were severely quashed. Indications of a different sort existed; France and Pakistan remained in SEATO in name only, and their respective leaders berated America for her war policy in Viet-Nam, as did a growing number of leaders and commentators around the globe. States whose security interests overlapped with those of the United States, either had to discount this growing tide inside and out of the United States and close ranks with their protector, as Thailand did, or they had to seek new sources of support for their statecraft, as the Philippines did.

Attitudes and the balance of forces in Southeast Asia itself were a microcosm of the larger arena. In 1965, Indonesia tightened her links with China, while Prince Sihanouk used a radical foreign policy stance to maintain Cambodia's independence; Lee Kuan Yew accused America of interference in Singapore's affairs to consolidate the island's unexpected and unwanted independence; and, General Ne Win, in contrast, used an internally radical policy to consolidate his hold on Burma. The United States felt sufficiently defensive to give urgent attention to the need for social revolution in South Viet-Nam; the "Honolulu Declaration" of 8 February 1966 proclaimed the need for land reform, radical political reform, and the like there. This had a strong impact on Manila.[1]

Fortuitously, the new American resolve in Viet-Nam in 1965 coincided with GESTAPU in Indonesia, which changed a great many things (though fewer than American policy-makers later attributed to it) and made moves toward Southeast Asian regionalism possible again. However much attitudes toward the war hardened against the Americans elsewhere, they proceeded differently after

1965 in Southeast and East Asia. The leaders of Singapore and Malaysia supported America, and the new regime in Indonesia, which was dependent on American aid, had no interest in a North Vietnamese victory. To the northeast, the Chinese nationalists and South Koreans were hard-liners on the war, and the Japanese government in private defended the American war effort, even more steadfastly than their economic benefits from the war would have suggested as prudent.

Both of these factors, systemic and regional, were more important for Thailand than for the Philippines. *Ceteris paribus*, a continental state will be more sensitive to systemic developments than island-nations. As an island-nation, the Philippines could afford to look at the decision on Viet-Nam on its merits; that is, in terms of what it saw the rights and wrongs to be, rather than in terms of contingent necessity. Continental states, necessarily more concerned with the balance of forces, tend to develop clearer notions of how international relations work. Small wonder Thailand takes such pride in her diplomatic tradition, and the Philippines has little such tradition.

Although Filipinos might have been less sensitive to general international and regional developments than the Thai, they were much more sensitive to developments in America, for good historical reasons. Many Filipinos also considered democracy, which they got from America, to be a vital interest, and understood the importance of the growing protest against the war in America much more clearly than did the Thai. There are many aspects of distance in foreign policy, spatial ones not necessarily being the most important.

States become involved in affairs outside their own borders not only because of the way they perceive the balance of forces, and the way it impinges on them, but also for reasons of history. Our second external source of policy is the *external ties*, in this case those each power had with South Viet-Nam and with the Americans there. We have already seen how important both of these states, Thailand and the Philippines, were in the founding of SEATO and how clear their views were as to the direction it should take. After the foundation of SEATO, the two countries began to occupy a peculiar position in American policy. They were, after all, the only potential American allies in Southeast Asia; as such, they were also the object of and, increasingly, the justification for, an American protective shield in Southeast Asia.

Washington justified aiding the French in Indochina on the basis of preventing Communist expansion in the area. "The neighboring countries of Thailand and Burma could be expected to fall under Communist domination if Indochina is controlled by a Communist government. The balance of Southeast Asia would then be in grave hazard," a National Security Council paper said in the early 1950s.[2] In his famous memorandum advocating the use of atomic weapons in Indochina, Admiral Radford proposed that, simultaneously to the air operations, "French Union Forces augmented by such armed forces of the Philippines and Thailand as may be committed would, in coordination with U.S.

Naval and Air Force forces, conduct coordinated ground, naval, and air action to destroy enemy forces in Indochina."[3] If (to American planners in the 1950s) the Philippines seemed less vital than Thailand, owing to Thailand's more vulnerable geographic position, this was evened out through the republic's greater operational involvement in American policy in the region. After all, the United States had been deeply engaged in the anti-Huk campaign of this period, and some of the actors there became involved in Viet-Nam, most conspicuously General Lansdale. The Philippines was a willing partner in and backup to Lansdale's "Saigon Military Mission." At one point, to prevent an anti-Diem coup, this mission diverted two potential accomplices to the Philippines.[4]

The Philippines was also engaged in more immediate and practical (as well as profitable) ventures in Viet-Nam, which helped to lay the groundwork for an expeditionary force. With clandestine American support, former aides to President Magsaysay and former guerrillas of the 1940s grouped to found the Freedom Company of the Philippines in 1954, later renamed (and privately constituted) the Eastern Construction Company after American support was withdrawn. Their purpose, in the words of the Pentagon Papers, was "unconventional warfare," for which they had an almost "untapped" potential. Tapped or not, they made themselves useful under American military assistance covers in Viet-Nam doing a variety of tasks that the Vietnamese could not do—including everything from instructing the Vietnamese army in administrative tasks to assistance in the writing of the Vietnamese constitution.[5]

One might conclude that Filipinos were mercenaries, as Senator Fulbright considered them in the 1960s. In the 1950s, after all, retired Filipinos would hire themselves out to do some of America's dirty work. If such name-calling was good American politics in this later period, it was bad social science. The Filipinos in the 1960s saw themselves as ahead of all Asia in economic and political development. They are good businessmen and had a comparative advantage in counterinsurgency-related activity from their experience in their own anti-Huk campaign; helping other Asian nations do the same thing was logical in terms of their experience, world view, and economic interest. Thanks to the productivity of their universities, they had a surplus of trained manpower, making the export of some of it even more economically sensible. It has also been observed that Filipinos seeking work in Viet-Nam considered that the lack of a Philippine contribution to the war effort "hurt their chances for employment there."[6] They would thus be another source of pressure on the Philippine government. Through all this, a considerable Philippine interest in Viet-Nam developed, without doubt sufficient to influence the decision to dispatch forces.[7] The fact that many of the Filipinos doing business in Saigon were former military and sometimes intelligence personnel tends to corroborate this.

In the early 1960s, Thailand became much more actively involved in the implementation of American policy in Southeast Asia than the Philippines was, although American use of Philippine facilities made the two reasonably equivalent in their utility to the United States. While discussions went on in Paris over the establishment of a Laotian neutral government, the Americans decided to increase the strength of advisors in the Laotian armed forces to the level of five hundred. A position paper circulating in 1964 carried the recommendation that Thailand "be asked to support our program fully, to intensify its own efforts in the north and northeast, and to give further support to operations in Laos, such as additional pilots and possibly artillery teams."[8] Detailed contingency plans, in the event of a breakdown of the ceasefire prevailing in Laos in mid-1962, included roles for Thai forces backed by the United States,[9] though these plans were made without consulting Bangkok. By 1964, Thai involvement in American-Laotian affairs had considerably increased. "Progress in Laos due almost entirely to T28 operations and Thai artillery," CINCPAC, the commander-in-chief, Pacific, telegraphed the Joint Chiefs on 17 August 1964.[10] By the end of 1964, the Americans had already worked out the basis for far-reaching cooperation and the use of Thai bases for the increasing American involvement in Southeast Asia.

Over all, however, external ties were a more potent factor for Filipinos than for the Thai with respect to direct engagement in Vietnamese affairs, despite greater distance and far less historical involvement in the precolonial era. Philippine business groups involved in Viet-Nam could influence foreign policy; extra-governmental groups in Thailand have seldom ever affected public policy— and business was largely in Chinese hands. Prior to the time that the Thai became intimately involved with the Americans in the defense of Laos and South Viet-Nam, one would infer that the only significant direct link they had to Vietnamese affairs was at the level of intelligence. To be sure, the historical intertwining of Thailand and Indochina increased Bangkok's feeling of involvement, which perception made the disparity between its and Manila's involvement in Vietnamese affairs less pronounced. Since the Philippine ties to Viet-Nam were less bound up in preeminently American strategic concerns, the Filipinos could make their decision on PHILCAG, as the Civic Action Group became known, less out of regard for American pressure than out of regard for their own interest.

It is usually assumed that the most important external pressure, or policy source, for both countries in these decisions was the "external input," our third external source, and specifically in this case the pressure exerted by the United States. Technically, of course, it is the government of South Viet-Nam that requested assistance, but it is not to its request that the Thai and Filipinos responded. As one wag put it in the *Manila Times*, "The simple fact of the matter is that the South Vietnamese are as much in control of the war in their country as the watchman at the Philippine National Bank building runs the [bank's] lending investment operation."[11] Partly because of this appearance of American control, neither state had contributed troops to the war effort in Viet-Nam before 1966. President Johnson wanted to have the presence of other

Southeast Asian troops fighting alongside Americans precisely to change this appearance.

Nonetheless, as early as 1964, the Philippines had taken steps to support South Viet-Nam in other ways, without American prodding. A bill approved in July of that year appropriated one million pesos for economic, medical, and technical assistance, justified on the basis that South Viet-Nam was (1) resisting Communist aggression, (2) under the SEATO protocol, and (3) enjoying support from other SEATO members, and (4) that the Philippines was committed to democracy and freedom; "PHILCON I" went to Viet-Nam later in 1964.[12] There is no doubt that such is precisely how the issue was seen by Macapagal and his administration. Prior to the commitment of American land forces to Viet-Nam, the Filipinos and Americans had already begun discussing a Philippine contribution of eighteen hundred men to serve there. The first high-level talks on this occurred during Macapagal's state visit to Washington in October 1964. Subsequently, Macapagal wrote privately:

President Johnson personally and through top advisors like the Secretary of State . . . Defense and the American ambassador . . . undertook steady persuasions as tactfully as they could to make my administration send a 2,000 men engineer contingent to Viet-Nam. More out of conviction than their persuasion, I recommended to Congress in 1965 the dispatch of the contingent.[13]

The whole effort was ill starred, mainly owing to the opposition of Marcos, then Senate president. Macapagal, however, "despite the continued persuasions . . . declined to certify its enactment in the two special sessions of Congress after the regular session failed to enact the measure." One suspects the reason is tied to his reaction to American policy. For in reply to the question of what kind of support from President Johnson he expected in return for sending the troops, Macapagal wrote:

It was not so much for my support of the project to send 2,000 men to Vietnam as on the basis of the general mutual cooperation between the two countries for the promotion of common objectives that I expected the Johnson administration to implement the terms of the Johnson-Macapagal communique of October 6, 1964, which could assist my administration. The implementation turned out to be lukewarm as indicated by the fact that the 100,000 tons of rice committed to be shipped to the Philippines in 1965 did not arrive and, I understand, was rerouted to Vietnam.[14]

By that time, Washington had, indeed, turned lukewarm toward him; it would seem clear that Washington preferred waiting out the Philippine elections of 1965 in hopes of getting PHILCAG through Marcos than getting it earlier with Macapagal.[15] As it turned out, Marcos won and reversed his stand on PHILCAG, on the negotiations on which we shall concentrate.

However warm the ties between Washington and Manila after Marcos's election, President Johnson could not be sure he would get soldiers without pressing. The proposal was certain to set off a great national debate, controversial as the war had already become in some quarters, despite the economic aid the Philippine government had already extended to South Viet-Nam in the preceding years.

Once Marcos had committed himself to support of a troop contingent, the legislature had to be pressed to authorize funds. Marcos himself was not *as such* pressed into a change of his position by the Americans but took his new reversed stand in support of PHILCAG for reasons of role, although he too would be sensitive to the type of subtle, implicit pressures that were the primary American input into this process. The *Manila Times*, however, editorialized that "the pressure on the Philippine government to send the military contingent to Viet-Nam is reminiscent of the drive to secure passage of the Bell Trade Act of 20 years ago. . . . The implication appears to be that no such aid can be expected if the condition is not fulfilled."[16] Senate President Tolentino denounced the "incredible pressures" put on Filipino lawmakers and noted that, although it was the South Vietnamese government which requested Philippine help, it was the United States which resorted to "intimidation" and other coercive measures to secure presidential support in the first instance.[17] Notwithstanding, it is Marcos who had to exert the pressure on Congress.

True, we can assume that the Americans did not sit idly by as the Philippine internal debate raged. Americans and many leading Philippine senators, however, insist that no arms were twisted (though it is those who were in favor of PHILCAG from the first who insist on the point most strongly). It seems clear that the really important pressure was more subtle; to a Filipino, sensitive to nuance and stubborn when overtly pushed, such would be more compelling. The Americans made a constant show of attention to the Philippines in early 1966. Vice President Humphrey came twice; Secretary of State Rusk and Ambassador Harriman came on the "peace offensive" that Johnson had dispatched to all parts of the globe; General Lansdale came in from Saigon to see his old friends, as did Congressman Zablocki from Washington. A Philippine-American Assembly took place in Davao, keynoted by William Bundy, which allowed frustrations to be aired, and convinced the Filipinos that the Americans still considered them important—and respected their desire for greater flexibility in their own foreign policy.[18] It was a shadow play of sorts, in which both sides spoke publicly of the high posture[19] of the other party and bargained privately, explicitly and implicitly, to see how intent the other side was.

From a positive point of view—which is how Filipinos would always look at such bargaining—what could the Philippines get from the Americans in return for their participation? What happens, they would ask, if the Americans are *utang na loob*, or indebted, to us? It would of course be a point of honor that no such consideration obtained; President Marcos not surprisingly stressed that PHILCAG was to be sent because it was a Philippine national interest. "It would be an insult to our people to insinuate that these convictions were imposed on us by any foreign power."[20] Hence the material incentives for the decisions had to be hidden. In his address to the nation, Marcos denied "vehemently" that the decision to ask Congress to appropriate funds for PHILCAG was made "for and in consideration of any additional aid whether in dollars or any other form from the United States.... Neither coercion, threats, blackmail, nor dollars have dictated this judgment. Now and in the future, only the national interest of the Philippines shall determine my decision."[21] This "high posture," as a State Department document termed it, was to cause trouble in time. However, it is easy to understand why, from the outset, Marcos "took the position that he did not want the Philippines to be placed in the position of having sent PHILCAG to Vietnam in return for U.S. aid," which was a good bargaining tactic.[22]

U.S. aid was indeed a factor despite this "high posture." The explicit American offer is summarized in the Symington report:

1. Equipment and logistic support of PHILCAG—c. $35,000,000
2. Overseas allowances
3. Replacement costs for a replacement unit in the Philippines
4. Two swiftcraft in addition to two already promised ($200,000 apiece)
5. Accelerated funding for three, already-promised, engineer construction battalions
6. Equipment with which "to strengthen Philippine forces at home": Engineering equipment, rifles and machine guns, follow-on support, packing, crating, handling, and transportation—or about three million dollars.[23]

Marcos proposed that items 4-6 not be *considered* as related to PHILCAG. For purposes of American accounting and in order to get the money out of service funds of the Defense Department, as "Viet-Nam related," these were considered as PHILCAG items. However, for purposes of Philippine pride, they were not so considered. Marcos declined to accept the third item. Had replacement units been provided for, there would have been little room left for honor; it would have appeared that the Philippines was providing nothing except Asian cannon fodder.

Having taken this tack, Marcos could bargain for all the traditional requests with which to increase his domestic strength. A month after PHILCAG was passed, for example, an American panel came to Manila for new negotiations on veterans' benefits, an issue previously closed by the American side. The Philippines got $31.2 million as benefits. To be sure, the negotiators on this issue did not explicitly link their discussions to PHILCAG. The question of veterans' benefits had been on the Philippine agenda for a long time. Yet in the view of one of the American negotiators, it is inconceivable that the Americans would have discussed the question were it not for PHILCAG. Agreeing to discuss it left the door open for all the favorite (and sometimes extraordinary) tactics that the Philippine side was accustomed to employ in dealing with important Americans.[24] Later in 1966, the American House voted to expand hospitalization and children's benefits for Philippine veterans of World War II. Two congressmen warned, however, that they would support no further benefits for the Philippines unless she began playing a larger role in Viet-Nam—as if any further comment needed to be made on the relation between the two.[25] Also, in 1966, it was agreed that the two sides would open discussions on the Laurel-Langley Trade Agreement. Such discussions were not an American interest, as the American side simply wished for the provisions to run their course in 1974, expecting no concessions from the Philippines (which in fact is what happened). There also was President Marcos's visit to Washington. Every Philippine president, save Magsaysay, has made a state visit to the U.S. Although the invitation would not have been a subject for explicit bargaining, such a trip would have been impossible without PHILCAG. The benefits to a Philippine president of a state visit to the United States, with addresses to joint sessions of Congress and ticker tape parades in New York, are incalculable. No president ever appeared to get more mileage out of it than Marcos: on his return he claimed (disingenuously) to have been promised $400 million.

Thenceforth, the Philippines did have the advantage in her bargaining with the United States. It is the Americans who had wanted a show of allies, and the Philippines had obliged. During the ensuing two years, no Philippine request was too large or too small to be discussed by the two parties. "The history of our relations thereafter was determined by our *utang na loob* to them," an American official commented.

The United States was able to get a civic action group out of the Philippines; but Lyndon Johnson wanted a still better show of Asian support in Viet-Nam. Demonstrating remarkable insensitivity, Johnson, in Seoul for a conference with the Koreans at the end of October 1966, was suddenly inspired to calculate that if the Koreans could send 50,000 troops, the Philippines, with a fifth larger population, could send a proportionally greater force, instead of its tiny battalion. This Ambassador Blair was instructed to request. Blair, a skillful diplomat, knew that it was not feasible, and that it grew less so daily. He therefore attempted to head off the request. Johnson, not to be deterred, instructed Blair to proceed. Blair and Marcos discussed it amicably, as Marcos knew Blair understood the impossibility of the request. Secretary of State Dean Rusk was also made a troop-recruiter; before his December 1966 trip to Asia, he was instructed to go to Manila and press Marcos. Rusk reportedly told officials that Blair was in the doghouse with the president for his failure to enlist more Filipino troops. Marcos found the whole thing preposterous, and knew a visit by Rusk would be counterproductive. All the American blank checks and presidential pressure could not change the domestic Philippine situation as it then stood; the American Secretary of State could not be welcomed in Manila.

The following summer of 1967, President Johnson sent General Maxwell Taylor and Clark Clifford, then a presidential advisor, on a tour of Asia to try once again to drum up further support, especially from the Thai. They were supposed to visit Manila (and said so publicly), but were advised by Blair, who had discussed it with Marcos, that, in view of the extremely delicate discussions then going on in the Philippine congress for the renewal of funding for PHILCAG, their visit could only be counterproductive. Ironically, they then did have to stop at Clark Air Force Base, owing to engine trouble. It was embarrassing to the American officials in Manila that two such important emissaries could not visit a close ally. The Thai, however, had no excuse to keep the mission away.

The first evident difference in the negotiations between the Thai and the Americans and the Filipinos and Americans is the difference in timing. The American commitment of ground forces to Viet-Nam and the first discussions about PHILCAG had occurred two years before the major negotiations in Bangkok (October 1967). Koreans, Australians, and New Zealanders were long since fighting in Viet-Nam also, and PHILCAG was already at work. The reason for the lateness derives from the strategic location of Thailand. As we noted earlier, American bases in the Philippines in the mid-1969s were still, for all intents and purposes, islands of American sovereignty, and not much in the way of additional permission was needed for a vast build-up on them; which was, in any event, generally welcomed, bringing as it did greater revenue. In contrast, as one American put it, the consent for every stage of the buildup of American bases in Thailand had to be "wrung out" of the Thai authorities. No blank checks were issued—though, in fact, they almost invariably agreed to American requests after a suitable quid pro quo was found, and even sometimes when it was not. Until the main U.S. bases had been developed and the substance of the backup operation achieved, the almost daily requests for additional cooperation from Bangkok were always more for strategic significance than for the psychological advantage deriving from a Thai contingent. Hence, the push for a great increase in the Thai troop commitment, above and beyond the first small ground combat unit, waited until after the Americans had gained the right to base B-52s in Thailand in early 1967.

Much of the idealism that had existed among the allied governments when the American commitment was increased in 1965 had gone out of the war effort by 1967. This idealism had coincided with the period when the Americans were getting base rights, not troops. By 1967, as one distinguished Thai put it, all that was left as far as Thai participation in Viet-Nam was concerned "was just a question of money—how much we could get out of it." Yet some principle remained in the Thai commitment. Following on a state visit to Canada in June 1967, the king himself had made a private visit to Washington and, during a discussion with President Johnson, promised that Thailand "would carry out her responsibilities and do her fair share" in Viet-Nam—meaning send troops to fight alongside (and under the command of) the Americans.

But the Thai beyond question did not really wish to send troops to

Viet-Nam—or they would have done so already. Ambassador Graham Martin, posted to Thailand between 1964 and 1967, testified quite straightforwardly that the Thai sent troops "in the full realization that it was increasingly uncomfortable for the United States to have massive deployment of U.S. troops with far less contingents from the other partners in the SEATO Alliance. . . . I do not believe that there was a firm conviction that the troops were actually all that important except for these reasons."[26] Thanat Khoman, in an admittedly less cordial period, commented later that "the situation worsened when the United States, feeling lonely in Viet-Nam began to induce other countries . . . to get into the quagmire that she was, to a certain extent, responsible for creating. . . . Thailand, *at the U.S. insistence*, had to send a full division of 12,000 men to join the American GI's."[27] The atmosphere in which the negotiations took place was thus very different—and much more cynical—from that in the Philippines, where a new president had just taken office and the war effort had not lost its momentum.

The first negotiations with Thailand were for a small ground combat unit of officers and men—2207 in all. This was agreed to in January 1967, and the men arrived in Viet-Nam in September. But American public opinion was becoming more demanding of results and increasingly curious that Asian allies were playing so modest a role. As the 1968 presidential elections drew nearer, and as Washington's intention of further escalation became apparent, the need for more troops became compelling. Consequently, the important negotiations came after the "Queen's Cobras" had already been agreed upon, i.e. negotiations for a substantially larger contingent, befitting the size of the Thai commitment to an Allied victory, as the Americans saw it.

In all negotiations between the Thai and Americans, permission for increased use of Thai facilities, or an increased Thai contribution of manpower, characteristically came after evidence of heightened American commitment in the war. The Pentagon papers reveal that, following the Gulf of Tonkin incident, for example, when a new American resolve was shown, "certain impediments" (i.e., Thai restrictions) to American actions were removed; hostile aircraft now could be engaged over or pursued into airspace over Thailand.[28] In 1967, the Thai, feeling that the Americans could "win" if only they made a sufficient commitment, did not wish to get any deeper into the Vietnamese "quagmire" unless the Americans escalated their effort. They very badly wanted the air war intensified, for example. After all, Japan had not surrendered in 1945 until atomic bombs were dropped, Thanom hinted.[29]

In July 1967 came the Taylor-Clifford mission to get more allied troops. They made a very strong and clever pitch, in terms of a greater American commitment, rather than directly in terms of the need for more troops.[30] This was the last period of self-confidence in Viet-Nam. President Johnson appeared blind to the obstacles ahead of him, and determined to press the war until "victory" was in hand. This reassured the Thai, who saw military victory as within the grasp of the allies. Some journalists wrote almost euphorically of the impending defeat and occupation of North Viet-Nam.[31] But before increasing the war's intensity, President Johnson would need a stronger show of support from Asian allies to balance the escalation, in domestic public opinion, the Americans said—an argument of which the Thai were to hear more. By the time Thai and American negotiators could get down to the conference table to bargain, Senator Percy and nineteen other senators would have introduced a resolution calling on President Johnson to seek a greater contribution to the war effort from America's Asian allies.[32]

The Thai were not fully reassured by the new American show of resolve. In order to keep the Americans on the defensive and to ensure that they had as strong a bargaining position as possible in the forthcoming negotiations for the supply of troops, they intensified their propaganda, airing their differences on the war in the wake of Clifford and Taylor's departure. "THAILAND AND AMERICA HAVE DIFFERENT VIEWS ON THE VIETNAM WAR ISSUE, PREMIER REVEALS," ran a headline in *Thai Rath*, a paper with good sources.[33] Thailand could not enlarge the contingent in Viet-Nam because it was "burdened with the task of maintaining national security and suppressing terrorists."[34] From the spring of 1967 on, columnists were slipped information about the Thai bargaining position. Writers often favorably compared Thailand's level of aid to Viet-Nam with that of the other allies, but then would decry the lack of sufficient American aid in a particular area: intelligence equipment so the government could keep its secrets (and presumably discover other people's). The need for ground-air missiles was constantly reiterated. Thanat took the hardest line, and noted that Thailand could increase its contribution to Viet-Nam in different ways from the dispatching of soldiers. "There are many other ways in military, political, and economic areas."[35]

This was effective. The day after complaints about insufficient electronic equipment for intelligence work, it was reported that the United States would grant an unlimited amount of financial aid for counterinsurgency and developmental projects in the Northeast.[36] "Unlimited" aid for the Northeast meant for all projects that were feasible and sensible, but this required planning that was a long way off. The Thai generals had grander—or at least more immediate—things in mind.

Negotiations began in the autumn of 1967, with the Thai digging in their heels in order to get everything possible—with consequences they would have cause to resent. On the American side was the new and very capable Thai-speaking ambassador, Leonard Unger. On the other side, the eminently practical Air Chief Marshal Dawee Chullasapya took charge; his attitude may be gauged by his reported statement that increased American aid to the armed forces could eliminate any difficulties for national security caused by sending a division of troops to Viet-Nam.[37] There was no input from the foreign ministry.

The main line of the Thai case was that, if they sent their best soldiers to

Viet-Nam, they would, in the State Department's words, "be weakening their capability to deal with the insurgency at home." The Americans "agreed with this analysis."[38] The American position thus was that the Thai should not have to pay any extra cost for sending their troops to Viet-Nam, but there was much room for negotiations over what constituted that cost. The Thai surely knew that, as a senior American put it, "We were under orders to get the troops into Viet-Nam and we weren't paying too much attention to the cost." The haggling lasted a long time. At the very end, Thanom still insisted that troops had not been committed, because "the additional aid the U.S. will give us is not yet to our satisfaction and negotiations will have to go on."[39] Meanwhile, Thanat and Pote Sarasin returned from the United States where they had been given further promises of extensive support; their line was softer. Prapat generally seemed to take a softer line too. He returned from South Viet-Nam arguing that an increase in troop commitment would be a good thing; South Viet-Nam was "badly in need of assistance."[40] In the end, the Thai got an additional $15 million military assistance (MAP) funds a year for two years for modernization of their armed forces to compensate for sending troops to Viet-Nam, which would "weaken the kingdom." It got the battery of Hawk antiaircraft missiles—enough to expand the missile battalion to brigade strength; it got full equipment, logistic support costs and replacement costs for the new division at home; overseas allowances; training costs; mustering-out allowances and representation funds for units: or about $50 million per year, according to U.S. government estimates.[41]

In addition there was a highly important negative external input by the United States, which pressed the American negotiators even more, and which made all the more financial incentive necessary as compensation. This was the growing attack on both allies by Senator Fulbright and others. At the time of the discussions for the Queen's Cobras, Fulbright referred to Thailand as an American colony; such a slur by a leading citizen of a great power is big news in a small country, and in this case it was even discussed in cabinet.[42] Thanat lost his patience, which provoked Marshal Dawee to bate him, saying that only Mao, Fulbright and Thanat were commenting on Thailand's alleged colonial status.[43] Thanat saw more clearly than his colleagues that this was serious. He grew increasingly nervous about the alliance. "He was the first to want in and the first to want out," one American negotiator commented.

For the Philippines there was also much bitterness and hurt feelings. Yet initially it seemed that they underestimated the importance of the American antiwar movement in a different way; being used to hyperbole in their own political arena, the Filipinos assumed that Fulbright's reaction was part of the ongoing, loud-talking democratic process. They soon learned differently. By 1969, Senator Fulbright could say at the Symington hearings that it was his feeling "that all we did was go over and hire their soldiers in order to support our then administration's view that so many people were in sympathy with our war in Vietnam. And we paid a very high price for it."[44] Fulbright and his colleagues continually asked why, if there was a considerable body of support for PHILCAG, as the American minister in Manila, James Wilson, had argued, the Philippines should have demanded a price for sending the expeditionary force. "Why they would insist on our paying these little amounts of a dollar a day allowance overseas and so on, to me only emphasizes the fact that we appear to be suckers who are willing to be bled in any and every pore. This is very offensive to me."[45]

The only response that makes any sense is the one the government officials at the hearings were most constrained from saying: at a time when President Johnson wanted Asian allies fighting in Viet-Nam, when the United States was vastly increasing its use of Philippine and Thai facilities in its war and steadily increasing its requests for cooperation, and when both of these countries had severe budgetary constraints at home and a growing need for the troops to maintain domestic order, it was hardly important that the allies would financially benefit from the operation. Johnson was willing to pay any price, and it is remarkable that he did not have to pay a higher one. The more substantial chunks of money, like the veterans' payments, were, in the Philippine view, monies owed anyway. The United States had helped finance the efforts of European and Asian allies in both world wars, not to mention the Korean War—where, in fact, the direct cost of the Philippine contingent had been higher than that of PHILCAG.[46] It was hardly precedent shattering, after lend-lease and all the rest, to pay the external costs for two developing nations' war effort. To be sure, alongside the apparent North Vietnamese resolution and sacrifice, the allies' attitude appears petty. But whatever else can be said, the Thai and Filipinos, unlike the North Vietnamese, were not fighting for the absorption of a different political system into their own system. That the allies should do well while doing good (as they saw it) hardly struck them as exceptional. Uncle Sam was throwing money around as never before, and an old Thai adage says, "Fill your jar while the tide is up."[47]

In all, as we have seen, a wide variety of pressures and incentives was used by Washington to achieve Thai and Philippine contingents for the war. It is worth noting, however, that for both Asian powers, perhaps the most important pressure was one not actively exerted at all, as is often the case in bargaining between unequal partners: the greater the disparity in size and resources, the less overt pressure the greater power will have to exert. The smaller power is only too aware of how much the greater power can do for him, and conversely of how much can be withdrawn if he does not go along. The big power can look out for himself: the small power often looks for ways to be helpful to the great power. When either partner needs help, whether as between states, groups, or individuals, and when there is a pattern of such cooperation in the past, the larger will be outraged if turned down, and in most circumstances can do positive damage, especially economic, to the smaller, while the smaller can only deny cooperation if turned down. These are differences of degree, rather than of kind, but they are nonetheless important. In the mind of every Filipino and Thai who had a role in the negotiations with the Americans was, What would the consequences be if his government refused to send troops to Viet-Nam, given the intensity of President Johnson's desires? Such a refusal would have constituted a very serious challenge to the relationship, jeopardizing at the very least the 100 percent increase in U.S. military spending that had already occurred in both countries since the escalation in Viet-Nam. As a gauge to American thinking between 1966 and March 1968, it is worth remembering that Washington resented the smallness of the Philippine contingent.

In all the negotiation that went on between Thai and Philippine leaders on the one hand, and Americans on the other, inequality pertained at the bureaucratic level as well. By 1966, the United States had a vast war-related data-producing and -processing capability in Southeast Asia, backed up an even greater capability in Washington. In any negotiation, the Americans started with highly specific needs and studies purporting to show the effect of whatever was being sought. One American involved in the negotiations in Thailand commented that the Thai could not even keep up with the flow of American paper, much less counter it. To be sure, it is possible for the smaller country to have an intuitive sense of whether or not a particular position will be helpful, but it is more difficult to counter it if the larger party can inundate the table with computer printouts purporting to demonstrate the appropriateness of its request.

Adding it all up, the Thai obviously got more in the bargain than the Filipinos, in specific Viet-Nam-related funds—as a result of their lengthy haggling and shrewd orchestration of their bargaining process. However, the Filipinos got more altogether when the indirect benefits are added up, especially when it is realized that they were contributing so much less in the way of manpower to the war. This does not mean, however, that the external input, American pressure, was more important for the Filipinos: perhaps it is the other way around. The Americans had to concede more to the Filipinos of a substantive nature, beyond the immediate payoffs to either of the two armed forces, because the Filipinos were less buyable, hence more expensive, thanks to the strength of other foreign policy sources. Philippine bargaining, after all, was done by a broad variety of agencies and departments of government, because a broad variety ruled in that country at the time. All of these were rewarded for their Viet-Nam-related efforts. In Thailand, where the military ruled, only the military was paid off, because it was perceived in Washington that they were the only ones that counted in making a key decision such as the one to send troops.

Perhaps, the strongest card of the Filipinos in bargaining with the Americans was their own weakness. They could do little actively for the United States, and in substantial measure they thought that what they had been asked to do was not going to be terribly useful, and might be harmful. Nothing the United States could do would induce them to send 50,000 troops; they had their own very clear views of what was needed, and knew their own limitations well. Other things being equal, their decision should have elicited more respect from Americans than the Thai decision, as it was openly, and less cynically, reached.

6

Societal Attitudes in Bangkok and Manila

Organized, conscious, structured lobbying on foreign policy issues and on a government's general foreign policy stance is a rarity in most less-developed countries, inasmuch as differentiation has proceeded insufficiently far in the modern sector, comparatively with more developed states.[1] We would call all such lobbying general-subjective, where those seeking to alter policy are conscious of their purpose and general in their objective, rather than sectoral, or particularistic. On the other hand, particularistic-objective sources of foreign policy in less-developed countries, where groups work for change largely unconscious of their effect on foreign policy, and are sectarian or ethnic oriented in their objectives, are plentiful. We can look at the decisions of the Philippine and Thai government to send troops to Viet-Nam in terms of these two types of societal pressures.

Pressure from the society—general-subjective policy sources—impinged greatly on the Philippine government in its decision to send troops to Viet-Nam, whereas there were few such pressures existing in Thailand to affect that government's decision. Likewise, particularistic-objective sources of policy were stronger in the Philippines than in Thailand, and affected the decision two ways. The state of the society—the amount of insurrection and general instability—counted much more in Manila than in Bangkok; insurgents thus affected foreign policy more in the Philippines than in Thailand. Secondly, widely held social attitudes did much to shape the general character of the Philippine contingent, whereas to the extent that there were public attitudes on such an issue in Thailand they affected policy less.

The radical nationalist movement is the first general-subjective policy source apparent in the Philippines. From the first it was able to ride the issue of the Vietnamese war toward greater strength in Manila. When President Macapagal's bill went to Congress in 1965, the then young organization Kabataan Makabayan (KM), a Maoist-oriented youth movement destined to grow greatly in power, provided much of the manpower and support for the June 18 rally of the Vietcong-supporting "Philippine Committee for Freedom in South Viet-Nam."

Countervailing forces supporting the American war effort and the South Vietnamese regime developed in reaction—although with only a tenth as many supporters as the KM. These were led by the "Anti-Communist Youth League" and a variety of similar organizations.[2]

Nine months later, with Marcos in power, much the same sort of activity transpired. A torch-bearing rally of about four thousand people, most of them students, was held outside Congress. Congressmen were upset when they were told that it was partly organized by extreme radicals from Madison, Wisconsin, who were members of the "National Coordinating Committee to End the War in Viet-Nam."[3] The day after the students had their day, however, thirty-five veterans' organizations held demonstrations in support of PHILCAG, reportedly dwarfing those of the students.[4]

Although Filipinos, broadly speaking, were and are, conservative and anti-Communist, and although they theoretically wished to help "defeat communism" in Viet-Nam, they nonetheless were deeply ambiguous about PHILCAG. A private poll in Manila taken after PHILCAG had left for Viet-Nam showed that 71 percent of greater Manila residents approved PHILCAG, 23 percent disapproved, and 6 percent had no opinion. On the other hand, it showed that only 44 percent would have approved sending "combat" troops, while 50 percent would have disapproved (the remainder having no opinion). As a State Department document noted:

There was strong feeling that the Philippines should not take up aggressive combat against the North Vietnamese and the Viet Cong who had never attacked the Philippines. Such action might conceivably open the Philippines to some unknowable retaliation; and certainly, they would foreclose a cherished Philippine hope that the Philippines by offering the hand of friendship, might some day play a role as peacemaker.[5]

PHILCAG must be kept in perspective, as other issues roused even stronger feelings. A survey by the Institute of Philippine Culture based on data gathered in the last half of 1969 measured various groups' perceptions of national problems. It shows that of the eight issues mentioned as "crucial" to national "influentials," or elite members, Philippine participation in Viet-Nam ranked seventh, with 22 percent, after land reform, foreign investments, the Laurel-Langley Agreement, the breakdown of traditional morality, the American bases agreement, and demonstrations against the Catholic hierarchy; only the prosecution of the Sabah claim, with 11 percent, was considered less crucial. Local influentials ranked the issues identically, with some slight variation in percentages.[6] A similar study in greater depth of attitudes of "influential respondents" showed a similar result, as shown in Table 6-1. Fourteen percent of national influentials and 26 percent of local influentials considered Viet-Nam "crucial," 75 percent and 63 percent "not crucial," and 11 percent of each as not an issue. By far the biggest age group considering it crucial were the young—45 percent for those twenty-five to thirty-four years old, only 5 percent for those over sixty-five. Ranked by area of influence, those in the professions considered it least crucial, with those in government, social justice, and religion considering it the most crucial (29, 30, and 33 percent respectively).[7]

One reason PHILCAG could stir such emotion, when it ranked relatively low among other issues, is precisely the perception that so many more important

Table 6-1

IPC/PAASCU influential respondents classified by selected variables, cross-classified by their opinion on the issue of Philippine participation in the Vietnamese war (1969-70)

Selected Variables	Crucial		Not Crucial		Not Issue		Total		No Reply	Not Asked
	N	%	N	%	N	%	N	%	N	N
Level of Influence										
National	27	23%	76	66%	13	11%	116	100%	8	46
Local	79	33	138	57	24	10	241	100	21	10
Total	106	30%	214	60%	37	10%	357	100%	29	56
Age										
25-34	13	45%	14	48%	2	7%	29	100%	1	5
35-44	21	26	47	59	12	15	80	100	5	6
45-54	30	30	62	62	8	8	100	100	9	15
55-64	22	32	39	57	7	10	68	100	5	10
65 yrs. and over	7	35	11	55	2	10	20	100	4	10
Age unknown	13	22	41	68	6	10	60	100	5	10
Total	106	30%	214	60%	37	10%	357	100%	29	56
Area of Influence										
Government	25	37%	34	51%	8	12%	67	100%	14	22
Economics	23	24	62	66	9	10	94	10	4	16
Education	15	33	25	56	5	11	45	100	4	5
Professions	12	16	52	70	10	14	74	100	5	2
Mass media	13	33	21	54	5	13	39	100	0	5
Social Justice and Welfare	10	43	13	57	0	0	23	100	0	5
Religion	8	53	7	47	0	0	15	100	2	1
Total	106	30%	214	60%	37	10%	357	100%	29	56
Occupational Area										
Government	32	31%	60	59%	10	10%	102	100%	7	28
Private	74	29	154	60	27	11	255	100	22	28
Total	106	30%	214	60%	37	10%	357	100%	29	56

issues *did* exist from which PHILCAG deflected governmental concern; note that the six issues in the first poll ranking higher were structural questions rather than foreign policy undertakings, despite the fact that three of them involved relations with the United States. The only one ranking lower, Sabah, was also a foreign policy *démarche*, and one that never elicited much international respect.

Participation in the war detracted from the possibility of solving other problems. Marcos had to use up much of the leverage that an incoming president has in order to get PHILCAG through the legislature; he might have accomplished much more in land reform, the inference seems to be, had he put the same energy there.

While PHILCAG started a "great national debate," the proposal to send Thai troops to Viet-Nam occasioned no public debate, and by all evidence little private discussion. The attitude seems to have been that there would be no negative implications to deepening the kingdom's involvement in Viet-Nam if the question were not broached. The State Department reported to the Symington Committee that the "Thai body politic, according to all indications, supports the deployment of troops to Viet-Nam. Later, during the 1969 Parliamentary Campaign, virtually no candidate took a stand against this participation."[8] Kuang Aphaiwong, a former prime minister and leader of what can loosely be called, in this nonconstitutional period of 1967, the loyal opposition, asked why the government was sending only a thousand men, which was like "throwing a can of water onto the fire."[9] A columnist in the *Siam Times* asked why combat soldiers were not sent the previous year—for it was "the Communists who are on the defensive . . . now," directly implying that it was time his country start backing the winning horse. The Thai press was full of reports that, for example, American intelligence estimates claimed that stepped-up pressure on North Viet-Nam would not bring a Chinese intervention. Thus the Thai argued that the "hawk" faction in Washington was growing in strength.[10]

The flavor of popular attitudes during the time of the first discussions on the Queen's Cobras may be got from a comment in *Siam Rath* on an incorrect, if prescient, American report that B-52s were stationed at Thai bases for bombing the North Vietnamese. The Royal Thai government denied the report, and the paper noted:

All the Thai people naturally believe statements made by their government because the Thai people are docile and always believe what is told them by persons in authority. Even though many Thais are able to read English and read American publications regularly, they are not interested in reports on which denials have been issued by their government. Thais are not like Americans who are stubborn and contradict their leaders as they please.[11]

The second basic type of societal source of policy, the particularistic-objective sources, was also stronger in the Philippines. The degree of dissidence and conflict existing in a country at a given time will obviously affect many foreign policy decisions. In the case of Thailand, a rebellion had broken out in the Northeast of the kingdom a year before the first request for troops, and by the time that the more important 1967 decision had to be made about troops for Viet-Nam, the rebellion had become much more serious. It was on the verge of spreading, or breaking out separately, in the north of the kingdom as well.

In contrast, when the PHILCAG debate occurred, although there was considerable nationalist ferment in the country, there was little problem of active dissidence beyond the low-burning flames of the old Huks in central Luzon. They were more interested in crime and pay-offs in the Clark Air Force Base area than in anything else.[12] The new administration had confidence in its ability to solve basic problems. To the extent that the governmental elites foresaw possibilities of dissidence in the future, the prospects for PHILCAG were strengthened, given the nature of the job envisaged in Viet-Nam and the uses such training would have back home in dealing with similar problems. Since the Thai had no such mission for their troops at the time, despite worsening rebellion in the Northeast, we must assume that they were far more vulnerable to American pressure and/or that they did not feel as concerned by the dissidence as they should have, which fact is corroborated elsewhere.

There were only a few indications to the contrary. *Siam Rath*, M.R. Kukrit Pramoj's paper, suggested that rather than send a combat unit to Viet-Nam, "It would be wiser for Thailand . . . to guard our border along the Mekong River thus giving the Thai people in the Northeast an increased feeling of security against the danger menacing from outside!"[13]

From all points of view, particularistic-objective forces were stronger in the Philippines. Indeed, with the birth of the Maoist New People's Army two years after PHILCAG's arrival in Viet-Nam, a very strong prop was kicked out from under the contingent. Partly as a result of this the contingent was soon brought home. By the end of 1969, all the troops were back, ready to be sent, as "PACAG," to Central Luzon, where peace and order were deteriorating apace, and where their assistance was apparently much sought.[14]

Among all the involved parties and in the public sector generally, the PHILCAG debate triggered emotions involving self-respect, and here we see another type of particularistic-objective forces as shaping the character of the national commitment to the Vietnamese war. Everybody knew that the pertinent request for Philippine support came from Washington, not Saigon. There were many unabashedly pro-American Filipinos ready to serve America (with the inherent financial advantages at least a partial factor). Congressman Pendatun, for example, on behalf of the Philippine Legion, publicly offered volunteers for Viet-Nam; he thought there would be 10,000-50,000 willing to serve. No doubt he was right. He did add, however, that the United States must finance those volunteers, just as it was financing the Korean contingent. Presumably the Filipinos would have been incorporated into the American army, as in World War II.[15] But the compromise reached between those Filipinos unreservedly "pro" and those "anti" PHILCAG was always based on national dignity. From the first, it was a question of preeminent interest as to whether the Philippines could contrive to avoid losing face in participating; Senator Morse, after all, had already said that if Philippine troops were sent, they would be "hired mercenaries," not allied forces.[16] What emerged was a genuine desire that the contingent be unmistakedly Philippine in character, mission, leadership, and financing.

When the Symington hearings, in late 1969, made public the extent of American financing, a tremendous crisis of confidence, and a self-perceived loss of face of sizable proportions, developed in the Philippines. Consequently, President Marcos withdrew the rest of PHILCAG more suddenly than had been anticipated. Although all this happened in 1969-72, it sheds light on how PHILCAG and international involvements in general were seen in 1966.

The contradiction that has to be resolved is, Why, when Filipinos are quick to glean benefit from their relations with larger partners like the United States (and this must be considered an adaptive trait), and when it was well known that Washington was going to be generous if PHILCAG were sent, should they have reacted so forcefully when details of the arrangements were discovered? Although President Marcos in the 1966 negotiations had insisted that as little as possible be said about Philippine benefits attendant to her dispatching of the battalion, there never was any secrecy about the fact that the United States was paying the external costs for PHILCAG as well as for those of the other forces from allied LDCs. The American probably most closely involved in the actual negotiations between the American embassy and Malacañang observed, somewhat hyperbolically, that "every Congressman had blackmailed Marcos into giving him a road, a dam, a payoff of some sort for his vote; so we were very much in debt to Marcos." It is hardly credible that any such congressmen could have been in doubt as to the gravy train's point of origin.

The Symington hearings published many details about the arrangements made, and numerous Filipinos received copies of the hearings. Nonetheless, Senator Salvadore Laurel, on 30 March 1970 (months after the hearings), demanded that "the truth be known"—whether the Philippine leadership had deceived the public, and had, as Senator Symington claimed, received altogether four times the amount for PHILCAG from Washington that the Philippines itself had appropriated, or whether Symington was slurring the Philippines. There was a great public outcry. Malacañang, and Marcos personally, hotly denied that any American money ever went to PHILCAG,[17] and even in private, senior officials who knew better maintained that their books would show no American funding.

A commission was formed to investigate PHILCAG, chaired by Senator Perez, whose report finally came out in 1972, having plowed the same old ground. It admitted that equipment used by PHILCAG in Viet-Nam had been borrowed from the Americans, and correctly insisted that it had all been returned. As administration officials had stressed all along, the commission accepted Malacañang's claim that checks endorsed by former defense secretary Ernesto Mata from the American Treasury, between 1966 and 1969, and totaling $3.6 million (Senator Symington had used these as proof of American PHILCAG funding) were *not* spent on PHILCAG, but that they had been used for intelligence and security projects whose nature could not be disclosed. It cleared the Philippines with respect to much of what was considered American PHILCAG funding (like that agreed upon for engineering battalions) by noting that it was charged, "for purposes of internal [America's] accounting,"[18] to Viet-Nam service funds: as if the fact that Washington *had* to consider it as Viet-Nam related, and the Philippines chose not to, made the support rendered any less of a quid pro quo. Indeed, the report concluded that "there was no quid pro quo arrangement between the Philippine and U.S. governments concerning the sending of the PHILCAG to Vietnam."[19]

The Philippine case hung on the slender thread of the $3.6 million, which the government could claim was not spent on PHILCAG (but which had been intended for it). Such was accepted as proof in the Philippines that honor was intact. There is, in fact, a high degree of fungibility in the Philippine budget; the president could transfer up to 25 percent of one department's budget into another under a different heading. What happened is that the money given for overseas allowances was indeed used for intelligence purposes (or whatever), and money from the same big budgetary pot was spent on PHILCAG's overseas allowances. Clearly it was extremely important to Filipinos that their honor be saved on this issue: important enough for Marcos to go to great trouble to avoid the appearance of a quid pro quo in 1966, important enough for senators, journalists, taxi drivers, everybody, to *believe* that, although the $3.6 million may even have been corruptly used, it certainly did not go for PHILCAG, despite the overwhelming evidence to the contrary.

The dichotomy between hard bargaining and honor is partly resolved by the realization that the psychological dependence on the United States at this point was still great. It was possible for Filipinos to consider it sufficiently honorable in terms of American demands that they appropriate the required 35 million pesos and no more, in view of domestic opposition and needs, and then compensate for this expenditure many times over in other areas. Societies differ on what is honorable, and differ on what is allowable in diplomacy. On both counts, Filipinos are unlike Americans, and the fact that the Americans, by publicizing secret agreements, for example, made it difficult for them to maintain their sets of distinctions, did as much as anything to add to the societally derived pressure on the government to become more self-reliant.

Although societal pressures did not affect the character of the Thai troop commitment to Viet-Nam, there was a fair amount of mostly negative feedback into the society as a result of the commitment. This affected future governmental options. It is clear from interviewing many Thai, particularly diplomats, that the fear of being involved too deeply with the Americans spread rapidly once the Queen's Cobras were sent to South Viet-Nam.

There were indirect repercussions to the troop decision that had a more immediate and measurable impact. Criticism of Thailand by American senators of the kingdom's ever-increasing role in the war led to a considerable increase in the calls in the press for self-reliance. Always close to the surface, these anxieties about excessive involvement with another power came up whenever a new, higher level of ties was reached. Thanat, always more sensitive to public sentiment than the rest of the regime, publicly chastised the American government for allowing revelations of Thai-American cooperation to come out and proposed a way that Thai foreign policy could become more self-reliant—by accepting less American aid and accepting more from other Western powers.[20]

A second effect made the Thai think more seriously about their form of government. *Prachatipathai* criticized Thanat for overacting to Fulbright's criticisms, and gave advice that was reminiscent of the policy of King Mongkut, who instituted judicial reform, for example, so that foreign powers would have no basis for demanding further extraterritoriality.

Thailand has made its decision to sink or swim with the U.S. Therefore, it is impossible for us to become a neutral. There is no alternative, *we must become a democracy.* ... The only practical way to remedy and overcome certain differences that are occurring between Thailand and the U.S. is for Thailand to become a true democracy as speedily as possible. Then Fulbright or Kennedy or Morse would be soft-pedaled.[21]

This was, of course, precisely the line of advice the American embassy was beginning to give in reaction to criticism in Washington. Many Thai intellectuals, in fact, thought that the Thai should be thankful to Senator Fulbright for driving home to them their need to be more self-reliant.[22]

A corollary to this reaction was the effect of learning about Thai affairs through the foreign press. This initiated increasing popular demands that the Thai press be less restricted. What Thai editors understood freedom of the press to entail, however, is unclear, judging from one paper's admonition of the American government for not preventing disclosures about the two governments' relations; the paper suggested that this omission meant that the American government did not take Thanat's warning against such revelations seriously enough.[23]

At the popular level, the only consequence to the deepening involvement with the United States was indirect—namely the question of American troops in Thailand, and the well-known problem resulting from vastly different standards of Thai public behavior and that of Americans on "R and R." Although indifferent to and highly tolerant of whatever private mores are chosen in personal life, the Thai deeply disapprove of any public show of affection, but no amount of briefing of U.S. soldiers on "R and R" in Bangkok, or of those stationed in the kingdom, could prevent at least a few instances of what came so naturally in the situation prevailing. There was a highly intelligent discussion and real attempts to understand why the *farang* behaved so oddly.

We should realize that Thailand has to depend on foreign military forces at present because we have a population of only thirty million, but our country has become a target of a country that has a population of over 600,000,000. Therefore, though the behavior of foreign soldiers may shock us at times, we should be willing to sacrifice our sensitivity; a much greater issue is at stake.[24]

In all, we find societal sources of policy stronger in the Philippines than in Thailand. Only in the broadest sense did the highly important question of sending troops abroad elicit a public reaction in Thailand, whereas in the Philippines, one of the most intelligently conducted public debates in the nation's history helped to shape the nature of that commitment. It might have been otherwise in Thailand, had a parliament existed. In fact, a parliament was created in the late 1960s partly as a result of pressures generated by the war and by the Americans.

Regardless of the effectiveness of societal pressures on policy, the Thai and Filipinos certainly had opinions about the wisdom of dispatching troops to, or otherwise aiding, Viet-Nam, as the opinion poll in Table 6-2, taken in mid-1965, demonstrates.

The data reveal not only a broad popular support for American policy in Viet-Nam, and broad popular support for their own plans to aid Viet-Nam, but a heightened reaction in the Philippines compared with Thailand. Of the whole group polled, there were 10 percent more Filipinos than Thai supporting

Table 6-2
Roper Public Opinion Survey

Question 32d. All things considered, do you approve or disapprove of what the United States is doing in Vietnam?[26]

	Thai.	Phil.	% Phil.	% Thai.
Approve	223	246	49	45
Disapprove	38	18	4	7
Don't know	26	14	3	5
No answer this question	213	222	44	43

Question 32g. Do you think the Philippines should or should not give help to the government of South Vietnam?

	Thai.	Phil.	% Phil.	% Thai.
Should	184	236	47	37
Should not	101	149	30	20
Don't know	48	33	7	10
No answer this question	167	82	16	33

Source: Roper Public Opinion Research Center, data collected for USIA sponsored attitudinal study, 1965.

national help to Viet-Nam, and 10 percent more *opposing* such help. Put differently, the number of Filipinos supporting such help was more than 25 percent greater than of Thai, and the number of Filipinos opposing such help was half again as large as of Thai. Not only did the Filipinos care more, one way or the other, but they were more able, as we saw in this chapter, to do something about their convictions.

7 Political and Governmental Structures

In looking at political and governmental sources of policy, we are looking at the views held by different components of the two governments on the question of troops for Viet-Nam, but we are also comparing how the *nature* of each government shaped the character of its commitments.

With respect to specific inputs into the Thai policy process, the military is the only group which had a role in the Thai decision, hardly surprising given the military's role in the government. There were strongly held views in other branches of government. Opposition on the troop question existed among some diplomats, particularly those of the old school whose well-developed notion of diplomatic self-reliance was being compromised. We must assume that their views were both strongly held and well known to the regime, inasmuch as several of their senior members (for example the permanent representative at the U.N.), were willing to state their anxieties about the Thai position to interested private and public Western parties. But in this decision they were not considered an important factor, and when actual negotiations occurred, Thanat and the foreign ministry were left out entirely.

However, in the Philippine foreign service, there was a brouhaha. The proclivity of Filipinos to leak classified documents to advance their cause (no doubt a technique picked up from their former rulers) once again helps us unravel what happened. Fifteen ambassadors who were in Manila for a general review of foreign policy problems, appropriately enough at the opening of a new administration, argued that the debate should be considered as part of Philippine security policy, rather than as an aspect of Philippine-American relations. Presumably they realized that this was a clever way of disarming the "hawks" among them, and their reasons for seeing the situation in this way were role-derived. They also rejected the "domino theory" in its absolute sense as a basis for policy, and proposed that nothing but humanitarian aid be given to Saigon.

The most eminent and most radical of their number, S.P. Lopez, a former foreign secretary (and later president of the University of the Philippines), was chairman of a special subcommittee to consider the question, part of the report of which was quoted verbatim in the press. "They shrewdly argued that if, in fact, the Philippines were to dispatch troops, 'this must be done with utmost dignity, i.e., the unit sent must be manned and financed by Filipinos. Otherwise, the troops would be nothing but mercenaries, and their presence . . . would only earn for us the odium of our Afro-Asian brothers.' "[1] Charges and counter-charges flew in the press as to what the ambassadors—all of whose appointments were in the president's power—truly thought. There was no doubt that they opposed a military contingent. "Personal adaptation" ultimately ensued. As one informed columnist wrote, "The high priest of the 'left-wingers' raised a wet right index finger high up in the air, felt the direction of the new wind of change at Padre Faura and followed this with his left hand in a final act of capitulation."[2]

Despite the great disparity in governmental influence between the military in the Philippines and Thailand, there are some senses in which it would be correct to say that the Philippine armed forces had more influence on the PHILCAG decision than did their Thai counterparts on their similar decision. Let us firstly look at the similarities, the most important of which was the experience to be gained. Armies are concerned with warfare, and there was a live war going on in Viet-Nam. Their counterparts in Saigon had urged the participation of the Thai and Philippine armies, as had their American military friends, in whose staff colleges they had trained and from whose arsenals they drew their weaponry. Both had growing national problems to which such experience might be pertinent. There was an insurgency in Thailand, which if not curbed might be susceptible to the same treatment the Thai troops would learn to use in South Viet-Nam, as at least the far-sighted Thai soldiers realized. In the Philippines, a great civic-action program in potentially dissident areas was under way, and a civic-action group in Viet-Nam had obvious spillover benefits. As a senior Thai military leader at Supreme Command Forward said, "Where else can we use and test live ammunition, gain training and experience of this sort? We also learn to work and coordinate with allies."

The other similarity was less important, and has to do with the material benefits to be gained from participation in the Vietnamese war, above and beyond the direct inducements given by the Americans to achieve the coopera-tion in the first place. Both armed forces participated in the Military Assistance Pacific Excess program (MAPEX). This was a fringe benefit of American excess, and both armies, particularly that of the Philippines, at first acted insulted by the offer of outdated, overstocked equipment usually in need of rehabilitation. But as the surplus-disposal program improved in efficiency and the armies grew in familiarity with what could be obtained so cheaply to their great benefit, they began taking advantage of it.[3]

Material benefits were a factor at every level. Among the prerequisites of service in Viet-Nam were PX privileges in Saigon. In many circles, the behavior of all the Asian allies were considered scandalous, so open was the abuse of this privilege; Filipinos, for example, spent more than their annual income at the PX, and the Thai were not very far behind.[4] Such behavior had considerable negative feedback in the United States, far transcending the actual costs involved. (It is not clear, however, what was expected by the critics of troops from countries whose *per capita* income was a twentieth of that of America's, who were ostensibly serving the same cause in Viet-Nam, and had this sudden opportunity to acquire a television set or to provide for a younger brother's education.) There were even less savory benefits of Vietnamese involvements. Working through the armed forces and the network established as a result of their presence, powerful Filipinos could obtain M-16s for private armies at a tiny fraction of the cost at home.[a]

These areas of similarity are less important than the areas of difference between the Thai and Filipinos in their deliberations over the contingents. General Yan, the Philippine chief of staff from 1966 to 1972, summarized the military's outlook and objective with respect to PHILCAG:

The AFP recognizes the importance of South Viet-Nam to the security of the rest of the Free Nations of Southeast Asia. The Philippines decided to send PHILCAG contingents in response to a specific South Vietnamese request for such . . . assistance. Since the AFP had limited resources but was well-grounded on the concept of engaging in civic action as an adjunct to military operations, the South Vietnamese request was well within the capability of the AFP to provide. . . .

By sending PHILCAG, the AFP helped to foster international understanding, cooperation and brotherhood—an objective that is often not readily grasped and understood. It also helped to prove that civic action (winning the hearts and minds of peoples) is a key adjunct to military operations in the battle to defeat Communism. . . .

For its part, members of the AFP who had the occasion to serve with PHILCAG broadened their perspective through their dealings with other peoples and gained considerable experience on weaponry, tactics, customs, tradition, etc. of other Armed Forces, both of allies and foes alike.[5]

General Yan also noted that the overall AFP (Armed Forces Philippines) attitude could well be gauged by the reaction of officers and men, since there were roughly five volunteers for every position in each of the PHILCAG contingents. What do we make of the idealism reflected in General Yan's statement? It is most difficult to imagine Marshal Dawee uttering such sentiments. One might hypothesize that the less powerful an organization and the less related to decision-making, the more idealistic it is likely to become: yet we know that the military played a very powerful role in shaping the character of PHILCAG. Senator Pelaez, among others, noted how carefully he and his colleagues worked with the military officers to determine what sort of contingent would serve Philippine objectives vis-à-vis the Vietnamese war, would be practicable, and would serve Philippine interests back home.[6] Since the start of Marcos's first

---

[a]The black market price was then under $100, or about a tenth of the open market price. Max Soliven, a highly competent and reputable journalist, wrote of how a Philippine naval vessel was purportedly bringing the last of PHILCAGs equipment, but in fact was carrying 153 high-powered automatic rifles, which, "unimpeachable sources informed me, are destined for delivery to a congressman from the North." Maximo V. Soliven, "By the Way," *Manila Times*, 12 March 1970.

term—though plans antedated it—the AFP's commitment to the concept of civic action within the Philippines had been substantial, and had to do with building up the influence of both the AFP itself as well as the influence of the government in peripheral or contested areas of the country. From the military point of view, PHILCAG was a perfect opportunity to test concepts of civic action in much more difficult terrain than that with which they expected to cope back home. It brought with it equipment from the United States for ten engineering battalions in toto, and by stressing civic action rather than battle plans, it made it possible for the Philippine armed forces to show their commitment not only to a non-Communist South Viet-Nam, but also to one less military oriented.

In contrast, the Thai military qua military had less to do with the character of the Thai contribution to the war than the Filipino military did with theirs. In their roles as national leaders, the military commanders of course shaped the decision. Essentially, the Thai responded to American pressure, and the only question in dispute was how many soldiers Thailand would send and what Thailand would get as a quid pro quo. On the latter question, the role of the military leaders was important. How the American pledges of support were given derived from the way power was divided among individuals in the kingdom—modern equipment for two Thai infantry divisions for one leader, a SAM missile battalion for another, and so forth. The Americans were hardly ignorant of the basic divisions in the ruling group and consequently were able to get the Thai commitment, we must presume, partly as a result of the manner in which they made their offer of aid—appealing to the individual leaders on the basis of what they could get out of it for their own area of expertise.

As previously mentioned, when Thailand made its decision, no parliament or legislative group of any kind existed. Contrarily all the pressures and interests involved in the Philippine decision were filtered through the legislature until an acceptable compromise, or mix of interests, was reached as to the nature, size, and function of a Philippine contribution. Within the Philippine system, greater independence of the executive obviously existed in the legislature than in either the foreign service or the military. Attitudes toward the bill broke down into three categories; "pro-American" supporters, radical and "anti-American" opponents, and a middle group trying to find an organizational structure that would express all the ambiguities felt in the Philippines toward the issue. In the first group was the Speaker of the House pro tem, F.K. Pendatun, who gave a speech in Congress entitled "Let Us Trust America." The late Vincent Crisologo, an Ilocano warlord from Marcos country in northern Luzon, volunteered for service and wanted to send combat troops to fight alongside the stars and stripes. He as well as other congressmen did, in fact, go. Senator José Roy, later the chairman of the foreign relations committee, considered it a duty to interpret the alliance with America broadly, as requiring a contribution.

The opponents of the war were much more vocal, and dominated the headlines. Typical was Senator Diokno, a delightful and brilliant lawyer of whom it would be inadequate (though not inaccurate), to describe as "anti-American" with respect to Philippine-American political relations. Of those opposed, he made one of the most logical and persuasive cases against the bill. It rested on five points. Firstly, that domestic needs were greater and that President Magsaysay had vetoed a similar proposed contingent for Viet-Nam twelve years earlier. Secondly, he pointed out that the Philippine diplomatic heads were against PHILCAG. Thirdly, it would be terribly expensive, at a time when budgetary restraints hurt. Fourthly, it would set a precedent, and further "seduction" would follow. And lastly, there simply was not enough in it for his country.[7] Others added the argument that even a contingent of engineers sent to the war constituted an act of hostility; they could not remain noncombatant, because a security detachment would be necessary if PHILCAG were to avoid coming under American command. Although this turned out to be untrue, it was assumed that Hanoi proposed to consider them hostile forces. Senator Salonga argued that the Senate had to declare war if it were to send such combatants; and in such a case, the declaration was up to Congress, not the president.[8]

A third group was basically dubious about PHILCAG and even more about America's conduct of the war, but felt that it was nonetheless a Philippine interest to participate in some way. This group had been severely critical of the bill a year earlier, and of the administration for being insufficiently briefed and attuned to Philippine interests. Some of these men, like Senator Manglapus, a former foreign secretary and a distinguished reformer, did not vote for the bill; others, like Congressman Pelaez, previously vice-president and a man of principle and of thought, supported the compromise measure. It was Manglapus's contention that in fact what the South Vietnamese had requested and most assuredly needed for the most part was nonmilitary; Filipinos had only recently come to realize that it was social reform that would count. The Vietnamese were being engulfed by the Americans, who overlooked this most vital aspect of the struggle—for men's minds. He claimed that Padre Faura, the foreign ministry, had not even bothered to translate, from French into English, that part of the official Vietnamese request which dealt with needs in the fields of pacification, fiscal reform, labor unionism, and the like.[9]

Others sought to examine the proposals to see what the Philippines could provide that would be distinctive and of service to Philippine interests. Emmanuel Pelaez pointed out that it had to be an engineering-cum-security unit if it were to be under Philippine command, as it must be to further Philippine interests. Doctors, moreover, were instructed to heal everybody, irrespective of ideology. It would be an identifiable Philippine unit that eventually would give the republic a voice at the peace table. Senator Roxas made his support conditional on making the expeditionary force independent, and on giving veto power to the commanding officer as to assignments.[10] Men like congressmen Pelaez and Roxas also noted their clear opposition to sending combat troops; by sending an engineering battalion, Pelaez commented, "We could let the Americans know, diplomatically, how we really felt about the war. It was our way of saying we did not agree with the American approach."[11]

These two considerations were, indeed, the nexus around which the compromise was worked out among the legislators and in conference with Marcos and the armed forces. PHILCAG, at least for a time, had the intended effect. The lack of enthusiasm for the war, as conducted by the Americans, was evident. War critics in America drew the obvious inferences about the size of the Asian contingents.

Having looked at external pressures, societal pressures, and governmental organization, what can we say about the two countries' leadership? This question is particularly important for the Philippines, inasmuch as President Marcos made an almost total volte-face in his position on PHILCAG between the time of his campaign and his election. It is worth noting the fortuity of the timing, as the PHILCAG issue arose in full force at the time of his inauguration. In the Philippines as in the United States, presidents have at least a few months' honeymoon. But Marcos was in an unusually good position: a supreme court decision nullified seventeen hundred "twilight" appointments by the lame-duck president, Diosdado Macapagal, leaving all of them to Marcos with which to tempt the patronage-starved congress. Marcos used his honeymoon period to achieve passage of the PHILCAG bill, and committed a considerable amount of prestige to its success.

Well before 18 May 1965 when the PHILCAG bill was passed by the House of Representatives, Senator Marcos's intention to contest the presidency in the November election was well known. His line on PHILCAG was that the nation's problem was "internal decay" thanks to the failure of government, rather than the threat of "falling dominoes" from Viet-Nam.[12] Yet Marcos was basically "pro-American" when Philippine politics divided on that issue, and his record on "standing up to communism" was clear. Even more outstanding than these two characteristics is the man's highly focused political instinct and ambition, which dominated his life from early on.[13]

Marcos would have been well aware that, in 1965, Macapagal was highly vulnerable after a somewhat lackluster term. He himself was in a solid position to get the nomination of the Nationalista party despite his lifelong activity in the ruling Liberal Party (thanks to the ease with which strong personalities could switch allegiance), and he would be unlikely to have as clear a shot as the presidency again. We must assume that his earlier stand on PHILCAG while Senate president was intended to help him win Malacañang more than to indicate belief. PHILCAG was not yet an issue of burning public importance, but it was one on which Marcos, could show his own power to wavering politicians and businessmen by frustrating the president. Simultaneously it would rally the support of certain left-leaning colleagues for his candidacy. Selective radicalism had other fringe benefits: the Lopez family, whose interests on few issues duplicated those of the United States, were to give literally millions of dollars' worth of support in money and radio time on their stations to Marcos's campaign, and were ready to "take to the hills" if he lost, according to one of them. A distinction must also be drawn between public attitudes toward sending an expeditionary force abroad and taking the actual decision. Marcos perhaps perceived that the latter would be full of controversy, but that once the decision was made whoever was president would benefit. Marcos clearly wanted to deny Macapagal that windfall on the eve of the election.

Almost before the ballots were counted Marcos had hinted a reversal of position. He attributed his reversal to the new determination of the Americans to "slug it out" in Viet-Nam, though that had occurred the previous summer at the latest.[14] What had really changed was Marcos's own role. Note how Marcos saw his priorities as president: his orientation was toward security-related needs, and he perceived that the law-and-order problem would worsen during his years in office. From the first he had worked on a plan that would modernize the military and extend its influence in the countryside, thus giving the administration a greater capability for governance.

There was no way of raising the funds required for this plan internally. Support had to come from the United States, as any Filipino president, elected within the existing system, would have seen it. It was America's hour of need, and no such support could possibly be forthcoming to the Philippines unless she helped the United States by a show of support in Viet-Nam. Thus Marcos could dispatch PHILCAG, "a token of a decision and resolve of the entire Filipino people that there is no price too high to pay for freedom," as he put it.[15] The important relationship is between PHILCAG and Marcos's entire program, which happened to have a military slant relative to programs of past presidents. The Americans would have exacted troops from any Philippine president by 1967, but the positive long-term results of PHILCAG stem from a particular, individual approach by the incumbent president, which drew in turn from pre-existing military plans.

Did the leadership as such have any effect in Thailand on the question of Viet-Nam? It is hard to see where, given how powerful external and governmental policy sources were. The strong personality qua personality, Thanat Khoman, had little influence on the decision to send troops to Viet-Nam. If anything, his influence was weighted on the cautious side, as he was by 1967 already anxious about the relationship between the two countries. What is important about the rest of the leaders is that they were military men, and looked at Viet-Nam through the lenses of vulnerable allies led by soldiers. The primary way personality impinged on the decision is, perhaps, through the personality of Marshal Dawee. A little more blunt, cynical, perceptive, and amusing than the rest, he probably drove a harder bargain than others would, and got more spin-off for the armed forces as quid pro quo. Marshal Dawee might be expected to look out for everyone in the armed forces; at that point he wore no ministerial hats. General Prapat, in contrast, might have dealt his Ministry of Interior, in addition to the army, a few good cards from the Viet-Nam deck had he been directly in charge of the negotiations.

What did these two Southeast Asian states get out of their involvement in the Viet-Nam war, above and beyond what they got as inducements to go in the beginning? The question is not just the "output" to the "input" which has taken up the preceding three chapters, but is also the feedback, positive and negative, which affected the two states in their overall efforts to adapt to the new regional and international environment. Involved in the question is the perception back home as to how well their men did, how much their participation affected allied strategy, and how greatly their participation did in fact affect their overall regional and international status.

With respect to the first question both Thai and Philippine forces in Viet-Nam did well, which stimulated a sense of pride back home, and which sustained support for the contingents. The soldiers' experiences, combined with the financial advantages, ensured that service in Viet-Nam remained a popular option when the next contingents were recruited. National leaders and journalists visited them often and made much of their contributions in speeches and the local press. In the case of Thailand the attractiveness of service was an important enough factor to keep forces in the field, despite all the other reasons for withdrawal. In some Thai military circles there was skepticism as to whether the troops would ever be withdrawn as late as 1971, though in fact they were withdrawn early in 1972. Thai soldiers could influence policy enough to prevent their withdrawal up to that point, well beyond when it was prudent. Even if service in Viet-Nam were, for the Philippines, as with Thailand only a part of the subjective commitment to the allied war effort, it is inconceivable that PHILCAG officers could have outweighed the Senate and other branches of government to keep the civic-action group in Viet-Nam against the general predisposition in Manila to withdraw it. To be sure, after PHILCAG was withdrawn Filipinos continued to serve in Viet-Nam; but this was in the context of pre-PHILCAG service (medical corps, for example) showing the Philippine's continued involvement and interests in the twenty-five-year-old war.[b]

The predisposition against PHILCAG stemmed from the initial opposition that we have surveyed in Part II. It is worth noting that funds were actually appropriated in 1966 for only one year, and Marcos chose not to go back to Congress for a renewal in 1967. With the clear knowledge of his own party

[b]The post-PHILCAG unit was in fact the same PHILCON V unit of doctors, dentists, and public health officials from the armed forces that had preceded PHILCAG. It included thirty-four officers and forty-nine enlisted men, working under the direction of the Vietnamese ministry of health. See Dave Baquirin, "RP, S. Vietnam to Ink New Pact," *Manila Chronicle*, 20 February 1971.

leadership, and presumably with the knowledge of the opposition as well, he used funds from the National Defense budget instead. As one senator put it, "We simply padded the defense budget in 1967 in order to have enough to keep PHILCAG in the field." In 1968 such was not possible. In the wake of Tet and growing opposition to the war in the United States, combined with increasing American criticism of Filipino participation, the issue had to be faced. Unquestionably there were enough votes in the house to get a bill through, but not enough in the Senate; not even Sergio Osmeña, Jr., possibly the most conservative solon, would touch the bill. American embassy officials were convinced that Marcos *could* have got it through, but that it was insufficiently high in his priorities by this time. The Americans also realized that they were hardly in a position to press; not only had they twisted too many arms the last time, as one of their members put it, but Washington had a different set of priorities and preferences.

Another factor had clouded the PHILCAG issue. In 1968 the Philippines once again began mounting a claim against Malaysia to Sabah. Despite Marcos's attempts in 1966 to defuse the claim, it once again became useful to Philippine politicians as a diversion, and perhaps as a part of strategy. The armed forces apparently became involved in testing contingency plans of the type one would imagine could be used in a forcible attempt to take Sabah from the Malaysians. A score or so Philippine Muslims involved in the training itself on the island of Corregidor were massacred in the "Jabidah affair." It was a messy situation, and the Malaysians were, alas for the Filipinos, the best-informed people in town. According to a highly trustworthy source, the Malaysian intelligence network functioned superbly at this time, even upstaging and outmaneuvering British intelligence substantially. The effect of this was that when the British tried to convince the Malaysians that there was no real danger of Philippine intervention in Malaysian affairs, the Malaysians were able to remind their exmentors of their own intelligence failure earlier that year. This, of course, severely limited the scope of British advice. It also gave to the Malaysians an indication as to how much they could trust Philippine intentions. It irritated them that Marcos and their prime minister had developed a cordial relationship, they had played golf together, during one of which times Marcos had reportedly assured his counterpart that his government had no intention of trying to seize Sabah. The Tungku at the time was in possession of the intelligence report on the training program on Corregidor.

General Carver in Hong Kong, moreover, spoke of the willingness of Her Majesty's government to defend Malaysia, while the Americans made clear, through the State Department's spokesman, that the United States would not be involved in defending the Philippines, if her ally got her fingers burned over Sabah. Knowledgeable and worldly Filipinos knew that the claim had no standing, yet it rankled to have the Americans unwilling—and worse, *publicly* unwilling—to support them. Francisco Tatad, who was later to become Marcos's press secretary, wrote in the *Manila Bulletin* on 24 July 1968 that there was no reason "why the Philippines must go on supporting American's military adventure in Vietnam, when America cannot even be persuaded to support the Philippines in the first and most important dispute that confronts it and its nearest neighbors. . . . Washington evades every opportunity to express its support to its former colony." General Yan, for his part, wrote that his country had "unequivocally declared it has no intentions of resolving the Sabah dispute by force. The relevance, therefore, of the RP-US Mutual Defense Treaty in relation to the Sabah dispute is hypothetical."

However, it must be pointed out that unlike in the case of SEATO, where the U.S. has officially limited its interpretation of external aggression in the Treaty Area to Communist aggression . . . no such provision is present in the RP-US Mutual Defense Treaty.[16]

There is some evidence that the AFP was involved more deeply in the Jabidah affair than is generally realized, and General Yan's comments at the very least confirm the resentment against the American position. It was one more reason why official circles in the Philippines felt little compulsion to pull American chestnuts out of the Vietnamese fire at this particular time.

Thailand and the Philippines dispatched expeditionary forces to Viet-Nam as a consequence of their assessment of both the present and future configuration of forces in Southeast Asia, and as a result of an historical association with Viet-Nam. They did not wish to be in the position of not supplying forces, with all that would have implied for the continuation of American military and economic aid programs; they wished to influence the ongoing strategy of the war as much as possible, and they wished to take part in the peace settlement that would eventually take place.

The Philippines always wished to strengthen the consultative framework that existed for the allies which, for the most part, they then used to try to downgrade the military side of operations; as the second smallest contributor, one not in a position to supply combat troops—but one protected by a bilateral American defense commitment—the Filipinos naturally tried to play up the solidarity of the allies. The Thai, for their part, minimized the importance of working with the other allies, and concentrated on influencing the policy of the United States in a "hawklike" direction. With over five times as many troops and a strong desire for a clearer American commitment to themselves, thanks to their geographic vulnerability, the Thai were much more realistic about the extent of the allies' influence than were the Filipinos. More important, the two governments were playing to quantitatively and qualitatively different audiences, the Philippine audience being far larger and more pacifically inclined; policy had to be more attuned to them than to the American audience, unlike the Thai case.

It was, therefore, the Philippines that took the initiative for allied consultation. We know from the Pentagon papers that Marcos had first sent an emmisary to Peking in July to enquire into the possibility of China's calling an Asian Peace Conference—which failed, owing to China's insistence that American withdrawal from Viet-Nam precede any such discussions. Having failed in this area, Marcos then, during his September state visit to Washington, pressed for the formation of the TCC (Troop Contributing Country) framework and arranged for its first meeting, the Manila summit in October 1966.[17] At home, Marcos played up this diplomatic success as an opportunity to press a political solution to the war, in contrast to the Thai, who took a hard, military-oriented line.

The Americans would not have supported Marcos had such solidarity not seemed advantageous at the time. President Johnson, however, played right into the hands of Marcos's domestic opposition, and made PHILCAG a political liability, when he, a head taller than his Philippine counterpart, put his arms around Marcos and called him his "strong right arm in Asia"; a phrase used frequently thereafter in Philippine circles at Marcos's expense.

Five TCC meetings in three years, and ongoing briefings by American ambassadors in Manila and Bangkok of top governmental officials, hardly constituted influence on American strategy. If anything, thanks to Washington's own frustrations in the war, Thai and Philippine participation in the war fed the fuel of official America's resentment against her allies. Nothing very important of a commendatory nature was ever said about the contingents. Much negative comment was made both publicly and privately.

It is difficult for a state to remain uninvolved in wars or turmoil taking place in its own region; impossible if its own protector demands as an unwritten condition of his continued protection that the smaller ally involve herself in the conflict. The question then is how to minimize the involvement without compromising the protection, which the Philippines did much more successfully than did Thailand.

The Philippines was in a preservative mode of foreign policy, if we use Rosenau's formulation, when the decision to dispatch PHILCAG was made. Ironically, President Marcos was able to use the contingent's experience promotively, as we have seen with his placing the returning soldiers into dissident-ridden areas of central Luzon, their Viet-Nam-derived experience proving a valuable asset in their new activity. In Thailand, the comparable decision was made when, with respect to foreign policy, the government could behave promotively. Yet the benefits were all subsystemic, as if the parameters on governmental action were of the preservative sort. In normative terms, democracy is a very valuable asset indeed, in times when great power-protectors make demands. The presence of autocracy only confirms to the great power-protector that the ally can indeed take whatever action she chooses, if only the right price is found.

In the next two chapters we examine the manner in which Thailand and the Philippines effected their change of stance in reaction to the American withdrawal from Viet-Nam, with all that those changes symbolized We also watch for evidence of whether democratic and autocratic regimes have the same virtues and failings in adjusting to great power contractions as they have in taking advantage of great power expansionary activity.

**Part III:
Adapting to the American
Withdrawal**

Introduction to Part III

In the mid-1960s, as the United States became more deeply involved in the war in Viet-Nam, it was clearly perceived in Manila and Bangkok that the United States needed their cooperation and participation in that war, more than the two Asian capitals needed American help, be it for economic, strategic, or for counterinsurgency purposes. At the very least President Johnson sought the appearance of allied help, and was, as we have seen, prepared to pay any price to obtain it. For the Philippines and Thailand, it was a buyer's market, in which situation with her open and plural political institutions the Philippines was able to obtain more benefits from such cooperation with the United States than was Thailand. This was despite the higher status Thailand enjoyed in Washington in this period. But what in a seller's market? Would democratic institutions prove so beneficial, with the tables so nearly turned around, given the centrifugal tendencies usually obtaining in developing countries with open political institutions? Had the two states preserved the same sort of regimes through the mid-1970s, and had the Thai regime successfully returned to a "promotive" stance and had the Philippines remained in a "preservative" stance, would the two states have differed in the same way in their ability to bargain with the United States, this time for her continued perceived umbrella of protection?

In fact the position of the two states was reversed. In 1973 Thailand moved very decisively toward an open political system, while the Philippines in late 1972 moved just as decisively in the opposite direction. By 1974 the stance of Thailand was purely preservative, with growing internal and regional pressures narrowing the margin of maneuver for whoever was elected—or whoever elected—to govern. In the Philippines, a strong leader brought the country almost singlehandedly from a preservative to a promotive stance, as quickly as such a switch can be made. Not only was domestic dissent quelled, but the press was silenced and long-pending legislation enacted by executive fiat. No longer were powerful senators able to thwart the establishment of relations with Communist powers, and no longer were business empires able to condition relations with the United States in a way favorable to them and unfavorable to foreign investment.

Washington was seeking a way out of the war in Indochina, while retrenching her position all over the world. Her alliances were tattered everywhere; some through the overpreoccupation with Viet-Nam, as in Europe; others, as in Southeast Asia, because of her own frustrations in Indochina. By the early 1970s Thailand had a bad name on Capitol Hill and in many Washington military and diplomatic circles. Opinion of the Philippines could only improve, and the conviction was slowly, but perceptibly, gaining ground, that the Philippines could become a more valuable ally to the United States. Thus by the mid-1970s the two states almost reversed roles in their respective relationship to, and standing with, the United States. After the democratic coup in Thailand authority was less concentrated, the opposite was true in the Philippines after martial law was instituted. Other things being equal, we would argue that in the circumstances of a seller's market, where the Philippines was promotively oriented and Thailand preservatively, the Philippines would have had the better bargaining position. In fact as President Marcos saw it, it was highly important for the Philippines to keep the American presence, both for economic and security reasons. For all his protestations in public, he made his determination clear to the Americans that he would not allow their military or economic position to be threatened. As Thai-American relations deteriorated in the mid-1970s, it might have been natural for Washington to scale down her huge presence. But of course the continuation of the war in Viet-Nam, for which the bases and headquarters at Nakon Panom had been the last American trump, and a growing need to maintain the bases for forward movement into the Indian Ocean and Persian Gulf, made it extremely important for the Americans to hold onto the bases in Thailand. The long-suppressed educated Thai elites, however, began demanding their withdrawal, even as the regime in Cambodia collapsed and that in South Viet-Nam surrendered. The contradiction led to the fall of one new Thai government after only a few days, and raised the question as to how long the newly elected civilian regime could sustain power, with so many threats to the kingdom's security. Thus Thailand's continued high bargaining power with the United States—at least with the American executive—was fortuitous; that of the Philippines was the result of long planning and hard work.

8
Soldiers, Students, and the Thai-American Alliance

As it intensified, the Vietnamese war brought Thai and Americans closer together in purpose and work than ever before. As the American phase of it—and hence the Thai part—wound down, Thai-American relations were to be subjected to more strains than ever before. At the interface of Thai internal and external relations during the period of adjustment are three successive crises, each of direct relevance both to the alliance with the United States and to the organization and structure of the Thai polity.

The first crisis derived from the American volte-face in Viet-Nam, when, after years of insisting that the United States would never withdraw until her aims had been achieved, American leaders were forced to begin bringing their troops home. For many Thai, the lesson learned was that it was necessary to return to the adaptive policies of past Thai statesmen, who never allowed their kingdom to become very dependent on any one power. The foreign minister, Thanat Khoman, began to seek a new policy, and a new set of relations with the powers of the region, particularly China. As the United States withdrew more and more of her troops and logistic support from Indochina, her potential support for Thai security in the future dwindled. The logical question was why Thailand should be further out on a limb than was absolutely necessary. In the mind of every Thai decision-maker was a giant graph, one axis measuring American support, the other the threat from North Viet-Nam and, to a lesser degree, China. When would they intersect? When would the credibility of American aid be so low that, even if the threat from the north were minimal, it would be too great to be compensated for by the low level of aid? At that point the Thai would ask the Americans to accelerate their withdrawal from Thailand, so that they could make as good a deal as possible with the erstwhile enemies. There was, of course, a great deal of controversy within the Thai government as to where they were on the graph at any given point. Thanat thought the lines intersected in 1968; the marshals and generals had become convinced that, despite the declining pertinence of American aid, Thailand would continue to be of sufficient relevance to American security interests to ensure that Washington would, in the final analysis, have cause to look after Thai interests.

In combination with the rapidly decreasing (and never large) tolerance the ruling generals had for the new semidemocratic institutions established to increase domestic support, the change of American policy and Thanat's search for a new policy led to a second crisis. The generals engineered a palace coup, threw out the parliament, hushed criticism of their profitable relations with the

United States, and served notice on Washington that cooperation would thenceforth be on their own terms. Their actions were to echo throughout the region in the ensuing several years, as other regimes—particularly those in Manila and Seoul—also found a new balance in their relations with Washington.

The cluster of policies adopted by the regime in the aftermath of their palace coup failed to take into account the continuing development of an educated and increasingly sophisticated middle class, and the accumulating flow of new ideas from abroad, leading to the regime's overthrow in October 1973. This third crisis brought a wholly new set of forces, hitherto submerged, suppressed, or ineffectual, into the foreign policy establishment, and before very long, a partial unravelling of the thick fabric of Thai-American relations.

President Johnson's abdication of 31 March 1968, was the first of many surprises and shocks to the Thai leaders—the first indication that, from their vantage point, the "Fulbrights of this world had won." Although he had foreseen what was about to happen more clearly than had his colleagues, Thanat Khoman was unable to hide his surprise and consternation from his SEATO colleagues in Wellington, New Zealand, where they were gathered at the time.[1] For the remainder of 1968 the regime was preoccupied by hopes of a Nixon victory. Nixon, it was assumed, could stay the course in Viet-Nam; by not listening to the loud domestic voices, he could exorcise them out of existence.[2] Once in office, Nixon almost immediately began indicating new directions in foreign policy. He realized that he had no choice but to wind down the conspicuously American parts of the war in Viet-Nam and hope for the best.

In these circumstances Thailand had three problems. Firstly, it had to try to affect American policy so as to preserve what it considered essential. Secondly, Thailand must hedge against an increasingly uncertain future and for the time being at least *appear* less dependent on Washington. Finally, the regime would have to consider its options in toto and decide how to adjust to the new position of China in the region. In regard to the first consideration, what Thailand wanted to guard against most of all was unilateral troop withdrawals by the Americans. Thus the regime began compounding the pressure it could apply on the Americans by every means available—which as was soon realized, was not much. All it could really do, so it seemed, was promise to be difficult (by, for example, becoming more intransigent than ever on a war settlement), and that could be ignored. When Thanat realized that the Thai position that no withdrawals could take place was untenable, he began insisting that those made should not be unilateral. The president, meantime, outlined an eight-point plan for peace in Viet-Nam—including withdrawals.[3] The Thai thought at this point that they had scored a victory.[4] Nixon assured the Thai government, said Thanat, that the United States would "continue to help maintain the freedom and stability of the Vietnamese people." Thanat praised Nixon's speech.[5] Thereupon SEATO foreign ministers met in Bangkok for their annual meeting, as did the ministers of the Troop Contributing Countries—mostly the same people, as it happened. Especially the latter conference was used to assure the allies of America's steadfastness. Secretary of State Rogers assured members that the U.S. would render assistance to Asian allies if SEATO failed to act, and insisted that American efforts to end the Vietnamese war did not imply a rapid decline of American interest in the defense of Southeast Asia.[6]

But Thanat picked up some contradictory signals and, thereafter, took two lines for safety. First came evidence of one of the most remarkable conversions since Saul was on the road to Tarsus—Thanat the hawk became Thanat the dove. The president's plan could work, he argued, and the withdrawals take place, because Vietnamese troops were becoming strong enough to take over from American forces; moreover, the Paris Peace talks were bringing progress. He began to add that he had long argued for Vietnamization.[7] But lest Nixon actually be contemplating unilateral withdrawals, Thanat also began stressing the unreliability of America in maintaining her commitments, and observed that he had asked other SEATO members to join Thailand in seeking contact with China. America, he told the foreign correspondents' club, would give up her status as the world's greatest power if she withdrew unilaterally.[8]

In early June, Nixon met President Thieu on Midway Island and announced the imminent withdrawal of 25,000 American troops, to be replaced by South Vietnamese troops. The stunned Thai cabinet discussed the implications for an hour, and was particularly bitter at not having been consulted, or even advised, in advance.[9] *Siam Rath* called it "somewhat sensational news."[10] Even the very special attention the president gave to the Thai in his visit there in early July did not reassure them. It was, in fact, at this precise point that they finally realized how serious their position was.[11]

Anxieties began to mount throughout the country, and particularly in Bangkok. Societal pressures for a change in policy mounted.

WE WILL SURVIVE!

Whatever is happening to the Thai people now!

They suffer from fear . . . a fear that has become a disease that is spreading rapidly. . . .

Fear is making my hair stand on end!

The fear that we will not be able to survive should America desert us.

If there were no America, would it be impossible for Thailand to remain in existence?

It is very true . . . we have to depend on it. . . . We have to march along with it. But that is no reason why we should make such a loud outcry, shouting ourselves hoarse, that we depend on it to such a great extent.

It puts all Thai to shame.

Thailand, the writer of this column said, could, but should not, become an object of pity. Could it not become self-reliant? Or had Thai politicians "throughout the time since we have had a democratic form of government" become dependent on aid from other people to safeguard independence, "thus completely forgetting that we, too, have feet on which to stand?"[12] The desire to return to the older values and to the old form of government and the discreditation of the present government was felt in many quarters. Some people, the same writer hinted, were planning to leave Thailand, with all their wealth. These were the people who had benefited from America's presence, it can be inferred. "Persons in power come and go. . . . But it is the Thai people who remain and who will continue in existence forever!"[13]

Thanat now had a basic need and an immediate motive to bring about the *appearance* of a change of policy for the survival of the government (and of his position in it). He needed a pretext, which he got in the form of the escalating furor in America over the war. So great was anxiety about American "overcommitment" in Southeast Asia that the withdrawal of troops seemed to exacerbate the problem. In 1964 the American and Thai governments had drawn up a top-secret contingency agreement, which principally specified the manner of cooperation between American and Thai forces in Thailand and Laos should the Pathet Lao forces immediately threaten the kingdom, as the Thai then feared they did. It was only indirectly connected with counterinsurgency within Thailand. The agreement, which required authorization of both governments before being used at any particular time, placed American forces, in an emergency, nominally under the control of Marshal Thanom.[14]

In his press conference in Guam, on 26 July, prior to his visit to Thailand, Nixon had denied the existence of a secret agreement with Thailand, and Thanat, during Nixon's visit to Thailand, similarly denied it. Alas for both of them, the Senate had already got wind of one of some sort; Senator Fulbright had appointed Senator Symington as chairman of a subcommittee "on United States Security Agreements and Commitments Abroad," whose talented staff had been gathering data from early 1969, and were to visit Southeast Asia during the summer. Defense Secretary Melvin Laird, acting on instructions, in reaction to Thai pressures not to release its contents, continually refused to show the document to a closed session on the Hill.[15] It understandably became a point of honor with the Thai government—but much more pertinently, with the United States Senate. Imagining America bogged down in another Asian land war—that is to say, in Thailand—as a result of commitments about which the public knew little, one senator after another began blasting the administration. Most of the critics, presumably, understood that such a secret agreement was merely the stock-in-trade of an alliance. By what other method might SEATO be taken seriously? They were obviously using the so-called secret agreement as a stick with which to whip the administration, to undermine Thai-American relations, and to make sure that, with or without such agreements, there would not be a deep American involvement in the kingdom in the future. It was a self-implementing constraint.

Thanat, meanwhile, began countermoves, firstly by suggesting, only hours after Nixon's plane had left Bangkok, that Thailand wished to withdraw its troops from South Viet-Nam,[16] and then by attacking the whole concept of foreign troops helping out another nation's counterinsurgency efforts. He emphasized, quite inaccurately, that this had always been the position of Thailand, who did not wish to have foreign troops, American or Asian, fighting her internal wars for her. The Senate was not wholly convinced: "Mr. Thanat observed, however, that the positions of Thailand and the United States did not rule out the provision of air and naval support by the United States for use against internal subversion."[17] Such caveats made the ambiguity in American commitments to Thailand yet more evident. Marshal Thanom, after all, had noted that the plan gave Thailand confidence that the United States would not desert it.[18]

Without forewarning, Laird showed he knew where his problem was—and so he disavowed the agreement. "I don't agree with the plan, I don't agree with using American troops without proper consultation and advice of the Congress."[19] What Laird's comments added up to was never made known as such. The administration claimed the pact had been shelved—but it had finally become clear to the Thai that the pact was not worth its paper so long as Congress felt as it did.

Thanat realized that Thailand looked foolish. Even if the pact were no good, there was much else at stake in the kingdom's relations with the United States and its foreign policy, not least an image of self-reliance and diplomatic subtlety. Thanat's *démarche*, a demand that the United States begin talks about the withdrawal of American troops in Thailand, showed a touch of genius, finding, as it did, a fit between very particular American and Thai needs without hurting either party. With the cessation of bombing of North Viet-Nam, Thailand was for the moment less crucial to the American war effort in Viet-Nam, but it remained vital to the steadily increasing military activity in the rest of Indochina, as many of those criticizing Thailand suddenly realized. The faithful Thai were actually asking the Americans to get out, or so it seemed. Now everyone took notice—of, among other things, the fact that the troops were in Thailand to prosecute the Indochinese war (or "America's war," as the hawks-turned-doves in Thailand began to call it), not the Thai insurgency.

Of greater importance was the indication that, for all the thickness of relations between the two allies, Thailand was still able to look after her own interests; once again, the larger power was being asked to keep her distance. Third powers—like the Soviet Union and China, both eager to strengthen their position in Southeast Asia—were signaled that Thailand was her old self, capable of dealing with more than one party at a time. An editorial in the *Washington Post* called the request a "blow to American diplomatic aplomb."[20]

To insure that the demand be taken seriously, Thanat orchestrated it with the usual Foreign Office accompaniment. An official there said that Washington had agreed to discussions on withdrawals, but since "the Thai government feels like having 48,000 U.S. troops withdrawn from Thailand, and such a total pull out is bound to have adverse effects on the part of the allies, the number of troops to be withdrawn must be decided." Moreover, "Thailand insists that Thailand withdraw its troops from Viet-Nam if there is no U.S. troop pull out." Finally, the spokesman—the director-general of the Information Department—noted that the move was a response "to the actions against Thailand of some American Senators, especially Senator J. William Fulbright who recently insisted that the Thai-U.S. secret military agreement be made public irrespective of Thailand's security and sovereignty."[21] Everybody knew how little policy was made in the Information Office of the Foreign Ministry—but it made good copy, and achieved its objective as a signal. Thailand was adapting very shrewdly.

This might not have worked had it not been reinforced by two other factors, namely American policy and Thai governmental homework. As for the former, the size of the American presence in Thailand was causing an increasing amount of anxiety to the embassy and to most of those concerned with Thailand in Washington, as Thanat well knew.[22] It was doubly convenient for the Nixon administration, which, according to Murray Marder, had just delayed withdrawing "a second slice" from Viet-Nam; the talk of withdrawal from Thailand would help to calm American public opinion.[23] The Americans also knew that the pressure for American withdrawal was from diplomatic, not military quarters, giving both sides much room to maneuver. "It would have been far more difficult to have worked this out had the Thai military wanted us out," as one American diplomat said.

Had the Thai government not been so well prepared, Thanat's first demand for withdrawal would have been dismissed, covered up privately by the prime minister, possibly with a joke about Thanat's famous temper. Without clear knowledge of the consequences of even a small withdrawal, the military would never have allowed the negotiations to take place, with how much they felt was at stake. As one of the most senior said, it was "Thanat talking too much as usual."

Then we discussed at Cabinet whether any troops could be withdrawn and we decided they could be as long as we didn't touch the Air Force and as long as we used it to provide more jobs for Thais and in effect squeezed out unnecessary Americans; on that basis we went along. Yes, it did have the effect of convincing everybody that we are not dependent on the Americans.

In any case, the infrastructural build-up at the bases was complete by this time—another reason for the military's willingness to go along with Thanat. But just to make sure nobody really thought that Thailand wanted to be rid of American troops (quite a separate issue from wanting an image of self-reliance),

Thanat began drawing back, once the Americans had agreed to the negotiations over withdrawals.[24]

The other reason the Thai were able to move forward toward negotiations on troop withdrawals is that they had been doing their homework on the effects of the war on their economy. At the Bank of Thailand, the Ministry of Finance, the National Economic Board, and at the American embassy, studies were complete, or almost so, by the summer of 1969, on every facet of war-generated spending—including the R and R expenditures of American soldiers in Bangkok, massage parlors in the base towns of the Northeast, and the indirect foreign exchange earnings coming through all the activities.[25] It was clear that, though the impact of an American withdrawal from Viet-Nam would be serious, it would not have a critical effect on Thailand if the government used its powers to reallocate resources where they were most needed (for example, in the Northeastern towns). A partial withdrawal in 1969 of American troops from Thailand, however, was seen as a useful preparatory exercise prior to the much larger withdrawal of both men and aid at some future date. Thailand would already have begun its process of adjustment, made on its own time.

The negotiations on the troop withdrawals themselves were perfunctory—form to the substance of the political agreement already worked out. The Thai military and the U.S. Military Assistance Command figured out where the most fat could be cut out without hurting the (down-played) counterinsurgency work of the Special Forces, the so-called secret war in Laos, and the American strike capacity for Viet-Nam. Thanat and Unger signed the agreement in late September, with the net result of an improvement in relations. The agreement, as best can be determined, had wide support in Thailand; if some were anxious that the American commitment to the defense of Southeast Asia (and Thailand) was smaller, they were more than compensated by the fact that their government apparently had a policy for coping with the kingdom's security dilemmas. There was no doubt that the leading bureaucrats approved, particularly those like Puey Ungpakorn, Governor of the Bank of Thailand, known to feel that the government was too dependent on the Americans. The real question was whether Thailand would continue to adapt in this manner, particularly to China's emergence as Asia's greatest power.

On the same day that the withdrawal agreement was signed there came a clear indication that the regime was now quite happy with its relations with the United States: it was announced that a Soviet-proposed civil air agreement and air route from Moscow to Bangkok had been turned down, ostensibly for reasons of security. The pursuit of economic agreements with the Soviets had always been an indicator of Thai pleasure and displeasure with her American allies, and if the timing here was partly fortuitous the signal was nonetheless clear.[26]

Stabilizing Thai-American relations through troop withdrawals was only a short-term solution to difficult, long-term problems relating to the essence of Thai security requirements. It diminished criticism of the relationship in both countries, but it did not provide a new policy. The search for a new policy in the ensuing three years took place on two levels. On the one hand Thanat Khoman sought to build a new basis of relations with China and, more generally, to reduce dependence on the United States. At another level, the men of "real power," the generals ruling the kingdom, wished to have the best of both worlds; they wanted to find a way of continuing to rule, with all the gratifications derived therefrom. They wanted no further American advice, but continued American aid; and they were willing to continue to permit American use of the great bases in order to get it. In Washington the need for the bases had increased, while the status of the Thai had declined. It made for a far more blunt relationship, one with a short fuse, for both parties.

Almost immediately after President Johnson's de-escalation in March 1968, Thanat began taking soundings within the government for a move of some sort toward China; in the summer of 1968, he made clear that it was time for some signals to Peking. At the SEATO meeting in Bangkok in May 1969, Thanat made a more serious pitch to his alliance colleagues, hoping for foreign support with which to redress the imbalance between himself and the ruling generals—and evidence in and of itself of the need for action. He clearly was encouraged for things started happening thereafter. The first was a search for an intermediary with Peking. Pridi Panomyang, who had been in exile in Peking until 1968, and who had subsequently moved to Paris, did not work out, for reasons that are not clear. France was a logical choice for the site of a meeting with the Chinese having recently made its own reconciliation with Peking and enjoying as it did at the time unmatched diplomatic prestige.[27]

China at this point was not interested in returning Thanat's signals. Thanat's various gestures throughout 1970 went largely unanswered. The only episode worth remarking is the debate over the Cambodian question of May-June 1970, when the question arose of whether Thailand should send an expeditionary force into Cambodia. There was a clear division in the cabinet, with Thanat staking out the far ground against intervention, and Prapat in strong support of an expeditionary force. It would have been characteristic of Thanat not to wish military intervention in any case in this period, but the hope of discussions with Peking and France's injunction added urgency to his argument. In the end the impossibility of dispatching a sizable force without American financing and an American backup was compelling. Some said the American refusal was the symbolic ending of the old relationship. On 1 June, the Thai cabinet decided merely to send some volunteers across the border.[28] No real obstacle to a Thai accommodation with China developed from the Cambodia crisis.

The rapidly spreading war in Indochina combined with the deterioration of Thailand's balance of payments and growth rate sufficiently worried the regime that the American embassy thought that a palace coup, of the sort that did finally occur a year and a half later, was in the offing. In fact all the government did at this time was to add some harsh taxes to consumer goods to improve the balance of payments.

There had been a series of eloquent messages from the Americans to the Thai leadership that they truly were de-escalating their part in the war; for Thanat, who had caught these signals and many others, the lesson was obvious—make peace with China or be caught trying to embrace an elusive United States. Early in 1971, when American signals began to get through—the Ping-Pong tournament invitation came on 6 April 1971—Thanat began having some success as well. But the Chinese first were interested in discovering what the Thai had to offer. According to Ross Terrill, Thanat wanted the government to commit itself to the removal of American installations once the Viet-Nam war was over—a sentiment paralleled in nearly all of Thanat's public statements in this period by his constant reiteration that the bases were there for the duration of the war only.[29] After Peking responded favorably to Thailand's peace feelers, Radio Thailand was ordered to cease propaganda against China. "Our differences have narrowed . . . Peking leaders have begun to understand us," Thanat said. Talks with Hanoi even began anew, through the Red Cross.[30] The possibility for change was very much in the air, or so it seemed. The *Bangkok Post* editorialized that Thailand was at the "most important crossroads in its modern history."[31]

Suddenly the brakes were slammed on, in a peculiarly Thai manner. Thanom's brother, General Sa-anga Kittichachorn, started reining in the foreign ministry, of which he was the deputy minister. Thailand had to be careful about seeking a dialogue with Peking, because "a small nation like us cannot push the event," he said.[32] Not for the first time, Thanat vented his frustrations on his natural allies, the press. The generals allowed the press to return the attack in full—in a style that no newspaper would have dared to use in discussing Prapat. For over a week Bangkok was regaled with satires and jokes at Thanat's expense written by numerous journalists, discrediting Thanat's policy.

What had happened? In the first place, the notion that an on-going debate had occurred within the regime, with Thanat on one side and the generals on the other, considerably overdraws the reality.[33] Thanat's influence was enough to get the question of China discussed at cabinet, but it is unlikely that, had the regime decided to shift its policy, it would be solely as a result of Thanat's efforts. What became still more apparent is that the regime was conservative not just ideologically, but also in temperament. It did not want to take the risk of having a Chinese embassy in Bangkok, and did not wish to disturb the uneasy equilibrium that did exist.

There is also a speculative factor. What did the regime really think American intentions were? Thanat often spoke of his irritation with Senator Fulbright, but the generals did not excessively concern themselves with antiwar sentiment in the United States—partly by inclination and partly because they genuinely believed the president of the United States when he said the United States would keep its commitments to Thailand; it is no accident that Nixon spent more time in Thailand than in any other country on his 1969 trip around the world. By early 1971 there were signs that the United States did indeed have plans for Thailand that extended not just beyond the contemporary phase of hostilities in

Indochina. Once the regime was adequately convinced that it was not Nixon's intention to cut and run—and, after all, the American role in the war was continuing at a very intense level several years after Nixon's first inauguration—they obviously could make their own calculations about American needs in the postwar period. If Nixon wanted a settlement on what they considered good terms—if he was prepared to stay the course as long as he could possibly get away with it in his own domestic arena, as he manifestly was—then he would want bases near Viet-Nam. In the meantime, they had their own nightmares about Laos. The likelihood of the removal of American forces from Viet-Nam to Thailand was publicly envisaged in May 1969, almost four years before it happened, by M.R. Seni Pramoj, the distinguished opposition leader.[34]

The leadership may have suspected more. Leaders are not wont to depreciate the importance of their own countries. The strategic location of Thailand did not go unnoticed in American discussions with the Thai regime. It is irresistible to conclude that, as early as 1972 when the Americans began to envisage a whole new need for the Thai bases, they communicated to the regime some rough notion of their own inchoate, but increasingly precise, concerns for American security interests in the Indian Ocean and the Middle East. Like Thanat, the ruling generals presumably were looking to the long term, but they did so less skillfully and more self-interestedly.

On the evening of 17 November 1971, the generals and field marshals ruling Thailand decided to dispense with illusions. There was what in the world press was called a coup d'état, by which was meant that the same people were to rule, but under a new "revolutionary" form of government. (The State Department referred to it as a "governmental reorganization" and Washington, owing to its weakened position in Thailand, made no comment.) The parliament was thrown out. It had begun to use its only power—that of the budget. The generals blamed the intricate relationship between internal and external events for their decision:

No matter how bad the outside situation, it would be easy to solve if there is internal peace and order. If there is confusion, divisiveness and dissension inside the country, it would be infinitely more difficult to solve both internal and external situations.[35]

The generous interpretation of their action is that they were losing what little sense of control they had had over their external environment, and sought to hold on to what they had internally. A blunter appraisal would add far greater weight to their own low threshold for criticism, their own failure to understand the point of democratic institutions, and their own arrogance at thinking they could remain in control.

New developments were occurring at this time in the American perspective toward Thailand, mostly because American needs were changing, but also because of what had been learned about Thai affairs in the years of close cooperation. The United States now needed to have a firm base in Thailand in order to conduct the war in Viet-Nam efficiently. As that need became more compelling, and as the margin of safety even for the declining number of American troops became thin, the Thai bases loomed steadily larger in short-term importance. But there was no more talk of the "heroic Thai," nor any deeply felt concern for Thai security, of the sort that "New Frontiersmen" of a decade earlier had so often voiced when discussing insurgency in the Northeast.

For the American image of Thailand had changed between 1968 and 1971. The "diplomacy of admiration" had given way to a diplomacy of disillusionment. Some of the criticism of Thailand in Washington was just a matter of kicking her while she was down—knocked down by senators looking for scapegoats. But anti-Thai sentiment began to grow within the bureaucracy as well. Richard Steadman, an accomplished senior official in International Security Affairs at the Pentagon, was known for his low assessment of the Thai contribution to the war and of the Thai spirit. Bunchana Attakorn, then the ambassador in Washington, tells of one encounter with Steadman, where the American repeatedly emphasized that Thailand should be more self-reliant, should commit more resources to the fight against communism, and should right her priorities; communism would remain a problem even if America and Hanoi reached a settlement. These were strong words to give to a gentle diplomat.[36]

As American capabilities became increasingly stretched, resentment grew against the consistently hawklike advice received from Thailand throughout the 1960s; more seriously, resentment multiplied at the price Thailand was exacting for her participation in the war, when Thailand had once identified victory there as a common interest. By 1971, a senior American official could ask whether, if Bangkok were encircled by the North Vietnamese, the Thai "would give us a ten percent discount on the aid they would charge us for saving them." A typical issue, however, was the question of a type of rice consumed only in Senegal and grown in Cambodia precisely for that market. The Americans requested Thai assistance in getting the rice out of the beleaguered Khmer capital, and by one high Defense Department account the Thai refused. Great powers always consider the rivalries between small powers as intensely boring and irrelevant, which is not how the small powers see it, and presumably the Thai did not propose to pull any more Cambodian chestnuts out of her fires than was absolutely necessary for Thai security—though Thailand was to give increasing aid to the embattled Lon Nol regime as the years wore on.[37] From the American point of view, such was petty politics; Thailand was still committed to an alliance in a war, the greater issues of which should have made the Thai think twice about quibbling over the small change of small-power rivalries.

All this meant that the Americans would simply try to maintain the existing equilibrium in Bangkok and continue to enjoy the great advantages deriving from a regime's inability to look to its own prospects for survival. Factions began to develop within the Nixon administration as to the wisdom of basing policy, toward a country of relatively large weight in an important region, on so unpromising a regime. To an extent the question also turned on whether one was willing to prosecute the Vietnamese war as vigorously as possible before American public sentiment precluded any involvement, but the issue was also discussed on its own merits. The lack of criticism of the 1971 governmental reorganization by Washington made it evident which faction had won.

In Thailand the leadership did not use the opportunity it had seized in 1971 to concentrate on the nation's survival, which had been the rationalization for its action. True, it decided to assert itself with respect to Washington. General Sirakit, one of the men of real power in Thailand at the time, went to Washington in late 1971 ostensibly to honor the retiring General Westmoreland. He came bearing a message: henceforth the regime would deal with its problems in its own way. It would need no advice from powers accustomed to dabbling in Thai affairs. Lots of aid, on the other hand, would be needed. The signal was unnecessary, because American leverage in Bangkok was diminishing rapidly anyway as her forces withdrew from Viet-Nam, and what was left was needed to sustain military privileges in the kingdom. The Thai bargaining position had strengthened, thanks to external factors, and the Thai rulers knew it. Whereas in the late 1960s Americans had pressed the Thai toward constitutionalism, when the generals turned the clock back in 1971 no regret was even muttered from the embassy or from Washington, much to the disgust of some American officials in both places. Thailand in foreign policy then was to have the worst of both worlds. It would not be innovative, it would not bend with the wind. It would continue to plan its strategy around the Americans, but it would not take any advice from them, nor in fact would the Americans be able to bail them out if there were real trouble.

On the domestic front matters were worse. There was no indication that the leadership had learned anything from the multiplying signals of dissatisfaction from the elites—students, bureaucrats, newspapermen. A few changes were made: the press was clamped down a bit tighter, as was a bit of the night life for which Bangkok had justly become famous. Between 1966, which was also the year in which American military spending increased so dramatically, and 1972, the performance was more checkered. Thailand lost the incentive to export. The military spending partly replaced the growing export sector, rather than added to it. This "windfall of foreign exchange" enabled the economy "to weather an export slump without the adverse effects on reserves that would otherwise have occurred."[38] Instead of searching for new rice markets as the market for rice declined dramatically with the "green revolution," Thailand let an ephemeral factor fill the gap. "Commodity exports as a percent of National Product declined from 14.5 percent in 1962 and 1963 to under 11.5 percent in 1969. This was not attributable to adverse movements in the terms of trade."[39]

Thailand had not lost the art of adaptation altogether, however. The year 1972 was her best ever in rice exports, partly because of vastly increased world demand and price, and partly because of focused Thai efforts to increase production. (See Table 8-1.) So narrow is the margin between success and failure that, after the successes of 1972, 1973 could be a disaster, thanks to both droughts and floods. By midyear rice exports had been banned, causing panic among Thailand's customers and endangering long-term markets. There was margin for this loss, for Thailand's reserves had also shot back up in 1972.

In all, the Thai coup of 1971 was not adaptive, though it opened the way to the democratic coup of 1973. The trouble then was that precious time when adjustments to new circumstances could have been made had already passed.

The forces within Thailand that had led the "revolutionary party" to take a few short steps toward democracy in the late 1960s did not cease to exist by virtue of the suppressive decrees issued after the 1971 coup. Students continued to attend universities in Thailand and the West. The intelligentsia and budding middle class of Bangkok grew in knowledge, and therefore in disenchantment with their government's shortcomings. The tensions resulting from rapid economic growth—urban unrest and lopsided growth, the gap between rich and poor, and rising expectations throughout the kingdom increased; resentment at the dependence on American support also grew; some resented the lack of any American criticism of the coup, comparing it unfavorably with the support given throughout the 1960s for building democratic institutions. It was by no means clear that the newly constituted group would be better able to handle these challenges, and the opposite proved true.

The generals, in their indolence and ignorance, vastly underestimated the internal forces that opposed them. The events that led to their demission in October 1973, and to the deterioration in Thai-American relations, bear examination, for the student-inspired revolution, the third and greatest crisis, was essentially an attempt to find a more adaptive response to the forces at work within and without Thailand. In the spring of 1973 a highly embarrassing incident occurred, in which a private—and illegal—hunting preserve was discovered in a national forest through the accidental crash of a helicopter; Thung Yai, it turned out, was a favorite spot of senior generals, where they took their women and brought back game.[40] They were already on the defensive, and thereafter their opponents were explicitly on the offensive.

Students had flexed their muscles in late 1972 in protesting Japanese

Table 8-1
Rice Exports 1965-72, Thailand

	1965	1966	1967	1968	1969	1970	1971	1972
(1,000 MT)	1,895	1,508	1,482	1,068	1,023	1,064	1,574	2,100
(Millions US $)	208	192	224	181	142	121	140	216

Source: Economic Survey of Thailand, U.S. Embassy, Bangkok.

domination of the economy—protests that the regime found useful in their dealing with the Japanese, and therefore had not quelled. In June 1973, some students were expelled by the regime for writing a satire on the decision of the regime's leaders to extend their term of office, entitled "The Animal Counsel of Thung Yai."[41] One of the largest demonstrations in Thai history thereupon took place protesting the expulsion, which was but a quiet overture to the events of October.

On 5 October eleven students and instructors were arrested for distributing leaflets calling for a return to constitutionalism. Within a few days Marshal Prapat (as by this time he had become) was claiming that a plot had been discovered against the government, and insisted on holding the group, along with two more, indefinitely. The number of protesters grew geometrically during the week. On Friday night, the 12th, the government offered to release them on bail, which was unacceptable, and on the 13th over 300,000 students demonstrated. For slogans they had quotations from St. Augustine, among others: "And so, justice removed, what are kingdoms, but great robber bands? And what are robber bands but small kingdoms?"[42] Late that night the students appeared to have won; they did not know how much they were to win. The king was instrumental in effecting the decision of the government to release the detainees unconditionally. Early on the morning of Sunday the 14th something ignited mass violence, probably a trigger-happy soldier, possibly orders from a regime figure. In any event, when word went around the milling and retreating students that blood had been shed they took off in all directions on a rampage, burning down the police headquarters and bravely facing platoons of soldiers gunning them down. By the end of the day there were at least sixty-six dead and hundreds of other casualties. The king asked for—and got—Thanom's and Prapat's resignations. With the atmosphere still tense and revolutionary, he sent them into exile and appointed his councillor, Judge Sanya Dhammasakdi, as the new prime minister. Colonel Narong Kittichachorn, perhaps the most despised man in Thailand, accompanied his wealthy father-in-law, Prapat, to Taipei. His father, Thanom, joined his daughter in Boston.

Now Thai-American relations, starting in bits and pieces, came unstuck. The duty-free import of privately owned vehicles for some military personnel was suddenly overruled by the foreign ministry. True, these were not covered by bilateral agreements. But then little had been so covered, by the design and convenience of both parties, so that on-going relations could truly reflect the balance of interests directly, without the lag that treaties might insert into the process. In the 1960s the Americans could get anything they wanted, and certainly a handful of automobiles would have been routine. At that time the Thai saw them as protectors. Now, the balance had shifted.

Bigger things were in store. Most American agencies had been wearing a low profile since the October revolution, but not intelligence at the embassy. Its officials were known to feel that the new government was not acting in

Thailand's best interests in all areas. It was argued that the learning curve of "Old Fatso," as Prapat had affectionately been known in the embassy, had steepened in recent years; if only out of a concern for his survival, he had become concerned with the Communist menace in the Northeast and was finally doing something about it. The new government did not even put dealing with the insurgencies on its list of fourteen priorities. This, combined with the Thai reluctance to shed Thai blood, even to interrogate professionally, might well lead to the destruction of the Thai counterinsurgency capability, they argued.

Sometime in December 1973 an American intelligence agent had a brainstorm. An "insurgent" in the Northeast would write to the press and to the government offering a ceasefire in return for a recognition of "liberated areas" by the government. This, surely, would sow dissension amid the insurgent ranks (this was the later explanation). More pertinently, it would advertise to the government and to the educated public that such things as "liberated areas" existed. The agent in Nakon Panom let the letters be posted by a local employee, who duly registered them, making it a fairly simple task for the papers and government to trace their origin.[43]

The CIA was vulnerable in Thailand. Students had for the most part not bothered to protest the American involvement in the kingdom, saving their attacks for the Japanese and the old regime; after the revolution they mostly aimed at the survivors of the old regime, like Air Marshal Dawee. True, when Senator Goldwater had argued in September 1973 that the United States could bomb Thailand to protect its oil lanes, the students had risen to protect Thai honor, and 25,000 pamphlets denouncing "American imperialism" were distributed.[44] But by and large the Americans were spared the students' attacks. The bases were not unpopular and they were a source of revenue. The CIA is an easy target; since little can be said by the embassy to counter attacks on it, little can be done to disprove allegations. Somehow in December students became aware of CIA activities in more precise form than theretofore; being helped by the Soviets,[45] if we are to believe the Bangkok press, and by outspoken public figures out of government.

There were warnings that some incident would be seized on. On 28 December, General Kriangsak Chanawan, the powerful chief of staff of supreme command forward, spoke of the problems in Thai-American relations. When the subject of the CIA arose, the interviewer, a visiting political scientist, noted that students were planning to protest the role of that organization, as several notables of the old regime were already doing. "It isn't just students who are upset by the CIA," General Kriangsak observed. Nor was it just the bureaucracy—it was the still-powerful military high command. He himself had just caught an American agent redhanded, trying to induce one of his own men to infiltrate Malaysian intelligence.[46]

American policy toward Thailand had been hotly contested in Washington for some time. One group, centered at the White House and the National Security

Council staff, was concerned with American strategic needs in Indochina.[47] If Thailand were willing to continue being useful, then why not capitalize on this and buy a little more time in Laos, Cambodia, and Viet-Nam by maintaining full use of Thai facilities? Others, principally in the State Department and at International Security Affairs in the Pentagon, wished relations with Thailand to be placed on a longer-run basis. This group thought little of the advantages the bases would give in Indochina, and thought that continued use of them would lead to a blow-up between Bangkok and Washington at some point, to the detriment of the longer-term utility of this century-old friendship. Added pertinence was given this view by the realities of the new regime in Bangkok: the newly emergent group of intellectuals elected to the interim national assembly were more skeptical about the seriousness of the insurgencies than anyone in the old regime.

A new American ambassador had been appointed just prior to the 14 October revolution, Dr. William Kintner, a well-known scholar with previous experience in the CIA and the army. A friend of Dr. Kissinger's, he seemed likely to take the "Indochina view" of American-Thai relations. In fact, in his new role he had reason to put Thai-American relations on a new, longer-term basis. From his arrival in Bangkok he worked to convince both his staff and the Thai that America's new role would be to respond to Thai initiatives for assistance, and otherwise not to meddle in Thai affairs.

The story of the faked CIA letter broke just after the New Year's festivities had concluded, before Kintner had had time to bring his team under control. Suddenly all the Thai frustrations pent up over the years of intimate collaboration with the Americans broke out. It was a serious infringement of Thai sovereignty. To recall Talleyrand's famous remarks, it was worse than a crime—it was a mistake as far as the Americans were concerned. Students demonstrated, demanding Kintner's withdrawal. New grievances were discovered; for example, some vacationing American students were caught climbing over statues of Buddha, a horrendous affront to the devout Thai. A radar station in a national forest, being built jointly by the two governments, and of great importance to the Americans, provided a new focus of furor, though it was quite routine by past standards of cooperation. "The deep appreciation felt by the Thai people of the friendship shown them by the U.S. in the past has vanished almost completely now. There is nothing that causes such great bitterness, resentment and hatred as the knowledge that we have been deluded by a treacherous friend who we formerly believed was our best friend," one journalist wrote. Another called the CIA the Cholera Institute of America.[48] Such protest was bound to die down, but things could never be the same again. Even before the letter incident embassy officials had observed that, after the Thai elections of 1974 or 1975 were held, the day would be gone forever when the United States could deploy large numbers of troops in Thailand.

The regard for America did not vanish completely, however. There were too many interconnections—students and administrators who had been educated in the United States, groups who had benefited from American economic aid, officials who remembered back to American good offices after both world wars. But the Americans were sufficiently stained by their association with the deposed regime to put them on the defensive. For the Thai, this same association made them look less favorably on the perhaps more constructive civil tasks their great power partner could undertake in the development of the kingdom thereafter. The Philippines was in the position of having aired her differences with the United States all along, and could thus go into the new phase of her relationship with the great power largely unhindered and unfettered by an unhappy past.

It was one of the more serious miscalculations in Thai history to have based policy on the assumption that America's commitment to Thailand was unshakable. At least from the end of the 1950s, it was Thai policy to convince the United States to strengthen its commitment to defend Thailand, and there was enough forward movement through 1965 in the direction desired to satisfy the Thai government. The Rusk-Thanat accord, the airlifting of troops to the Mekong of 1962, the contingency plans laid out between then and 1965 for the defense of the kingdom, and the constant reiteration of support and sympathy from the embassy and from the highest officials of the State Department and the Pentagon, not to mention the personal word of the president of the United States, convinced the Thai government. There was, moreover, a historical background of good will between the two governments, and a vast fund of credibility from which America could draw as a result of its actions in the 1940s.

However, from 1965 on, signs and signals of an ambiguous purpose in America had multiplied. A great wave of antiwar sentiment had gathered force, and caught Thailand in one of its eddies. To the extent that the Thai had taken all this into consideration prior to March 1968, it would appear that it was only to snap back at such American adversaries of Thailand as Senator Fulbright. The fact that the Thai kept pressing for assurances—and became more sensitive on the issue as time went on—does show that they were aware of a basic problem in the American commitment. A Louis Harris poll in May 1969 for *Time* magazine asked a sampling of Americans whether they would favor sending troops into Thailand for its defense were it invaded by outside Communist military forces. Only 25 percent favored it.[49] But their method of dealing with it did not go at causes. Asking for a firmer commitment from the American government, when the real question was whether any commitment could be *honored*, did not help at all. The Thai learned this too late.

How could they have made this mistake? It flows logically, as foreign policy must, from the nature of the kingdom, its decision-makers, and the pressures on it. There are a number of human tendencies such as to see action elsewhere through the same lenses as used at home, and not to notice processes, especially latent ones, that do not exist at home; or if one does notice these, to underestimate their importance. The further the Thai had gone with the Americans, and the more frequently they had stopped to consider whether they should get out or go on, the more difficult it became to turn back. By 1971, it was still possible to back-pedal a little and to try to protect themselves from too much damage, but more basic change was needed. In fact, the full realization of how far America had changed only came later after it was seen that President Nixon could neither, by some magic, bring back the status quo ante, nor even keep a residual force in Viet-Nam.

The men in power were incapable of understanding the dilemma adequately. They were sufficiently compromised in other areas to limit their freedom of movement: they were not only "selling out to the Americans for a lot of sophisticated military equipment," as one Thai official put it, they were selling out in order to keep the very substantial economic opportunities open to themselves which flowed, directly or indirectly, from the enormous American military presence, and which had made all of them very rich men. At least some of Thailand's best servants understood the basic dilemma—perhaps only because they were viewing it from afar. At least by 1967, some of the critics, as we have already noted, stated their belief that Thailand was in "much too deep" with the Americans, and was much too compromised. They wondered whether the military leaders understood that relations between nations are different from relations between individuals.

A former editor of a Bangkok newspaper accounted somewhat cynically for the growing demand for a return to a Thai foreign policy of balance. The recent foreign policy was a "most profitable venture," but was in contrast to the "traditional policy of caution which enabled Thailand to survive unscathed both the colonial period and the second World War."

By the mid-1950's, it appeared that the Thai ruling generals had put all their eggs in the U.S. basket with a view to profiting from the tension reigning in South East Asia and U.S. efforts to retain some control over the area. Any restraints to this policy of total commitment were of form, not of substance. As a result, Thai-American relations became an exercise in mutual deception, with the deceivers slowly realizing today they had been the deceived.[50]

Although Thailand as a polity responded with remarkable innovation in deposing the regime and electing a new government between 1973 and 1975, its foreign policy problems were great. With noncommunist regimes in Indochina collapsing in 1975, the Thai were hardly eager to ask the Americans to vacate the bases. But domestic political forces had been suppressed for too long. The only way M.R. Seni Pramoj could put together a ruling coalition after the January elections was by promising that the Americans would withdraw from the bases within eighteen months. Within days he was out of office; his more conservative brother M.R. Kukrit, put together a slightly more stable coalition, but only after shortening the lag of the American withdrawal to twelve months. True, he pegged the withdrawal to the security situation in Cambodia, which left many means for stretching out the period if circumstances required, and left much to bargain about with the United States.

The Americans had hoped to keep the bases for two reasons. Firstly, until the massive North Vietnamese advance began in March 1975, there was always the possibility that Washington would use its remaining strategic base at Nakon Panom as a last trump card if Hanoi moved too fast; in the event the United States chose to do nothing in response to the North Vietnamese victories, thus showing that her retention of the Thai bases was a bluff as far as Indochina was concerned. Secondly, growing doubts about access to the Indian Ocean by way of Europe made Thailand America's furthest forward base for a westward approach to the Persian Gulf, increasingly the critical theater of world politics.

But where was the trade-off? If Washington could and would do nothing to save Indochina, what would it do for Thailand? Giving up the bases for the Thai had once been a bargaining chip for dealing with Hanoi, but the time had passed where that counted for anything. The Americans could not help Thailand in fighting her growing insurgencies. The new Thai regime did not have sufficient support for a bold policy, but it was difficult to see what comfort they could take from the continuation of parts of the old policy whose utility was finished.

It seemed as if the old duality in Thai statecraft, that had existed throughout the period of this book, had come back to haunt the kingdom more strongly at the end of the period than ever before. The people who were running Thailand, mostly survivors from past military regimes who had put up vast sums in the 1975 elections, understood how grim was the security position in the region. The combination of that perception, and their own extensive interests, and involvements with the Americans, made them hope that, in the final analysis, the United States would help them in a desperate hour. They therefore immediately enabled the Americans (for example) to recover the aircraft flown in by South Vietnamese pilots upon the collapse of President Thieu's regime in Saigon. In contrast to the powerful faction led by Deputy Prime Minister General Pramarn Adireksan, the civilian political faction led by Prime Minister M.R. Kukrit Pramoj seemed to wish to speed up the accommodation to the new rulers in Indochina and to find a new policy. But neither faction was strong enough—and the chief irony was that in the new circumstances, neither faction could effect the support of its desired external partner—the Americans for the one, the new Communist rulers for the other.

9

The "New Society" and Philippine Adaptation

However different the situation in the Philippines was from that in Thailand, she too faced the possibility of an American withdrawal in the 1970s, at the same time as societal pressures built up in some quarters for reform, and for revolution in others. New policies based on the new realities, external and internal, were in order.

Bases were certain to be closed down throughout the archipelago as the Vietnamese war wound down and American interest in Asia slackened, with many implications for the economy and the nation's defense strategy. Beyond that, changes were required in direct Philippine-American ties. The military bases agreements themselves badly needed updating and possibly restructuring, to allow for Philippine sensitivities.[1] Most obviously, the Laurel-Langely Agreement was to run out on 4 July 1974, leaving uncertain the access of Philippine goods to the American market; or so it seemed in 1970.

As his second term began at the end of 1969, Marcos was increasingly convinced that the partnership with the United States would assume more importance for the Philippines than it had had in two decades, if rapid development was to occur and if key bottlenecks in the economy were to be opened. In these circumstances, when he knew that the Americans were unimpressed by his reckless election spending in 1969 and realized that he was dependent on them in the short run, he had to transform the American interest into a longer-run one; with the U.S. government once again committed to long-term development plans and American business willing to bring in substantial new investments.

Domestic events reinforced foreign policy needs. Thanks to the domestic political crises, Marcos envisaged the possibility of proclaiming martial law and ruling by executive fiat, something linked doubly to foreign policy. In the short run martial law might disturb relations with the United States; in the longer run it might permit the massive reforms in the economy and social-political institutions and structures that could make the Philippines a more attractive haven of foreign investment, while giving the country the self-confidence to strike a fair balance in her dealings with larger powers. Though no doubt his own continuation in office was foremost in his mind when he first began contemplating martial law—which is at least as early as 1970—and though the problems martial law was designed to ameliorate were partly of his own making, he from the first tied it to basic reform, and his staff drew up hypothetical plans right from the start.[2]

The gravest crisis of the young republic, which led to the proclamation of martial law in September 1972 and to the transformation of the Philippine system, was acted out on three stages in the first three years of Marcos's second elected term. The first was in the streets, the second in a epochal feud with the Lopez family, until then the nation's most powerful group, and the third in a constitutional convention, where all the contending forces could work. The backdrop of each stage was foreign policy.

The first few months of Marcos's second term were rocked by the worst urban riots in the nation's history. Dissatisfied students and youth, catalyzed by well-organized members of the Kabataan Makabayan and representatives of the Maoist New Peoples' Army, demonstrated in front of Congress the day of Marcos's State of the Union address, almost preventing Marcos from making his speech. They were fired upon by troops. Within a few weeks and a few more demonstrations every window front in Manila and Makati was boarded over with plywood—something of an overreaction. Marcos had good reason to fear for his security, and it is a fair inference that, in the months ahead, he saw himself surviving, to a certain extent, courtesy of new American equipment for use in presidential security and intelligence. Several thousand M-16s were bought for hard cash—something new in the military relations of the two powers.

Matters went from bad to worse during 1971 and 1972. The New Peoples' Army was able to take over nearly every village in Isabella Province. In Mindanao, the long-festering resentment of the Muslims intermittently exploded. Crime in the Manila area got worse, as a sense of fatalism began to settle in. A hand grenade thrown into a 1971 Liberal party rally attended by almost every prominent member of the opposition critically wounded eight senators; and added to their fortunes at the polls in November, while adding to Marcos's woes.

It was not only urban terrorism and revolution in the countryside that threatened the government. A monumental power struggle in 1970-72 occurred between Marcos and the great ruling families of the Philippines, principally the Lopezes. Nor was this struggle entirely separate from the terrorism and revolution in the streets, as the government had strong grounds for suspecting at least several of its rich opponents of aiding dissident groups, both urban and rural.[3] Although the immediate issue was who was going to rule, the stakes involved went far beyond that, deeply affecting foreign policy options for the future. The nature of the alliance with the United States, and the importance and character of economic nationalism were closely allied to that question.

Although the Lopezes had supported Marcos in 1965 and 1969, they were at the breaking point by late 1970. Marcos's oil policy catalyzed their opposition; as Marcos put it in accepting Vice-President Lopez's resignation as Secretary of Agriculture, their opposition came from his own refusal "to approve their project for the establishment of a lubricating oil factory, a petrochemical complex, the purchase of CALTEX, and the use of the Laguna de Bay development project for reclamation of areas to be utilized for an industrial complex."[4] More important was Marcos's own growth in power concurrent with a massive increase in Lopez capabilities and appetite. They were among the most innovative and dynamic empire builders in Asia, so powerful that they had seriously considered "having nothing to do with government—taking care of all our own needs," as one of their number put it. They were a state within a state.

On the oil question the really important long-term issue was whether oil prices would rise along with international prices, as Marcos correctly realized was necessary. A raise would hurt jeepney drivers and other small businessmen, which would be politically expensive. In the shorter term the issue was control, and the Lopezes suspected Marcos of trying to gobble up the oil industry for himself; which might be true, but was unrelated to the larger and longer-term question. In early 1971 the drivers went on strike for a rollback in prices, which they achieved, temporarily at least. Marcos accused the Lopezes of aiding the drivers, of "fomenting unrest and inciting the already militant and impassioned groups."[5] The Americans were equally convinced that the Lopezes were financing the strikes. The protest movement was very powerful indeed as students had joined the jeepney drivers.

The issue of economic nationalism was vital. Marcos wished to see foreign investment flow in to help solve the nation's economic problems. He did not wish to see the great families getting still more powerful, and thus all the more capable of vetoing his ambitious programs or sabotaging his personal interests. Foreign investment unlike local investment would be controllable by the state.

The Lopezes and their allies had different interests, and for a long time had helped through their newspapers to create an atmosphere in which such a foreign investment flow would be unlikely. The Lopezes were hardly against foreign investment as such; loans from American banks, the Import-Export Bank, and other foreign banking institutions, provided the basis for Lopez's acquisition of many of their properties, particularly the Manila Electric Company. Like Marcos, they sought only foreign investment that strengthened their position; Marcos, as head of state, had broader interests, and it is thus possible to argue that the nation could benefit more from his policy than from that of the Lopezes. They wanted an outflow of foreign control, which would leave well-equipped companies behind for them to buy. Throughout 1971 the Lopez press hit away at Marcos, at "imperialism," and at foreign control of the economy.

Interestingly, a survey conducted by the Asia Research Organization and published in the *Manila Chronicle* (the Lopez family owned newspaper) showed that public perceptions of the cause of the unrest and demonstrations were different from what might be expected. Thirty-eight percent attributed them to the high cost of living; thirty-one percent to the need of reform in government and corruption therein; "feudalism/facism/imperialism of government" was less than one percent, as was foreign control of business and "American imperialism."[6]

The near-anarchy that pervaded Manila between January 1971 and September 1972 was primarily caused by long-neglected social forces, communist organization, and Marcos's mistakes and overconfidence. This atmosphere threatened not only his development plans but also threatened to overthrow the republic itself.[7] But by which side was to take over—the New Peoples' Army and its affiliate the Kabataan Makabayan, or the armed forces? Marcos's strategy was to provide a third option, one closer to the second, but which allowed for an eventual return to constitutionalism.

The real scene of struggle between contending forces was not in the streets, but at the Manila Hotel, where a constitutional convention began meeting in 1971. A popular movement in preceding years to replace the old constitution written in 1935 when the Philippines was a dependent commonwealth, the convention reflected the idealism still present in public life. A national plebescite disbarred elected politicians from eligibility for election to the "con-con," so great was public cynicism about the political sector. There was never an elected Philippine gathering about which cynicism was more justified than con-con. The anti-Marcos forces—particularly the Lopezes—succeeded for a while in using the convention as a club with which to beat Marcos. Marcos, knowing the state had more ammunition than any conceivable internal group of opponents, if only the guns were skillfully aimed, bided his time while the debates droned on. In the summer of 1972 it was clear that he would be able to buy off more of the delegates than his opponents.

In 1971 Marcos suspended habeas corpus after the bombing at the Liberal party rally, giving the country a foretaste of what was to come. As disorder spread in 1972 martial law became increasingly inevitable. Interestingly, the prime objective of student demonstrators in early 1971 was to obtain a promise from Marcos that he would not find a means, quasiconstitutional or otherwise, for running for a third term (not permitted by the old constitution) or for simply remaining in office by force of arms. Marcos's mechanism for holding onto power was to get the convention to propose a parliamentary form of government, in which he could be the prime minister, then to proclaim martial law and rule indefinitely without parliament.

Order deteriorated further in September. The New Peoples' Army offered the Liberal party an alliance with which to bring down the government, but according to high Malacañang officials, Senator Roxas, the party head, never even considered it. Senator Aquino, feeling the noose already around his neck, reported the same offer to Defense Secretary Enrile; which was not enough to save him. An assassination attempt on Enrile's life on 22 September provided the excuse (nowhere considered genuine) to institute martial law.[8]

Under the shadow of martial law, the constitutional convention dutifully voted in a new form of government, one in which they themselves, along with incumbent senators and congressmen, would be the parliamentarians—if they voted for Marcos's proposal. But the Prime Minister would not have to convoke the parliament until he felt the urge. Even the ratification of the new "constitution" was a bad joke. In a measure that evoked memories of Sukarno, Marcos disallowed voting, and instead held plebescites by discussion in the barrios. Members of the armed forces reported the results to him. They were favorable. In such a manner did Marcos bring to an end Philippine democracy, which had been its significant political contribution to the world in the postwar era.

The full economic benefits of political rule could now be reaped by Marcos, his family, and his entourage. What happened to the Lopez family is not representative, but indicates the extent to which the Marcos forces were willing to go to attain their ends. Eugenio Lopez Jr., theretofore the most powerful younger member of the family, was incarcerated on grounds of plotting against the life of the president. Though the government was not without evidence, it was believed in many circles that the real reason for jailing him was the crudest possible, namely, to have a hostage to be held for ransom when negotiations for the disposal of Lopez assets took place. The Lopez family was squeezed financially and their empire came unstuck. Control of their brightest jewel, the Manila Electric Company, passed to a foundation headed by Marcos allies. The sparkling new headquarters and plant of the *Manila Chronicle* were taken over by other regime forces.

But Executive Secretary Alejandro Melchor now brought out of his files his long-laid plans to restructure the government, economy, and society. By his own account, on the eve of the proclamation of martial law he had drafted a long memo to his president, asking rhetorically whether he would use the new situation to shock and transform the nation; whether he would not merely use the military to clean up rebellion and dissidence, but use the civil sector to rebuild the society. The Philippines in one day had gone from preservation to promotive adaptation, at least internally.

Marcos and his aides from the first saw the link between internal reform and change in foreign policy, particularly with regard to the United States, much as their Indonesian counterparts had a half-decade earlier. Melchor wrote that the "establishing of the New Society in 1972 had the effect of cutting the Gordion knot; it demolishes a vicious cycle in which the Philippines found itself, and set it off on an upward virtuous cycle of development. But all this required decisive, dramatic changes at home which had to be backstopped by an equally decisive development diplomacy abroad."[9]

Marcos had to develop a cluster of policies to elicit the desired response from the United States. The true character of his policy only became clear in 1974, after he had had time to develop a personal style of rule by martial law, and it obviously reflected a combination of planning begun in 1970 and a taking advantage of events as they unfolded.

There were short-, medium-, and long-term problems that had to be solved in

Philippine foreign policy for the reorientation to take effect. The short-term problem was simply economic survival. Marcos had cashed in all his chips to win reelection in 1969; he was the first Philippine president to be successful in so doing. Philippine elections always leave the country with a balance-of-payments problem, none more so than in 1969. The deficit resulting from the sixty-nine election, in combination with export shortfalls, was large enough to disgust high-level American officials in Washington; those in Manila had long seen it coming. Reserves dwindled to $150 million, against short-term liabilities of $190 million—at a time when Thai reserves were almost a billion dollars.

The Filipinos had been far-sighted in a sense. A Marcos family emissary and the governor of the national bank had gone to Washington prior to the election asking if the American government would buy pesos for their Philippine needs a year in advance. Washington's negative response frightened Marcos, and foreshadowed future American diplomacy. Hence, after the election, foreign exchange spending virtually ground to a halt, while the reelected administration attempted to find sources for its ongoing needs in the New York and European banking community. They achieved two things—an $80 million loan, and a restructuring of $247.4 million in short-term loans. The terms of this financing showed how bad their credit was. Half of the new loan was obtained in effect by mortgaging the cash flow coming from American veteran payments and the like in the Philippines; the other half, borrowed at the Eurodollar rate plus 2 percent, came via the American oil companies in the Philippines, working back in a circular chain to the New York banks. The banks stretched out the short-term loans by lending the republic her own money. The Philippines thus paid a 2 percent charge in order to avoid withdrawing Philippine funds, which would have looked bad to creditors. The resulting stretch-out to seven years meant for the bank that unsecured loans were outstanding for only the first four years. "Marcos was surviving courtesy of American and European banks," as one American official put it; and the banks were not doing badly themselves. Philippine debt to American financial institutions was, in toto, about a billion dollars.

That only solved the immediate crisis. To sort out the economic muddle for the medium term, American officials told the Filipinos that they would have to go to the International Monetary Fund, and take whatever strong medicine was prescribed—knowing full well it would be devaluation of the overvalued peso. The IMF approved a third credit tranche of $27.5 million, and Marcos disguised the devaluation of the peso, which he had promised never to do, by floating it rather than by devaluing it outright. It went from 3.9 to around 6 to the dollar before long, about where the black market rate had hovered in the preceding months.

The IMF's action in forcing the peso's devaluation had put the country over the first hurdle in 1970. Thereafter the Americans could say "the Philippines had joined the international community," in reference to the fact that it had had to find its salvation internationally rather than through some special American accommodation. "Joining the international community," or, analytically, interacting in terms of a wider number of units in the international system, had a multiplier effect. On American urging, the World Bank formed a Philippine Consultative Group in April 1971 to assess needs and to make recommendations, showing that the Bank's view of the Philippines had vastly changed.[10] The formation of such groups historically has tended to stabilize aid flows, and to allow host countries to make more accurate long-term economic development plans, not to mention to play off donor countries against each other at the new higher level. The Philippines had not seen these advantages, owing to its close ties with America. "Why bother" was the attitude. There was a lag before it was realized that the United States was not in a position to fill—and was not filling—the role she had once played and that the international financial community could play.

"Philippine Government adherence to the financial stabilization program recommended by the IMF has placed the World Bank—chaired Consultative Group in a strong position to endorse increased development assistance from the international community," wrote Thomas Niblock, the American AID director in Manila.[11] By 1970, assistance from international organizations equalled $73.9 million, compared with $7.9 million in 1966, Marcos's first year.[12] There was also great elasticity in the amount of aid. The limiting factor was the lack of considered Philippine proposals. To be sure, this is often true of a developing country; well-worked-out proposals usually find financing whatever the political considerations. But few countries had so sympathetic a reception with aid donors as the Philippines.

Joining the international community initially had chiefly economic connotations for the Philippines. Thus, in February 1973 the Philippines decided to join GATT in order to compete unhindered in world markets and to prepare for the end of the Laurel-Langely Agreement in 1974. Diplomacy itself was cast in economic terms: "Development diplomacy" was the cliché of the year in 1973, but it was one increasingly wedded to action. As Marcos saw it, the Philippines could immensely benefit from the "interregnum of détente" among the great powers, and use these years, however few there might be before Philippine security needs might necessitate new policies, to increase economic prospects.

For the long term, there had to be a complete restructuring of foreign policy, a change in the parameters within which Philippine foreign policy operated. For at least half a decade it had been American policy to attempt to force the Philippines to cut her apron strings with the United States, while somewhat contradictorily preserving all American privileges in the archipelago. It had long been Philippine rhetoric to announce its intention of doing so. But from Manila's point of view in practice there had been no reason to do so, both from the realities of American commercial and military ties with the archipelago, and from the myopia that prevented Filipinos from peering into the future and seeing how rapidly these ties would disintegrate under new circumstances. Although the efforts of Marcos's government "to go it alone in its international relations"[13] would not be without backward glances to see if Uncle Sam were indeed still peering over their shoulders (part of what Melchor called the "colonial hangover"[14]), the key men around Marcos now clearly saw what their predecessors had failed to see, namely, the necessity of broadening their international contacts, of practicing "self-reliance,"[15] and of building a solid basis for Asian regionalism. Without this they would have neither the confidence of Washington, nor the vast financial support they sought.

The broadened base of Philippine foreign policy was the framework within which changes in the partnership with the United States could work. The actual restructuring of ties with Washington took place on a number of fronts. The foundation had been laid as early as 1966, during Marcos's state visit to the United States, when he had astutely obtained specific commitments to such programs as rural electrification for the entire archipelago. The commitments were implicitly linked to pledges of Philippine participation in the Viet-Nam war, which the Philippines had honored. At the time, it had appeared that Marcos was going to be more a problem-solver than a fortune-builder; Washington was forever seeing a new Philippine president as a knight in shining armor. The Americans, alas, had to wait three more years before Marcos had accumulated sufficient personal wealth, and before the domestic scene was ready, for a concentration of the government's considerable energy and talent on a resolution of the country's vast problems.

The changes in Philippine relations with the United States came in the diplomatic, commercial, and military arenas. A good example of the new style of Philippine diplomacy is the work in Washington on the new Sugar Act in 1971.

By 1970 Marcos had become anxious (with good reason) lest Latin Americans principally, but others too, increase their sugar quotas at Philippine expense. As it turned out, the Philippines did very well indeed with the new bill. They took a small cut in the maximum quota, but they in fact had never supplied as much sugar as the new act allowed. From that point of view, considering the pressures on Congress to decrease their quota, it was a Philippine victory. Losses to other powers would have hurt psychologically and redounded to the detriment of Philippine-American relations.

How, after the terrible beating the Philippines had taken in the American press that year, do we account for this success? First was Philippine diplomacy in Manila, at its improvised best. The Philippine leadership had been late in waking up to the dangers posed by an American cut. However, the eleventh-hour preparations succeeded which says much about how the world of international relations works. A series of gestures toward the United States was undertaken to bring policy in line with contingent necessity. Marcos began long talks with Ambassador Byroade, and strengthening his diplomatic arms in Washington. The consequence of this, in combination with the new American assessment of its long-term interests in Southeast Asia, was a new American readiness to accommodate Philippine needs.

The second component was Philippine diplomacy in Washington. Given the financial situation in the country, the Philippines had no greater interest in Washington than in preserving its sheltered sugar market. Marcos appointed a shrewd old sugar hand, Ernest Lagdameo, even though he was of the wrong party. (Indeed Lagdameo was related by marriage to the Lopez family.) Lagdameo's knowledge of, and interest in, the sugar industry was surely in Marcos's mind when he appointed him in early 1969. Lagdameo did his job in the tradition of General Romulo, entertaining, briefing, and pressing congressmen and their staffs. "He did his homework and he didn't oversell. He made a solid, convincing case," said one State Department officer. In an open diplomatic capital like Washington, a little good will on the part of self-confident and genial envoys goes a long way, which few developing countries have learned. Not everything worked smoothly; one Philippine emissary became convinced that the State Department was working for a quota cut, when the opposite was true, according to American diplomats. But the damage was not great. There was no such unpleasantness as after the veterans' bill eight years earlier.

The third factor was the State Department itself. It was the general view, up to the highest level, that 1971 was not the year to restructure the quotas. No particular staff work had been done to argue for a different apportionment. Moreover, Philippine-American trade was roughly in balance, and cuts in the quota would jeopardize Philippine imports from the United States.[16] The Philippines, it was felt, could "make it" economically with a little luck, and could not stand the strain of serious cuts. Philippine stability, it was finally being perceived, was a "plus" for the American policy at a time of national ferment over American policy in Southeast Asia. "We worked hard on the bill to keep the boat from being rocked at this time," a department official said. Some of the same men who had laughed at the Philippines for years were now working on its behalf. The department as a whole weighed Philippine interests as being of a higher priority than those of Latin American claimants. The same was true in Congress, where Wilbur Mills was of the same mind as the State Department.

The very dealings with foreign governments, in foreign capitals or in Manila itself, became more professional. Marcos saw that the Philippine image and hence its bargaining power could be improved by improving the reputation of the nation's chief officers. From the first he had recruited a talented group of young technocrats, and in his second term in order to project an image of progressiveness and efficiency he brought in more and raised the standing of those already present. The effect of the new team was remarkable. Dr. Hannah, administrator of AID, visited Manila and conferred with Marcos and his key assistants and secretaries at Malacañang; he told a senior American official afterward that this was the first time he had sat in that cabinet room with anything other than political hacks. He let the word go around that any well-thought-out project would have a solid chance of funding from his agency. A commitment to give $20 million to the republic for rural electrification came shortly thereafter, and though the homework long since done on that was important, the speed and ease with which the commitment was made is attributable to the new Philippine image. (Note also the help coming from distinguished public servants in such a case; Senator Pelaez, one of the greatest politicians of this period in the Philippines, had long interested himself in rural electrification, and did much to bring about the consummation of the project.)

In the commercial arena Marcos's actions were promotive also, and paved the way for the desired vast inflow of foreign investment. Two factors beyond economic nationalism had been scaring away foreign investment. The first was uncertainty, which is the greatest inhibition for business investment. Prior to martial law, the American embassy had polled American businessmen in Manila asking if they could continue to operate in the existing environment; the response had been affirmative, if there were assurances that the situation would deteriorate no further, which looked impossible. It was business doubts, not actual policy, that were at issue. Thus an oil exploration bill, long debated in the Congress, had been passed in the House but not in the Senate. With martial law the bill was declared enacted, and the oil companies could get to work. "Philippine stock shot up on Wall Street," a banker at the Morgan Guaranty Trust Company said after the proclamation of martial law.

The other factor was the question of vested American rights, tied up with the old battle cry of parity, and given precise form in the so-called Quasha case. The parity amendment of 1946 among other things had given Americans the right to own land in the Philippines. Would title remain good after the passing of the Laurel-Langley Agreement in 1974? If not, could the government confiscate American businesses that owned land in the archipelago? A successful American lawyer named William Quasha, who had spent most of his career in the Philippines, went to court to test the title of the land on which his house in Forbes Park, Makati, was built.

On 19 August 1972, just after the great typhoon that destroyed so much of Luzon, and only a month before martial law, the supreme court ruled against Quasha, to no one's surprise. The press was jubilant. Radicals on the fringe of the "legitimate" political system now demanded that escheat proceedings get under way immediately, to confiscate without compensation all American-held land, both private and corporate. The establishment radicals, like Senator Diokno, did not go quite so far, but advocated that recompense be strictly tied to concessions from the United States: ironclad assurances on the Philippine sugar quota for ten to twenty years, minimal duty on other imports into the American market. To the vast discomfiture of the economic nationalists, Marcos almost immediately assured Americans that recompense would be paid. Diokno, who had less than a month of freedom left, accused him of overruling the Supreme Court.[17]

The Quasha decision gave Marcos something with which to bargain in fashioning his cluster of policies with the U.S. But in the immediate period following the proclamation of martial law he had to provide some free goods to the Americans in order to spur on foreign investment—and thus economic results.

The foreign business community was too battle-scarred itself, and needed incentives. So Marcos gave himself and his chief advisors at the Economic and Development Authority and at the Board of Investments negotiating leeway with which to find attractive terms for investment. The long-studied governmental reorganization plan, which had been stalled in Congress, was immediately declared in force, making it far easier for business to sort out its problems with the government. The whole banking system was similarly reformed by executive decree, something the IMF had recommended but which had been held up by the great families in control of most of the banks. The terms on which foreign capital could participate were made more precise and generous. A completely revised custom and tariff code and a new oil exploration law allowing foreign corporations to enter into production-sharing service contracts also speeded up investment. The liberalization of central bank regulations on capital repatriation and profit remittance, and the decree encouraging multinational companies to establish regional headquarters in the Philippines, the liberalization of the Investment Incentives Act and of the Export Incentives Act, all helped. These were all "free goods." The result was an almost two-and-a-half-fold increase in investment applications at the Board of Investments in the first year after martial law. The tenfold increase in stock transactions in the stock market better reflected the actual increase in business confidence in the economy as a whole, as did the near quadrupling of foreign exchange reserves between the proclamation of martial law and the end of 1973.[18]

How the question of American land titles ultimately would be resolved was not clear. But as the U.S. embassy had anticipated over a year in advance, the final draft of the new constitution, which Marcos pushed through under the martial law administration, declared land titles acquired in the parity period to be valid against private persons, but left the status of these titles negotiable after July 1974. Corporations required to have at least 60 percent Philippine ownership by that time meanwhile managed very nicely to increase Philippine participation, by issuing stock to employees, separating foreign and domestic operations, and a variety of other techniques, most of which had the effect of shaking up the corporate structure in a way that stimulated efficiency and benefited foreign stockholders.

"Self-reliance" in the military field reinforced autonomy elsewhere. As the reality of American withdrawal began to sink in, Marcos began more ambitious plans to make the Philippines self-sufficient militarily for when the United States would be no longer around. Thus a whole military-industrial complex was to be developed to support the defense effort; almost a billion dollars were to be invested in the manufacture of weaponry. It was hoped that within five years the country would have its own self-sustaining defense establishment. That target was ambitious, but by 1974, a plant was under construction to build M-16s. Tactical radios and radar equipment were among the increasingly sophisticated equipment already being made in the Philippines. They were diversifying supply. Twelve training aircraft were brought from Italy.

Marcos worked on other fronts to strengthen the order-maintaining function of the armed forces. The American program of public safety—aid to the police—distributed more money. Effectively the Philippines became a testing ground for new weaponry and techniques of urban riot control—all the panoply of urban guerrilla warfare—much as Thailand had been the testing ground in the early 1960s for rural counterinsurgency techniques in general. Marcos appointed General Fidel Ramos, a graduate of West Point, one of the most competent men of the republic and his own cousin, head of the Constabulary—the National Police—in order to maximize its effectiveness. The result was that, when martial law was proclaimed, Marcos had a trustworthy and professional ally in the most crucial position for maintaining public order.

"Self-reliance" had two other catalysts in the military field. The armed forces had always had to coordinate their plans closely with the Joint U.S. Military Advisory Group, if only because they were so dependent on American military aid. It will be recalled that the Philippine Congress had on occasion refused to appropriate funds for the armed forces, and had always held them hostage to political considerations in promotion of officers. With martial law, they had a dependable supply of money for the first time. They got their greatly increased budget for 1974 on the first day of the new fiscal year, months before their American counterpart was to get its. Although the Pentagon had always tended to downplay Philippine forces and the alliance in general, they had, in 1970, "straightlined" their projected military assistance for five years, at around its current $20 million level. As the Philippine budget increased, this became a smaller proportion.

Necessity was the most important factor in building self-reliance. From September 1972 the armed forces administered martial law throughout the archipelago, and especially from March 1973, had to fight a tough war against secessionist groups in Mindanao and Sulu. Despite fears to the contrary in certain American circles, the Philippine military got no direct assistance in either of these endeavors. (It is an interesting commentary on American apprehensions that the civic action involvement of small companies of armed forces personnel transferred from Okinawa upon the closure of bases there could elicit fears of "another Viet-Nam." It was widely thought that the men in question were "green berets," which is not true. Teams of from thirty to forty men, from the army's first civil affairs division, at the request of appropriate Philippine agencies and with the approval of the ambassador, would work with Philippine armed forces personnel in nonsensitive areas, bringing in medics to eliminate rabies from an area and the like; no weapons were brought in.)

The longer-term picture of Philippine-American military collaboration was less evident in 1974 than it was in other areas, so far as this pertained to external defense and American base rights.

During 1972, as public pressures on him mounted, Marcos had had to adjust the rhetoric of policy to the new realities. Opposition to the American position in the archipelago, always a vocal and influential small minority, when combined with all the other problems to which solutions were difficult to find, became pertinent enough for the first time to elicit apparent presidential approval. Whereas in 1971 Marcos was using every stratagem to convince Washington to keep the bases at full force as long as possible, by mid-1972 he was having to change his tune, if only publicly. Mainly to defuse the sense of crisis in Manila, Marcos agreed with radicals that the bases should go. The history of Philippine demands in public and negotiations in private ensured that it would be a long time before that would happen, even if Marcos were serious—but that was, for the first time, the direction in which events seemed to be moving. By waiting until there was no conceivable alternative, so that the new policy would be understood in Washington, Marcos ensured maximum sympathy there. Had his policy been the reverse, that is, supporting the radicals in 1970 or 1971 on the bases and then using what margin he had brought from them to hold on to the American presence in 1972, he might have got neither—no support from nonbelieving students and a feeling of sell-out from the Americans, who at that point were still unsympathetic. Marcos was privately assuring the Americans that he had no intention of phasing out the bases; it was the Americans—as he correctly feared—who were more eager for a phase-down. After martial law, there was no more talk of changing the terms on which the Americans used the bases. That was bound to come once Marcos had settled the conflicts in Mindanao and built up the economy still further. The panels appointed for the renegotiations of the base treaties, which had met intermittently between 1970 and 1972,[19] did not meet again until after the fall of Cambodia in April 1975.

Thus by strategy, and by taking advantage of circumstances and contingent necessity, the Philippines had vastly increased her international status. As is always the case, there were exogenous forces at work conspiring either to favor or hinder such changes in status. In this case circumstances worked for the Philippines, particularly in her all-important relations with the United States.

The most important fortuitous factor is systemic. The importance of other Asian countries to the United States was declining rapidly, while nothing was happening *pari passu* with the Philippines to lower its position in the American hierarchy. Consequently her position rose relative to the rest, the exact opposite of what had happened in the 1940s after her independence. The United States was withdrawing from Indochina; by 1970 Indonesia was relatively stable. Nixon was in a stew about India, whose war with Pakistan at the end of 1971 gave him an excuse to cut off American aid. Though this happened after aid to the Philippines had already increased dramatically, it made available a vast new source of funds to sustain the increased flow of resources to the archipelago. Philippine luck then in effect matched that in 1961 when the Cuban sugar quota was cut out and reallocated to countries still friendly to the United States. Moreover, as the Philippine economy took off, becoming as important a trading partner with Japan as with the U.S., and as the government obtained as much aid from Japan and other, generally multilateral sources as from Washington, bargaining between the two parties became less one-sided. Both parties wanted concessions and the increasing equality made for much greater Philippine self-confidence.

If proof be needed of the Philippine gain in status, at least in American eyes, it can easily be seen in the astonishing rise in American aid as seen in Table 9-1. In 1967 aid officers had piously proclaimed that the Philippines could not use any more aid than it was getting—and that such was the parameter, and the explanation, for the puniness of the American program. As we saw with relation to Thailand (when the case was the reverse), such considerations are seldom pertinent. Absorptive capacity will be ignored if political considerations obtain. Five years later the regular aid program was $62.7 million, or about seven times the 1967 program, despite the fact that American aid was declining globally and the United States was withdrawing from Southeast Asia. Not only that, total American aid flows, thanks to the devastation caused by the 1972 typhoon and floods, the worst national disaster in Philippine history, were at their highest level ever. About $80 million in additional funds went to the Philippines. Thus with military aid included, the grand total in 1972 exceeded $170 million. Bureaucrats in Washington still cracked jokes at Philippine expense for a little while longer, but something obviously had changed, unless we assume that such an incredible jump could be purely fortuitous.

True, the great rise in American aid came prior to martial law. But so did

Table 9-1
U.S. A.I.D. Assistance to Philippines (Millions of U.S. Dollars)

	FY1968	FY1969	FY1970	FY1971	FY1972	Estimated FY1973
Total	21.1	19.6	27.2	39.3	62.7	154.9
Technical Assistance Grants	6.0	5.6	9.0	10.7	9.5	10.0
(Family Planning)	(1.1)	(1.4)	(4.9)	(5.0)	(5.5)	(4.2)
PL480 Title I (Loans)	6.8	9.3	5.1	5.9	8.1	18.5
PL480 Title II (Grants)	–	–	10.1	20.3	20.0	50.0
Regional Grants	.5	.8	2.2	1.4	1.6	1.5
Development Loans	6.7	3.1	–	–	20.0	20.0
Excess Equipment	1.1	.8	.9	1.0	2.5	2.5
FY1973 Disaster Grants						52.4

Source: U.S. A.I.D., Washington, D.C.

Marcos's intentions to transform the republic, and so did the perception by the Americans in Manila of that intent. By early 1971 certain of the most senior officials at the embassy believed that Marcos would continue to improve the position of foreign investment at the expense of the entrenched national elites; would continue with his increasingly successful pilot land-reform program under way in Nueva Ecija; and would move relations with the United States on to a new, self-confident base that would be far more beneficial in the long run for the excolonial power. In fact, the people who were running the government in 1974 were in exactly the same positions in 1971; but with the removal of the politicians their effect was far greater. They were, in conjunction with the armed forces, running the country.

From the beginning of martial law Marcos made a link between structural reform in the society, civil peace, and foreign policy. "Letters of instruction" went out raising the wages of the *sacada* (the sugar workers), thus reallocating economic values; forbidding other than essential foreign travel; reallocating social status values (and increasing regime control). Decrees went out forcing private owners of the media to sell a majority interest to the government, firing inefficient followers of the great families from the bureaucracy, and so forth. Worth mentioning is a fortuitous factor in the growth of Philippine status in Washington. Henry Byroade happened not only to be well suited for the job at the particular time, but to wish to make the Philippines once more a showcase of economic growth and stability. Well connected throughout official Washington, knowledgeable of how Washington worked, and perhaps seeing the Philippines as a chance to cap a remarkable career with something bigger, Byroade brought great drive to his job and convinced Filipinos that the American aid program could be more substantial and that cooperation in a variety of fields would be profitable. While not neglecting American interests, Byroade was able to advise the Filipinos as to both tactics and strategy in increasing the aid program. Official Washington was very much aware of what Byroade was up to, and approved.

Land reform was the anchor of the "New Society," and looked like one of its earliest successes. Building on the capability acquired in the pilot project in Nueva Ecija during the preceding two years, the government went all out to redistribute rice and corn lands, starting with one hundred-hectare estates, working down to the more difficult fifty- and twenty-four-hectare farms. Secretary Melchor used his computer system to maximize efficiency. The Constabulary prevented recalcitrant landlords from stalling. As of early 1974, 259,081.98 hectares had been transferred to 144,424 recipients.[20] Land-reform experts thought progress in the first year was as great as had been achieved in the first year of the postwar land reform in Japan, Korea, Taiwan, and, later, Iran. Through all this President Marcos was building a new constituency.

It was such progress that elicited vast new inputs of foreign aid—not the land-reform program as such. The successful handling of such a program encouraged donors to give for other purposes. American aid, for example, was to a certain extent keyed to performance, though we have carefully noted that politics was the major determinant of aid allocations during the period this book covers. Inequality and low income generally during this period was perceived in Washington to be a major determinant of civil strife—a highly inaccurate perception, as it turns out, but one strongly felt nonetheless.[21] A willingness of governments to deal with inequality through reform of economic and social structures usually resulted in a greater predisposition of the American govern-ment to aid the country. The general perception in Washington that some relationship existed between perceived social problems within developing coun-tries and political stability was not inaccurate, however. And the perception that the existing maldistribution of rewards within the Philippine system would have to be changed before the country could cohere was correct. Social progress and stability had once again elicited aid, as it had done before for Thailand.

Philippine economic essential structures began improving about the time those in Thailand started their downhill slide. The devaluation of 1970 had as big an effect as was hoped for, and the economy continued to pick up steam thereafter. The real growth rate in 1971 was 6.5 percent, and instead of the 1970s deficit of a billion pesos there was a surplus of P539 million. In 1972, despite a turndown in the terms of trade and continued inflation, real growth continued at the same rate until the disastrous floods of July and August. These, combined with the massive expenditures, would produce the biggest government operating deficit ever, even bigger than that of 1969, which forced the peso's devaluation. Fiscal measures taken to counteract this—a permanent export tax, revision of the Tariff and Customs Code, higher excise taxes on various consumer items—would bring about an 8 percent increase in revenue, a World Bank mission thought. Part of the reason the world financial community was not excessively gloomy about the deficit was that the country's trade position showed an extraordinary turnaround—from a deficit of P560 million in the first half of 1972, to a surplus of P1559 million in the same period for 1973. By mid-1973 most economic experts on the Philippines were confident that the economy would continue its real growth. So much was in flux in the immediate aftermath of the proclamation of the New Society that it was not possible then to see how lucky the country would be in benefiting from greatly increased international commodity prices, or how successful the government would be in managing the economy. What first became evident was that the cluster of policies the government would use was to be far different from that in the old order.

The luck factor must be seen from two perspectives. It was extraordinarily good fortune for President Marcos's martial law administration that, after the floods and chaos of 1972, an upturn in international commodity prices should reverse the previous decline in the Philippines' terms of trade (between October 1972 and October 1973 the wholesale price index of exports advanced 70.2

percent, against 39.9 percent for imports). It was this more than anything else that pushed Philippine foreign exchange reserves beyond the billion-dollar mark for the first time. From another point of view such luck could be considered in terms of the opportunity, deserved or undeserved, it would give the administration to consolidate rule during a time of rapid inflation (26 percent in consumables in 1973) and rebellion in the south. With such vast reserves there would be little foreign exchange problem in obtaining necessary imports for continued economic expansion, not to mention weaponry with which to fight wars against Muslims. More important was the economic planning that the regime undertook, for it was on the success of this that the good luck in commodity prices could be taken advantage of for the long term. A complete restructuring of the economy was under way in the first few years of martial law, and it was by no means clear how it would end; it could hardly make things worse. Given the high level of sophistication involved in the planning mechanism and the freedom on the part of the planners to implement desired policies (much like that of Delfim and his colleagues in Brazil who achieved that "economic miracle"), it seemed likely to prove a great success. Though the actual harm done to democratic institutions amounted to annihilation, and some of the most eloquent spokesmen for Philippine democracy languished in prison, genuine social and economic reform began to be undertaken, which left open the possibility of a fuller and wider democracy in the future.

Whether, in fact, American officials should have used their influence to inhibit Marcos's moves toward martial law and the consolidation of his own power is another matter entirely, and beyond our scope. It was never very likely that they would have been so inclined, cynical about the workings of Philippine democracy as they were; in an era of retrenchment generally in Asia, with the Nixon doctrine as a guide. It was even less likely that they would work against what they saw as a solid chance for the building of a stronger partnership with their oldest ally.

10 Democracy, Stability, and Foreign Policy

Apart from their normative value, which in this volume was taken as given, we have seen that democratic institutions function in relation to foreign policy in different ways, relevant to different national moods. The Philippines, in its preservative mood of the 1960s, bargained more successfully with the United States than did Thailand, whose promotively oriented regime had fewer demands internally with which to countermand those coming from the United States.

Democratic institutions keep the nation's guard high: where an external power has compelling needs, the presence of democratic institutions will vastly strengthen the bargaining power of the state. When the needs are reversed, democratic institutions are unlikely to be of help. Thus in the Philippines the leadership could only get substantial support for internal programs where these were perceived to be tied to the Vietnamese war. True, democratic institutions have a symbolic, at times even ideological, significance, but such is pertinent in the way that they mold relationships between parties over the long term, not as a point at issue, or as a direct advantage, in bargaining.

The problem is that developing countries wish to develop rapidly. They seek financial support with which to develop. Here the value of democratic institutions tends to become negative. In the Philippines prior to martial law, and in Thailand to a certain extent after the 1973 coup, it was difficult to reconcile the needs—and characteristics—of a democratic policy with the requirements for stability of foreign investors and lenders. Franklin Weinstein found much the same thing for Indonesia, where he examined the differences between a period of "competitive" and "noncompetitive" politics:

Given the prevailing perception of a hostile world, a competitive situation creates strong incentives for carrying out a foreign policy emphasizing defense of the nation's independence, while the liabilities accompanying a policy designed to serve the needs of economic development are formidable; in a noncompetitive political situation, however, the liabilities of a development-oriented foreign policy can easily be overcome, while the political incentives to carry out an independence policy are reduced.[1]

While Philippine ranking in international financial circles shot up after 1972, that of Thailand declined after the 1973 coup—though the fundamental soundness of the economy and the resilience of the system as a whole tended to compensate for this.

Stability has various utilities for foreign policy; societies with coherent and

155

stable social structures will be able to focus more productive effort on finding a good fit between internal needs and external pressures. There is also a shorter-term relationship to foreign policy. Stability elicits external admiration and respect. It also elicits aid. Thailand, as a much admired "island of stability in a sea of crisis" during the 1960s, was able, rightly or wrongly, to make herself an important anchor of American foreign policy. In the early 1970s, as the American conviction spread that Thailand was pretty much incapable of solving her principal societal problem, the insurgencies, Washington for the moment tended to write Thailand's chances off. There only remained the American short-term need for bases in the Indochina war. It is thus not entirely accidental that the Washington faction which viewed relations with Thailand in strategic terms was undisturbed by the short-term character of Thai-American relations.

When a region, or any international subsystem, is characterized by rapid change and uncertainty, which is certainly descriptive of Southeast Asia in the 1970s, *purposeful* autocracies appear to do better in their relations with great powers, particularly when the powers are seeking to diminish their regional involvement. The Philippine leadership was able to increase American aid and support very substantially by fashioning a new image, and even by appearing to reduce her psychological dependence on the United States. True, Filipinos were helped by the reduction of American alternatives in the region, but image is still a more critical variable. The Thai regime, during most of the period of this book, was an autocracy, but an increasingly unpurposive one as time went on. Its image of stability and promotive behavior internally in the 1960s brought it economic rewards, and the leadership thought it was also bringing a long-term security guarantee. Because its perceptions of American intentions were incorrect, and because of its own economic interests, it did not adjust its foreign policy to the new realities. Even in 1970 when congressional action was taken to prevent the administration from dispatching combat troops to Thailand, nothing was done, though Thai diplomats saw the contradiction clearly. Democratic institutions would surely have served Thailand better than those she had, for then groups would have made their own convictions of the changes needed more salient. For foreign policy purposes in times of rapid change, democratic institutions are better than preservative autocracies, but less adaptive than wise and promotive autocracies.

What can we conclude about the value of democratic institutions for a developing country, in cases of its bargaining with a greater power who purports to value these? On the face of it the conclusion is hardly reassuring for those who choose to think that the United States should reward those regimes that build or strengthen democratic institutions. The record is fairly clear. The United States almost exclusively allocated rewards to the Philippines in terms of strategic needs and perceptions of stability in the archipelago. In the 1960s, only when American needs were great—as with the wish for at least symbolic support in the Vietnamese war—was Philippine bargaining power great. The financial support rendered the Philippines in return was resented as much by the giver as by the recipient. A large aid program began anew only when it was perceived that President Marcos would make the internal changes deemed necessary to increase national coherence and stability, and martial law little affected—indeed, it postdated—this judgment. Other than in communiqués and July proclamations, the United States never paid much attention to the common adherence to democratic values. Although many American officials questioned the wisdom of the policy, Washington generally accepted martial law as a happier solution to Philippine problems than the old political system. The country team at the embassy, with some conspicuous exceptions, was enthusiastic about the regime and its results through early 1975. It is hard to find any negative component in Philippine-American relations that flowed from the institution of martial law. This is hardly surprising; in the duel between radical Philippine "nationalism" and the technocrat-military-American alliance, the latter had won.

The Thai case is equally instructive. In the 1960s the United States pressed the regime to develop democratic institutions and bolstered those nascent and incipient ones. But the value was not for the democratic institutions as such: rather, in that day of "Title IX" and "political development," given the prevalent assumption in Washington that *stability* came with democratic institutions, the concern was over the survival of a Thai regime sufficiently friendly to the United States to permit her continued access to the great bases. The need for the bases increased, fortuitously, as the conviction that there was a relationship between democratic institutions and stability declined. The two trends intersected at about the time of the maladaptive Thai coup of 1971. Thus as the strategic balance in Asia changed and the United States became dependent on the Thai regime for continued access to the Indochinese theater, Washington became silent on the deficiencies of what was a highly unattractive system. By 1973, it was argued in Washington that only a Communist government would make any difference to it: in fact the administration in power had recurrent difficulties dealing with third world democracies.

A decade of intense involvement in the developing world had indeed caused a revolution in American thinking. In 1959 Walt Rostow could argue, from the position that American security was directly related to the preservation of democratic regimes throughout the world.[2] The searing experiences of the 1960s left little room for that sort of concern. It does not follow that Americans had come to devalue democratic institutions themselves; on their domestic front the opposite was happening, as previously underprivileged groups established their rights within the system and a mood of national reform swept the nation, as a disgraced Richard Nixon was swept from office. The Americans had discovered the relative detachment of foreign policy and domestic affairs. They had discovered how modest was their ability to affect domestic affairs in other countries, and also that, as long as a foreign power inclined toward neither communism nor radical socialism, its own attachment to the United States would derive primarily from an identification of its own security and personal interests with it.

Nor did Philippine and Thai elites seek to preserve their ties with the United States for purposes of preserving democracy. True, Thai of the old school looked to the West for reinforcement after the democratic coup, but not to the United States as such. American support of the old regime hardly helped. The Thai did look to America for the preservation of a pattern of relations indirectly related to democracy, in that their security needs remained compelling; to preserve their autonomy they saw continued close association with the United States as important. With the Philippines, America had compromised her own principles, in the eyes of those who cherished the old system, by supporting Marcos's martial law administration. But shared historical memories, mutually supportive security ties, close and beneficial trading relationships—these, the stuff of which international friendships are made, preserved a closeness between both these Asian powers and the United States, at least at the official level.

This is not to say that these patterns would be the same whether or not the United States was a democratic state, only that we must separate abstractions characterizing political systems from the determinants of relations between states. Regimes interact in terms of their perceived interests, and the very manner of diplomatic interaction insulates or at least separates their own domestic institutions from their direct foreign policy implementation, though choices are molded in the longer run by the nature of their institutions.

Who did better in foreign policy in this period, with reference to the United States—the Philippines or Thailand? It is difficult to find quantitative indicators, and the question is complicated by a subsystemic dimension of the problem, the "who benefited" one. A state's overall adaptational capability is clearly closely related to which elite controlled the state, and to how it allocated scarce resources accruing to it. It is not easy to be objective on this question, given the presence of ideological preferences among so many observers as to who *should* benefit, and as to which elite could best maximize the state's overall benefits derived through foreign policy. Thus we are back to the "preferred roles of foreigners," which was at the heart of the conflicts in both the Philippines and Thailand. The question is not just the preferred roles of foreigners, but the preferred roles of *nationals* in their benefits derived from relations with foreigners.

Thai generals, for example, found their own rule consolidated by accepting the American view of the dangers of war in Viet-Nam. They also found themselves richer, a dimension (and consequence) of foreign policy choice that is usually too sensitive to be investigated in the developing world, and yet often is one of the most important variables. As in Thailand, the results often are felt on the most important social structures. Traditional and relatively stable patronage patterns had been greatly altered by the 1932 coup, and successive military coups continued the alteration in favor of the armed forces. The massive increase in the amounts of money going through the hands of the generals and marshals in the 1960s took things much further, leading "in some cases to unbridled behavior . . . and frustration and resentment on the part of those left out in the cold (mainly civilian bureaucrats)."[3] The point is not that American military aid was responsible as such for the institution or the continuation of military government, as has been argued.[4] The military were already in power when the first American military aid went to Thailand. The Americans pressed the Thai to write a new constitution and to reopen parliament in the 1960s, which they did, only to throw these institutions out when the American bargaining power began to decline. The argument is rather that the massive increase in money available to the regime so increased their ability to allocate values authoritatively without need of inputs from traditional sources of influence and advice that they could remain blind to their most important problems—building a broader base of support and adjusting foreign policy to the new realities in the region.

As the generals and the Americans became more determinant in the direction of Thai foreign policy in the 1960s, the foreign office, and the traditional elite in general, became less so. The foreign office's opposition to the military regime and to the excessively important role of the Americans was both a function of its perception of the need for Thailand to keep her options open, as in times past, and of its own relative loss of position. After the 1973 democratic coup, diplomats talked euphemistically about the "demilitarization" of foreign policy, and celebrated the new, higher position they held in the central decision-making elite.

Efforts were also made to restructure Thai society as a whole. The National Student Center of Thailand, which had been instrumental in overthrowing the old regime, lost no time in announcing its intention to launch a campaign for a "change in social values."[5] Students demonstrated outside luxury goods stores; forced a cancellation of a contract made for a new airport with Northrop, an American company, in which many leaders of the old regime had reportedly taken sizable cuts; and started organizing groups to educate peasants in the countryside as to the issues in the 1975 election. In 1974 the students were generally considered the strongest political force in the country, though their decline was rapid. They spoke with exactly the voice of those social scientists who had argued that the whole socioeconomic system would need to be restructured before Thailand could *develop* (as opposed to merely "modern-ize").[6]

In the Philippines, the dominant political elite had benefited from a vaguely radical anti-Americanism, because with it went an outflow of American investment which they, in their primary role as rich businessmen, could buy up. Technocrats emerged in the 1960s, partly because of the trends in Philippine education and partly because of Marcos's particular desires. They found themselves unable to administer the country efficiently because of the opposition to central control by these very powerful subsystemic elements, some of which were rivals of the state itself in power in certain areas. Marcos and his technocrats worked closely with the Americans, and used American aid, much as Thai generals had, to strengthen their own control. Whether it was granted for purposes, ironically, of increasing "political development" under Title IX or of furthering decentralization (as AID officials so often said), its result was almost uniformly to reinforce the power of the state—either in building up control and intelligence mechanisms through the armed forces, or in strengthening the bargaining power of Malacañang palace vis-à-vis traditional provincial political elites, by giving it more funds to disburse. If one misconstrues the *primary*, that is, economic, function and true interests of the political elite that was replaced, it is easy to understand Marcos's assertion of power, and the use of American aid, as "refeudalization."[7] Thus one can also misconstrue the overthrow of democracy for autocracy, of a group willing to "stand up" to America being replaced by one subservient thereto, as "refeudalization."

Plot theories of history aside, what happened is that the technocrats, reinforcing Marcos's will, asserted themselves and, buttressed by the army, began ruling in his name, dispensing with the old political system in the process. Like the Thai generals, they became more prosperous and more powerful in the process; unlike them, they were using their new largesse from abroad, and their new resources derived from their greater control of the system, for productive ends. Whether they should have been the ones so benefiting, there can be no question that the central authority of the state would have to be reinforced before the Philipines could cope as a modern effective state system, whatever one's ideological preferences. If the power of the army, bureaucracy, and presidential family was increased, the power of the state mechanism itself was vastly augmented. In economic terms, this was done at little financial cost to the old elite—as the state's new resources were largely derived from the expansion of the economy, which soared as foreign investment flowed in. In political terms, of course, the process was vastly expensive to the old elite, just as this process has always been in every country in the process of modernization and development.

Another problem in comparing the performance of two states is settling on a temporal point. As entities, societies have their own timers, ticking differently from one another on many issues, no matter how comparable they are on static indicators, no matter how much they are mutually influenced by international trends. There were also such great uncertainties in the political situation of both countries that it was not easy, at the conclusion of this period, to make a judgment, for such requires peering into the future and predicting trends emerging from the existing structures; both states were in the midst of the greatest transformation of these structures in a generation. Marcos for his part had constructed a system that might lay the basis for a broadly based democracy, but the success of which, such as it was, for the moment depended on the fragile basis of his own survival. Were he not to live until a stable succession was assured a scramble would ensue between his family, leading generals, and old politicians, ending the stability he had brought at least to the central government. But it was also difficult to be confident that the young Thai soldiers who took over the leadership of their armed forces from their retiring leaders would feel bound in 1975 by the oaths of their predecessors never to intervene in the polity, should the new democratic government flounder.

In all, from an internal perspective, Thailand appeared to have done rather better, emerging at the end of this period as she did with a new elected government, with some of her most talented subjects at the helm, after deposing a corrupt, inefficient, and lazy regime. One was bound to have misgivings examining what had happened to the Philippines, no matter how impressive economic progress was thought to be, no matter how much law and order had improved (everywhere but Mindanao). The imposition of martial law, the imprisonment of some of her most distinguished citizenry, the silencing of the press, the ever-increasing enrichment of the president and his family, all cast a heavy pall over the archipelago.

Yet in looking at foreign policy, and relations with the United States in particular, the Philippines appears to have done rather better than Thailand. It was with a foresight rare in the world of statecraft that Marcos had transformed Philippine ties with the United States, supporting the great ally in her wars, getting American support in return for his country's various efforts, all the while laying the basis for a more autonomous position in the international system. The protection of the China sea from the raging wars of Southeast Asia was an additional happy factor in the Philippine future. Thailand, on the other hand, had insurgencies around her periphery moving slowly but seemingly inexorably toward the center, to which threat her new ruling elite was insufficiently attuned. Beyond her frontiers, epochal wars had been waged, and came to their unhappy conclusion in 1975. The fall of Cambodia meant that Thailand's 600-mile Eastern border was now also insecure, for Marxist-Leninist cadre across the frontier were unlikely to be able to contain their own revolutionary ardor. As loyalist troops fled into Thailand, Khmer Rouge troops jeered across the border, "threatening to march on Thailand."[8] Thai leaders in the past had gambled on American protection but, unless American needs—and the Congress's perception of these needs—changed, this gamble might well be seen to be lost. Small wonder that students burned American leaders in effigy and the Thai government demanded an apology, when the U.S. used a Thai base for routine logistic purposes in the retrieval of a merchant vessel seized by Cambodian forces. Six years before he briefly became prime minister for the second time, M.R. Seni Pramoj showed that he understood the dilemma perfectly. "We have let U.S. forces use our country to bomb Hanoi. When [the Americans] go away, they won't take that little bit of history with them."[9]

Notes

Notes

Preface (pp. xi-xvii)

1. See Peter A. Corning, "The Biological Bases of Behavior and Some Implications for Political Science, Individual Societies, and for the International System as a Whole," *World Politics*, XXIII, April 1971. Adaptation, however, seems to me to be an appropriate approach with which to begin building theory, but I can only give a tautological "reason"—because I accept in part Corning's notion that "the same Darwinian criterion—reproductive efficacy (and all that it entails)" is applicable at both micro (individual) and macro (systemic) levels. "The theory of evolution should be applicable at all levels of analysis.... We should be able to evaluate the systemic behavior of nations, groups of nations, and various international organizations in terms of its survival consequences for individual societies and the international system as a whole."

2. James N. Rosenau, *The Adaptation of National Societies: A Theory of Political System Behavior and Transformation* (New York: McCaleb-Seiler Publishing Company, 1970), p. 15.

3. Quoted in Herbert Phillips, "Some Premises of American Scholarship on Thailand," mimeo, 1971. See Norman Jacobs, *Modernization Without Development: Thailand as an Asian Case Study* (New York: Praeger, 1971), p. 25, for a comment on scholarly admiration of the Thai.

4. Phillips. 1971.

5. See, for example, Bruce M. Russett, *International Regions, and the International System: A Study in Political Ecology* (Chicago: Rand-McNally, 1967), p. 70.

6. J.C. Pierce and Richard A. Pride, "Cross-National Micro-Analysis: Procedures and Problems," in Pierce and Pride, *Cross-National Micro-Analysis, Procedures and Problems* (Beverly Hills: Sage Publications, 1972), p. 13.

7. Bruce Russett, *Trends in World Politics* (New York: Macmillan, 1965), p. 127. Philippine per capita income in 1960 was $220, while that of Thailand in 1963 was $113. In 1970, largely owing to a devaluation of the peso, Philippine per capita income was about $126, while that of Thailand in 1969 was $180. The difference was not as great as it seemed, as real growth rates in both countries were relatively high. See also C. Taylor and M. Hudson, *World Handbook of Political and Social Indicators II*, First ICPR edition, 1971; Bruce Russett, *World Handbook of Political and Social Indicators* (New Haven: Yale University Press, 1964), p. 156; "Economic Summary of Thailand," American Embassy, Bangkok, July 1971; K. Davis, *World Urbanization 1950-1970*, Vol. I (Berkeley: University of California, 1969), pp. 71-72.

8. For Thailand, see, in particular, David Wilson, *Politics in Thailand* (Ithaca, N.Y.: Cornell University Press, 1962); Fred Riggs, *Thailand, Modernization of a*

Bureaucratic Polity (Honolulu, East-West Center Press, 1966); Frank C. Darling, *Thailand and the United States* (Washington, D.C.: Public Affairs Press, 1965). For the Philippines, see Jose Veloso Abueva, and Raul P. de Guzman, eds., *Foundations and Dynamics of Filipino Government and Politics* (Manila: Bookwork, 1964); Frank H. Golay, ed., *The United States and the Philippines* (Englewood Cliffs, N.J.: Prentice-Hall, 1966); Jean Grossholtz, *Politics in the Philippines: A Country Study* (Boston: Little-Brown, 1964). For comparative studies of the two, see Frank Darling, "Political Development in Thailand and the Philippines: A Comparative Analysis," *Southeast Asia*, Winter-Spring 1971; Jerrold Milsted, "National Formation, Social Mobilization and Assimilation in the Philippines and Thailand," mimeo, 1972, and "Political Development: The Philippines and Thailand," mimeo, 1972. See also Bernard K. Gordon, *Dimensions of Conflict in Southeast Asia* (Englewood Cliffs, N.J.: Prentice-Hall, 1966).

9. Thanat Khoman, "Which Road for Southeast Asia?" *Foreign Affairs*, July 1964, p. 635.

Chapter 1
Historical Background (pp. 3-24)

1. See Thomas A. Bailey, *A Diplomatic History of the American People*, 7th ed. (New York: Appleton-Century-Crofts, 1964), pp. 473-74. David Steinberg writes that the "Americans in their effort to justify imperialism as altruism and to blunt revolution by evolutionary nationalism, naturally made alliance with the *ilustrados*, giving them access to power and wealth in exchange for collaboration. . . . Neither side ever regretted the decision to collaborate." In "An American Legacy: Years at War in the Philippines," *Pacific Affairs*, Vol. 45, No. 2 (Summer 1972), p. 174.

2. Theodore Friend, *Between Two Empires* (New Haven: Yale University Press, 1965), p. 266.

3. A point I owe to Friend, in ibid.

4. See U.S. Department of State, *Foreign Relations of the United States*, 1945, Vol. VI, pp. 1240ff., passim.

5. George Taylor, *The Philippines and the United States* (New York: Praeger Press for the Council on Foreign Relations, 1964), p. 235.

6. Hearings before the Subcommittee on United States Security Agreements and Commitments Abroad of the Committee of Foreign Relations, United States Senate, 91st Congress, 1st Session (September-October, 1969), Part I, pp. 89-90. (Hereafter to be known as *Symington Report, Philippines.* Part II to be known as *Symington Report, Thailand.*)

7. *Symington Report, Philippines*, p. 348.

8. Interviews, Manila and Quezon City, 1970. JUSMAG influence was not all negative. "It is generally believed that members of the mission also had

something to do with the adoption of the new program of social and economic reform that was an essential part of Magsaysay's approach to solving the Huk problem." Taylor, p. 150.

9. *Symington Report, Philippines*, pp. 95-96.

10. See "U.S. A.I.D. Assistance to the Philippines, 1946-1970," U.S. A.I.D., Manila, September 1970, p. 1.

11. See David Wurfel, "Problems of Colonization," in Frank Golay, ed., *The United States and the Philippines* (Englewood Cliffs, N.J.: Prentice-Hall, 1966), p. 156.

12. Ibid., p. 158.

13. U.S. A.I.D. Philippines Program Office, "Remarks by Thomas C. Niblock, Director, U.S. A.I.D./Philippines at Mirador House, Baguio, Wednesday, February 17, 1971, before the Bishops' Conference" (mimeo), p. 3.

14. "The Strategy of the Thai/Aid program," mimeo, no source given, but clearly a publication of USOM, Bangkok, np.

15. See "RTG Support for the USOM Program," mimeo, no source given, also presumably a publication of USOM, Bangkok, np.

16. "Aid and Modernization in Thailand, Prospectus for a Dissertation," by J. Alexander Caldwell, The Woodrow Wilson School, Princeton, New Jersey, 6 December 1969, p. 5.

17. Quoted in M.W. Meyer, *A Diplomatic History of the Philippine Republic* (Honolulu: University of Hawaii Press, 1965), p. 193.

18. *United States-Vietnam Relations, 1945-1967* Book I, Part IV, A.3, pp. 3-5, U.S. Government Printing Office, Washington, D.C., to be known as: Pentagon Papers, U.S. Government Edition.

19. Stanley Hoffmann, *Gulliver's Troubles, or the Setting of American Foreign Policy* (New York: McGraw-Hill, for the Council on Foreign Relations, 1968).

Chapter 2
Dealing with a Foreign Presence (pp. 25-40)

1. Robert L. West, "Economic Dependence and Policy in Developing Countries," in C. Fred Bergsten and William G. Tyler, eds., *Leading Issues in International Economic Policy* (Lexington, Mass.: D.C. Heath, Lexington Books, 1973), p. 178.

2. Ibid., p. 171.

3. Ibid., p. 171.

4. Ibid., p. 172.

5. Ibid., p. 158.

6. Herbert P. Phillips, "Thai Attitudes Toward the American Presence," Center for South and Southeast Asia Studies, University of California, Berkeley (September 1971), p. 4.

7. See George Tanham, *Trial in Thailand* (New York: Crane, Russak, 1974). Also see *Foreign Affairs Bulletin*, Bangkok, December 1965-January 1966, pp. 309-10.

8. July 27, 1972, AID, S.O. 1017.1, Thai Information Center #04149.

9. Tanham.

10. Memo of John W. Limbert and J. Sheldon Turner, 29 June 1965.

11. See also J. Alexander Caldwell, *American Economic Aid to Thailand* (Lexington, Mass.: D.C. Heath, Lexington Books, 1974), pp. 86-87.

12. Phillips, p. 4.

13. "Facts About RP-US Relations," No. 9-a, U.S. Embassy, Manila, 16 November 1970, p. 2.

14. José D. Ingles, Undersecretary of Foreign Affairs, Letter to the Editor, to *Manila Chronicle*, 25 March 1970.

15. See *Manila Chronicle*, 15 November 1968.

16. See José V. Macaspac, Jr., "Mendez-Blair Pact in Force," *Manila Chronicle*, March 29, 1970.

17. "Background on the Holman Case," mimeo, U.S. Embassy. The source is biased, but independent checking turned up no contraditions in the embassy paper.

18. See in particular the daily articles in the *Manila Chronicle*, throughout March, April, and May 1970 ("Filipino Servility," Edit., 17 May 1970; "Byroade Proves U.S. Can Do It," Edit., 24 March 1970; "Dealing With Natives," I.P. Soliongco, 17 May 1970.)

19. Francisco de Leon, "Our Courts Mean Business," *Manila Chronicle*, 1 April 1970.

20. Court Order, quoted in "Background on the Holman Case," underlining of the court, p. 5.

21. "Background on the Holman Case," pp. 10-11.

22. See "Secret Alterations of Base Pact Bared," *Manila Chronicle*, 7 October 1971.

23. George M. Guthrie and Fortunata M. Azores, "Philippine Interpersonal Behavior Patterns," IPC Paper No. 6, Ateneo de Manila University, Quezon City, 1968.

24. Guthrie and Azores, pp. 55-57.

25. Ibid.

26. *Pentagon Papers*, U.S. Government Edition, Book 2, Part IV.B, p. 54.

27. Ibid., Book 3, Part C.2, p. 31.

28. Arthur Schlesinger, *A Thousand Days* (Boston: Houghton, Mifflin, 1965), p. 163.

29. See *Symington Report, Thailand*, pp. 614-15, for background to the Rusk-Thanat accord.

30. *Pentagon Papers*, U.S. Government Edition, Book 3, Part C.2, p. 31.

31. Interview, Ambassador Kenneth Young; see also George K. Tanham, *Trial in Thailand*, (New York: Crane, Russak and Co., 1974).

32. Hearings, House of Representatives, Foreign Assistance Act, 1967, p. 737.

Chapter 3
Interstate and Transnational Interaction (pp. 41-56)

1. Samuel Huntington, "Transnational Organizations in World Politics," *World Politics*, Vol. XXV, No. 3 (April 1973), p. 333.

2. Samuel P. Huntington, "Foreign Aid for What and for Whom," *Foreign Policy*, Vol. 1, No. 1, Winter 1970-71, p. 179.

3. Unpublished paper, Bangkok, 1970, mimeo.

4. Alexander Caldwell, *American Economic Aid to Thailand* (Lexington, Mass.: D.C. Heath, Lexington Books, 1974), pp. 51-52.

5. See Horst Mendershansen, "The Diplomat As a National and Transnational Agent: A Problem in Multiple Loyalty," *University Programs Modular Studies* (New Jersey: General Learning Press, 1973), for a modern essay on an old theme.

6. Interview, Ambassador Kenneth Young, 1971.

7. See George K. Tanham, *Trial in Thailand* (New York: Crane, Russak and Co., 1974), pp. 71-93, for a development of the theory.

8. Tanham, p. 85.

9. Ibid., p. 86.

10. Peter Braestrup, "How the Guerrillas Came to Koh Noi," *Sunday Magazine, New York Times*, 10 December 1967.

11. See Tanham's earlier works on guerrilla warfare, particularly *Communist Revolutionary Warfare, From the Vietminh to the Viet Cong* (New York: Frederick A. Praeger, 1967).

12. *Symington Report, Thailand*, pp. 910-11.

13. Herbert P. Phillips, "Thai Attitudes Toward the American Presence," *Center for South and Southeast Asia Studies* (Berkeley: University of California, September 1971), pp. 22-23.

14. Memorandum to the Ambassador from USOM, 15 May 1963, T.I.C.–02749.

15. *Second Joint Thai-USOM Evaluation of the ARD Project*, Vol. 1, Bangkok, July 1966, p. 125.

16. Caldwell, p. 9.

17. "Brief Report of Central Government Officials Orientation for ARD in the Board of Changwads," 9 February 1965, Government House, Bangkok.

18. Memorandum, notes on CARD meeting, 11 August 1966, from Frank Shepard, Jr., 2 September 1966, Thai Information Center, 03850.

19. Quoted by permission from Foreign Affairs, October 1969, Vol. 47, No. 1. Copyright 1969 by Council on Foreign Relations, Inc., pp. 121-122. Emphasis added.

20. PERM Team Annual Report, October 1970-September 1971, Office of ARD, RTG, Bangkok; ARD "Luck," *Far Eastern Economic Review*, 6 May 1972.

21. Ibid.

22. Paul Trescott, Fred von der Mehden, and David Wilson, "Thinking About ARD," Memorandum #2-1971, for United States Operations Mission/Thailand, April 27, 1971, *The Academic Advisory Council for Thailand*, Bangkok.

Chapter 4
Personal Centers in Manila (pp. 57-69)

1. See, in particular, General Edward G. Lansdale, *In the Midst of Wars; An American's Mission to Southeast Asia*; N.Y., Harper and Row, 1972.

2. "Rural Development in Asia," House of Representatives, Committee on Foreign Affairs, Subcommittee on Asian and Pacific Affairs, 25 April 1967.

3. Lewis Gleek and Harold Koone, "Land Reform in the Philippines," *USAID Spring Review* (June 1970), p. 1.

4. Frank H. Golay, *The Philippines, Public Policy and National Economic Development* (Ithaca: Cornell University Press, 1961), p. 274.

5. Gleek and Koone, pp. 2, 3.

6. Office of the President, Republic of the Philippines, "Nueva Ecija Land Reform Integrated Development Program," Office of the Project Director, December 11, 1970, p. 1.

7. Gleek and Koone, p. 77.

8. See Thomas R. McHale, "Sugar in the Seventies," *Solidarity* (May 1971), p. 7.

9. It should be pointed out, however, that the world market was historically a dumping ground. See Robert MacDougall, "The Linkage Politics of the Philippine-American Sugar Trade," M.A. thesis (unpublished), The Fletcher School of Law and Diplomacy, April 1971.

10. Frank Golay, p. 134, fn. 23. Between 1952 and 1967 the sugar windfall was twice the amount of American foreign aid to the Philippines. See Frank Golay, "The Case for Disengagement," *Graphic* (Manila), 5 July 1967.

11. Nicholas Berry, "Representation and Decision-Making: A Case Study of Philippine-American War Claims," Ph.D. thesis (unpublished) University of Pittsburgh, 1967, p. 78.

12. See Ibid., and also *Symington Report, Philippines*, p. 263. Fulbright stated that "Philippine interests sent a substantial sum of money to their lobbyist, who with their ambassador distributed it very wisely among Members of our Congress." This would not have been the last time Philippine money was involved in American politics. A $30,000 contribution was made to the Nixon Re-election campaign by former Philippine ambassador to the United States Ernesto Lagdameo, but was, surpisingly, returned, as it was illegal under American laws. See *The Philippine Times*, 16-31 March, 1975, p. 21.

13. Perla G. Makil, PAASCU/IPC Study of School and Influentials, 1969-70, Final Report, Part I & II, Summary of Findings and Conclusions.

14. For background to the case see *Manila Chronicle*, 28 April 1969, 28 March 1970.

15. Interview, Juan Ponce-Enrile, Manila, 1970.

16. Interview, U.S. Embassy, 1970 and 1971. See "Clark Used as a Nuclear Arms Depot?" *Manila Chronicle*, 16 April 1970, for one of the rare discussions of the nuclear issue.

17. Note 297, American Embassy, Manila, 23 April 1969.

18. Nicholas Berry, "Representation and Decision-Making."

Chapter 5
Pressures from Washington (pp. 75-90)

1. See Senator Raul S. Manglapus, *Asia: Revolution and Ideology*, pp. 180-85.

2. NSCD 64, 27 February 1950, in *Pentagon Papers*, U.S. Government Edition, Book I, Part II, A, p. 36.

3. Memorandum of Admiral Radford to Secretary of Defense Wilson, May 26, 1954, in *Pentagon Papers*, U.S. Government Edition, Book 9, p. 491.

4. Report of the Saigon Military Mission of General Lansdale, in *Pentagon Papers*, Gravel Edition, Vol. II, pp. 643-649, esp. p. 648. (Boston: Beacon Press, 1972).

5. Ibid., pp. 135-136.

6. Michael Onorato, "The Philippine Decision to Send Troops to Vietnam," *Solidarity* (November 1971), Vol. 6, No. 11, p. 4.

7. Op. cit.

8. *Pentagon Papers*, Gravel Edition, Vol. III. p. 681, (Boston: Beacon Press, 1972).

9. NSAM 157, 29 May 1962, in *Pentagon Papers*, U.S. Government edition, Book 12, p. 467.

10. *Pentagon Papers*, Gravel Edition, Vol. III, Document 179, pp. 542-45, (Boston: Beacon Press, 1972).

11. *Manila Times*, 15 January 1966.

12. *Official Gazette*, Republic of the Philippines, 17 July 1965.

13. Macapagal to W. Scott Thompson, 20 April 1970.

14. Ibid.

15. One State Department official noted, however, that the strategy backfired; there was less opposition to PHILCAG in 1965 and a stronger commitment from the Philippines could have been obtained.

16. *Manila Times*, 8 February 1966.

17. *Manila Chronicle*, 18 April 1966.

18. See Frank H. Golay, ed., *The United States and the Philippines* (Englewood Cliffs, N.J.: Prentice-Hall, 1966).

19. *Symington Report, Philippines*, p. 359.

20. Ferdinand Marcos, "The Battle for Peace" (Manila: Government Printing Office, 1966), p. 13.

21. Ibid.

22. *Symington Report, Philippines*, p. 356.

23. Ibid.

24. Ibid., p. 260. See also *Manila Times*, 2 September 1966, and *Philippine Press Analysis*, Vol. 14, #16, 11 October 1966.

25. Ibid. The Congressmen were Representatives Chamberlain and Gross.

26. *Symington Report, Thailand*, p. 905.

27. Address by H.E. Dr. Thanat Khoman before the American Chamber of Commerce in Thailand, July 15, 1970, mimeo. Emphasis added.

28. *Pentagon Papers*, Gravel Edition, Vol. 3, p. 191.

29. *Bangkok Daily News*, 22 August 1967.

30. See *Siam Rath*, 1 August 1967.

31. See for example the column of Theh Chonkadidji, "Keeping Posted," in the *Bangkok Post*, during this period. Theh, a prominent journalist, was known to reflect the thinking of Thanat Khoman.

32. See "23 Senators Ask Asian Help in War," *New York Times*, 16 October 1967, p. 1. As the *Times* pointed out, "Some confusion developed over whether the Administration had tacitly approved introduction of the resolution."

33. *Thai Rath*, 31 July 1967.

34. *Siam Rath*, 31 July 1967.

35. *Siam Times*, 29 July 1967.

36. *Siam Nakorn*, 1 August 1967.

37. *Bangkok World*, 23 October 1967.

38. *Symington Report, Thailand*, p. 625.

39. *Siam Rath*, 26 October 1967.

40. *Phim Thai*, 2 November 1967.

41. *Symington Report, Thailand*, p. 657. See also Chinese Press, 10 October 1967, Bangkok (USIS Translations).

42. *Chao Thai*, 6 October 1967. See also *Siam Rath*, editorial, 3 October 1967.

43. *Siam Rath*, 7 October 1967.

44. *Symington Report, Thailand*, p. 261.

45. Ibid., p. 266.

46. Ibid., pp. 36, 267. The cost of support for Philippine troops on Korea was $47,907,630.40. As of October 1969, PHILCAG had cost the United States only $35 million.

47. Quoted by M.R. Kukrit Pramoj in his column in *Siam Rath*, 31 January 1969.

Chapter 6
Societal Attitudes in Bangkok and Manila (pp. 91-100)

1. Little work has been done on this subject. For an exception, see Jorge Dominguez, "Public Opinion on International Affairs in Less Developed Coun-

tries," paper presented to the International Studies Association, New York, March 1973.

2. *Manila Times*, 26 March 1966.

3. Ibid.

4. *Philippine Free Press*, 5 March 1966.

5. *Symington Report, Philippines*, p. 360.

6. See Supra, p. 60. PAASCU/ISC Survey of Influentials, Institute of Philippine Culture, Ateneo de Manila University, Quezon City, Philippines.

7. Ibid.

8. *Symington Report, Thailand*, pp. 625, 758.

9. *Prachatipathai*, 15 January 1967.

10. *Siam Times*, 14 January 1967.

11. *Siam Rath*, 2 January 1967.

12. See Eduardo Lachica, *The Huks: Philippine Agrarian Society in Revolt*, (N.Y., Praeger, 1971).

13. *Siam Rath*, 2 January 1967.

14. See *Manila Times*, 27 June 1970.

15. See "The Listening Post," by Oscar Villadolid, *Manila Bulletin*, 22 January 1965.

16. Quoted in *Philippine Herald*, 21 January 1966. See also "The Philippines and Vietnam," *Manila Bulletin*, 15 February 1966.

17. *New York Times*, 20 November 1969. See also *Washington Post*, 28 March 1970.

18. "In Anger or in Shame?" Privilege speech delivered by Senator Salvador H. Laurel on the floor of the Senate on 30 March 1970. Courtesy of Senator Laurel to the author.

19. Ibid.

20. *Lak Muang*, 23 August 1967.

21. *Prachatipatai*, 15 October 1966, emphasis added.

22. See Montri Chenviykakarn, "Senator Fulbright and Thai-U.S. Relations," *Journal of Social Science*, Bangkok (April 1970).

23. *Thai Rath*, 12 July 1966.

24. *Daily News*, Bangkok, 14 June 1966.

Chapter 7
Political and Governmental Structures (pp. 101-112)

1. *Manila Times*, 19 January 1966.

2. *Philippine Herald*, 18 January 1966. The reference presumably is to S.P. Lopez.

3. Interview, American Embassy, Manila; JUSMAAG, and A.F.P. Headquarters, Quezon City, 1971. As of early 1971 the Philippine Navy had hauled in a total of 1873 short tons—442,907 cubic feet—of cargo. See David Barguirin, "Bonus From Vietnam War," *Manila Chronicle*, 7 March 1971.

4. See *Manila Times*, 7 July 1968.

5. Memorandum, General T. Yan, Chief of Staff Armed Forces, Philippines to W. Scott Thompson, 15 June 1970.

6. Interview with Senator Emmanuel Palaez, September 1970. Colonel Banzon, Military Attaché in Saigon and well acquainted with many congressmen and senators, flew in during the debate and made a series of sophisticated and effective presentations to Congress. See *Manila Bulletin*, 1 February 1966, and *Philippine Herald*, 2 February 1966 and 4 February 1966.

7. Interview, Senator Diokno, Manila, 1971.

8. See José D. Ingles, "The Philippine Position on the Vietnam Question," *Philippine Studies*, Vol. 14, #4, October 1966, p. 647.

9. *Manila Bulletin*, 25 March 1966. See also Raul S. Manglapus, *Revolution and Ideology* (1966), pp. 180-89.

10. Interview, Philippine Senate, 1970, and *Manila Bulletin*, 3 March 1966.

11. Interview, Philippine Senate, 1970.

12. *Manila Chronicle*, 19 May 1965.

13. See C. Spencer Hartzell, *For Every Tear a Victory: The Story of Ferdinand Marcos* (New York: McGraw-Hill, 1964), for a description of Marcos's career.

14. O.F. Villodolid, "Listening Post," *Manila Bulletin*, 1 December 1965.

15. "The Symbol of Filipino Faith—Speech Before the PHILCAG," 11 September 1966, in *A Battle for Peace* (Manila: Government Printer, 1966), p. 14.

16. Manuel T. Yan to W. Scott Thompson, 15 June 1970.

17. *Pentagon Papers*, U.S. Government Edition, Book 12, Part VI, A., p. 28, and Chester Cooper, *The Lost Crusade, America in Vietnam* (New York: Dodd, Mead & Co., 1970).

Chapter 8
Soldiers, Students, and the
Thai-American Alliance (pp. 117-136)

1. According to a senior American diplomat with Thanat at the time. Thanat's own doubts about the wisdom of Thai reliance on the Americans began circulating privately as early as 1966, at the Manila Summit.

2. The Thai confidence in Nixon had deep roots. All senior members of the regime interviewed emphasized their belief that Nixon was sympathetic and supportive: thus their determination in the early 1970's to stand by Nixon whatever he decided in Viet-Nam. See *Siam Times*, 5 July 1969.

3. *New York Times*, 15 May 1969.

4. Interviews, Ministry of Foreign Affairs, May 1969. Thai diplomacy worked, as usual, at all levels to communicate its views. The author, interviewing in Bangkok at the material time, found most of his sessions with Thai diplomats turned into "signals" to Washington of the Thai position.

5. *Chao Thai*, 17 May 1969.

6. All Chinese papers (as cited in United States Information Service translations), Bangkok, 24 May 1969.

7. See all Chinese morning papers, 23 May 1969. Senior American diplomats stressed, however, Thanat had only urged that South Vietnamese pilots be permitted to carry out the bombing of North Viet-Nam. This was a common theme among all of America's Asian allies. This position was more a symbolic issue concerning Asian competence, than an advocacy of Vietnamization.

8. Chinese Press, 24 May 1969, and *Siam Rath*, 9 June 1969.

9. See *Siam Rath*, editorial, 13 June 1969.

10. *Siam Rath*, 17 June 1969.

11. See "Political Corner," *Kiattisak Bangkok News*, 5 August 1969.

12. *Naewna Daily News*, 5 August 1969.

13. "Foreign Policy," edit., *Chao Thai*, 17 July 1969. The call for Thanat's resignation was strong enough that his supporters had to be called into action. *Chao Thai* cautioned against reaching the conclusion "too hastily that politics in this part of the world can be completely changed in the twinkling of an eye." And should Thailand's foreign policy be changed and realigned, it would mean that "the Prime Minister and whole government would have to be changed," not just the foreign minister.

14. See *Symington Report, Thailand*, pp. 653-55, 746-47. See also Murray Marder, "Thai Pact Feeds Fears on Hill," *Washington Post*, 17 August 1969.

15. See "Pentagon Again Balks Fulbright Committee on Pact with the Thais," *New York Times*, 13 August 1969.

16. See "Thailand Wants to Pull Troops Out of Vietnam," *Washington Post*, 2 August 1969.

17. Quoted in "Pentagon Again Balks Fulbright Committee."

18. Quoted in Murray Marder, "Laird Views on Defense Plan Surprise Thais, U.S. Officials," *Washington Post*, 22 August 1969.

19. Ibid.

20. *Washington Post*, 24 August 1969.

21. *Ching Hua Jih Pao*, 25 August 1969.

22. *Symington Report, Thailand*, pp. 767 and 769. Ambassador Unger later testified that he had long been so concerned that he had communicated this feeling with Washington. From the fall of 1968, after all, the Thai had asked for a "trade-off for any additional Americans that we were going to bring in," which effectively put on a ceiling. "The more Americans, the more potential incidents; the more the Thais would feel defensive." This is credible: Unger perfectly understood Thai sensitivities, and ran as quiet an operation as possible. Still, it

was Thanat who made the public proposal "at a time when he had the feeling that the presence of American forces in Thailand was being seriously misunderstood" in America, Unger said.

23. Murray Marder, "Laird Views on Defense Plan Surprise Thais, U.S. Officials," *Washington Post* 22 August 1969.

24. See *Chinese Press*, 28 August 1969.

25. See, for example, "Analysis of the Economic Impact of the Vietnam War," Department of Fiscal Policy, Ministry of Finance (in Thai), 1969; Hermann Hatzfeldt, "The Impact of U.S. Military Expenditures on the Thai Economy," unpublished, Bangkok, 1968. See also the study of this subject and extensive bibliography in Bunyaraks Ninsananda, "Economic Aspects of the De-escalation of the U.S. Military Presence in Thailand," The Fletcher School of Law and Diplomacy (unpublished); also *Thai Daily*, 20 June 1969.

26. See Chinese Evening Papers, 30 September 1969; for background to the troop withdrawal negotiations see *Symington Report, Thailand*, pp. 768-70. See also *Hsing Hsien*, 24 September 1969.

27. France's sine qua non of mediation was an improvement of Thai-Cambodian relations. This makes sense, France being concerned about Cambodia's security, Cambodia being sensitive to Thai attitudes, and Thailand being in debt to France for this favor. See the *Far Eastern Economic Review*, 12 June 1969. Relations with Cambodia had been broken in September 1968. See *New York Times*, 1 October 1968.

28. See *Prachatipatai*, 3 June 1970.

29. Ross Terrill, "Report and Comments: Thailand," *Atlantic Monthly* (October 1972).

30. "Thailand has Second Thoughts on China," by Leon Daniel, *Manila Chronicle*, 29 May 1971. See also "Thanat Views Red Links," *Bangkok Post*, 7 May 1971, and "Peking Dialogue a Step Nearer," by Theh Chongkhadikij, Ibid., 14 May 1971.

31. "Time for Self-Reliance," *Bangkok Post*, 19 April 1971.

32. "We Can't Push for Dialogue—Sa-anga," *Bangkok Post*, 25 May 1971.

33. See, for example, Ross Terrill's otherwise excellent "Report."

34. See *Siam Nikorn*, 18 May 1969.

35. *Bangkok Post*, 18 November 1971.

36. *Memoirs*, Bangkok, 1972. I am grateful to Mr. Somkiati Arayaprucha for translating pertinent sections of the memoirs.

37. Subcommittee on U.S. Security Agreements and Commitments Abroad of the Committee on Foreign Relations United States Senate, *Thailand, Laos, Cambodia, and Vietnam, April 1973*, U.S. Government Printing Office, Washington, 1973, pp. 30-31.

38. Emile Benoit, *Impacts of the End of Vietnam Hostilities and the Reduction of British Military Presence in Malaysia and Singapore*, (New York: Asian Development Bank, 1971), p. 364.

39. Ibid.

40. It was called "Bangkok's Watergate" at the time. See *Far Eastern Economic Review*, 1973.

41. Ibid.

42. I am grateful to Mr. Robert Zimmerman for providing this quotation and translation.

43. See W. Scott Thompson, "Thai Students Waving Bogus Letter, Chip Away U.S.-Thailand Relations," *Christian Science Monitor*, 16 January 1974.

44. *New York Times*, 11 September 1973.

45. See "Enter the Russians," editorial, *Bangkok Post*, 11 February 1974.

46. Interview, 28 December 1973, Supreme Command Forward Headquarters.

47. See W. Scott Thompson, "Thai-American Relations," *Bangkok Post*, 8 March 1974.

48. *Bangkok Daily*, 21 January 1974 and *Thai Rath*, 11 January 1974.

49. *Time*, 2 May 1969.

50. Alessandro Casella, "U.S.-Thai Relations," *The World Today*, Vol. 28, No. 3 (March 1970), p. 124.

Chapter 9
The "New Society" and Philippine Adaptation (pp. 137-154)

1. See W. Scott Thompson, "America Renegotiates with the Philippines," *Pacific Community* (July 1971), Vol. 2, No. 4.

2. Interviews, Malacañang Palace, 1970, 1974.

3. Most conspicuously, Senator Aquino had good working relations, by his own account, with NPA leaders, who used Hacienda Luisita, the huge plantation owned by his wife's family, the Cojuangkos, as one refuge. The Lopez family was widely believed to have funded many demonstrations, though they denied this in interviews.

4. *Manila Chronicle*, 15 January 1971. Note that Lopez spokesman denied seeking to buy out CALTEX (see ibid.), though it is generally assumed that such was their intent.

5. *Manila Chronicle*, 15 January 1971.

6. "What the People Think," *Manila Chronicle*, 24 July 1970.

7. See, as an example of how the international press saw the situation in this period, Henry S. Hayward, "Gathering Malaise in Philippines," *The Christian Science Monitor*, 20 February 1971.

8. Martial law was proclaimed on the 23rd, but the papers were drawn up on the 21st. See "Korea and the Philippines," November 1972, a Staff Report, Committee on Foreign Relations, U.S. Senate, 18 February 1973, pp. 1-4.

9. Alejandro Melchor, Jr., "Development Diplomacy," *Ambassador Journal* (1973), p. 4.

10. See "U.S. A.I.D. Development Assistance to the Philippines," A.I.D., Manila, 1971, p. 4.

11. Ibid.

12. "U.S. Overseas Loans and Grants," House Foreign Affairs Committee, 14 May 1971, p. 182. 1966 was a bad year—but grants in the sixties still averaged less than a third of their 1970 level.

13. Melchor, p. 3.

14. Ibid., p. 14.

15. Ibid., p. 3.

16. A point well realized by the Philippine community. Interview, Ramon Nolan, Manila, 1971.

17. See *Manila Times*, 29 August 1972.

18. *Business Day*, 9 January 1974.

19. See Thompson.

20. Cited in *Highlights of Agrarian Reform, Program Accomplishments, January-December, 1973*, Department of Agrarian Reform, Quezon City, 7 January 1974.

21. See John V. Gillespie and Betta Nesvold, eds., *Macro-Quantitative Analysis: Conflict, Development, and Democratization* (Beverly Hills: Sage Publications, 1971).

Chapter 10
Democracy, Stability, and Foreign Policy (pp. 155-161)

1. Franklin B. Weinstein, "Uses of Foreign Policy in Indonesia," *World Politics* (April 1972), Vol. 24, p. 380.

2. Walt Rostow, *The United States in the World Arena* (New York: Harper & Row, 1960).

3. Jerrold K. Milsted, "Thai-U.S. Relations, the Nixon Doctrine and the Test of Transition," unpublished paper, Harvard University, 17 January 1972, p. 40.

4. See Frank C. Darling, *Thailand and the United States*, Public Affairs Press, Washington, D.C., 1965.

5. *Bangkok Post*, 30 December 1973.

6. See Norman Jacobs, *Modernization Without Development, Thailand as an Asian Case Study* (New York: Praeger, 1971).

7. Robert B. Stauffer, "Philippine Martial Law: The Political Economy of Refeudalization," paper presented at Association for Asian Studies, Boston, 1-3 April 1974.

8. Andrew Malcolm, "Shooting and Shouting Incidents Heighten Tension in a Thai Town on the Border Facing Cambodia," *New York Times*, 24 April 1975.

9. Quoted by M.R. Kukrit Pramoj in his column, *Siam Rath*, 31 January 1969.

Index

Accelerated Rural Development,
52-56, 69
Acheson, Dean, 13
adaptation, xii, 128, 165n
Adulyadej, Bamibol (King Rama IX).
See Bamibol
agreements, bases, 65
aid, absorptive capacity of, 39, 59,
150; increase to Philippines, 156
American, aid to Philippines, 150;
ambassador, 26, 41, 67; dependence
on, 129; image on Thailand, 127;
military aid, 159; role of embassy,
42-43
Aphaiwong, Kuang. See Kuang
Aquino, Benigno, 12, 140, 177n
Armed Forces Philippines (AFP),
103-104, 110
Attakorn, Bunchana. See Bunchana

bargaining power, xi, xvi, 6, 7, 35-38,
87-89, 97, 116, 128, 155-156
bases, Philippine, 12
Bell Trade Act, 80
Bell Mission, 59
Benoit, Emile, 176n
Berry, Nicholas, 62, 69
Blair, William McCormick Jr., 11, 57,
82, 83
Bohlen, Charles E., 57
Bamibol Adulyadej (King Rama IX),
130
Bunchana Attakorn, 127
Bundy, William, 80
Burma, 3
Byroade, Henry, 10, 26, 32, 57, 58,
60, 144, 151

Caldwell, Alexander, 53
Cambodia, 3, 124, 127, 135, 161
Cassella, Allessandro, 177n
Central Intelligence Agency (CIA), 50,
130-132; in Thailand, 43
Chakri Dynasty, 3
Chamman Yuvpurna, 47, 53
Chanawan, Kriangsak. See Kriangsak
Charusathien, Prapat. See Prapat
China, People's Republic of, 21-22,

23, 117-119, 124, 125; support of
Thai insurgents, xiv
Chonkadidji, Theh. See Theh
Chulalongkorn, King Rama V, 3
Chullasyapa. See Dawee
Civilian-Police-Military (C-P-M), 46, 50
Clark Air Force Base, 7, 27
Clifford, Clark, 82
Communist Suppression Operations
Command (CSOC), 43, 49-50, 56
Community Development Depart-
ment, 45
Constitutional Convention, 140
Controlled American Source (C.A.S.),
43-44
counter-insurgency, 18; in Thailand,
46
Crisologo, Vincent, 104

Darling, Frank C., 21
Dawee Chullasyapa, 85, 86, 103, 107,
131
democracy, xi, 98, 158
democratic institutions, 115, 155-156
Department of Local Administration,
Thailand (DOLA), 46, 48, 49
Department of Technical and Eco-
nomic Cooperation (DTEC), 53
de Silva, Peer, 48, 49
de Venecia, José V., 67
Dhammasakai. See Sanya
Dewey, George, 4
Diokno, José, 105, 146
domino theory, 101
Duncanson, Dennis, 55

élite, xii, xv, 5, 128, 158-159; ilustrados, 4

Fluker, J. Robert, 42
foreign policy, 132, 141, 157-159;
defined, 25; external sources of, 21;
moods of, xiii; Philippine, 142, 143;
societal sources of, 91, 99; sources
of, xi, xii, 78, 94
Friend, Theodore, 5
Fulbright, J.W., 44, 62, 77, 86, 120,
122, 125, 133, 170n; criticisms, 98

179

About the Author

W. Scott Thompson is an associate professor of international politics at the Fletcher School of Law and Diplomacy, Tufts University. He attended Stanford University and received the D. Phil. in politics from Oxford University, Balliol College in 1967. Dr. Thompson is the author of *Ghana's Foreign Policy, 1957-66* and is a member of the editorial board of *Orbis*.